New Korea

New Korea

New Land of
the Morning Calm

Kyung Cho Chung

*Illustrated with photographs and a
map of Korea*

The Macmillan Company   New York

Macmillan New York, London

A Division of The Crowell-Collier Publishing Company

Dedicated
to those who sacrificed their lives
to protect human rights and preserve
real democracy in Korea
and also
to those who rendered great service
and assistance in the cause of a uni-
fied, independent, and democratic
Korea

Preface

In the five years since *Korea Tomorrow* was published, many readers have written to me. I have received letters from every corner of the world and from all kinds of people in every conceivable occupation. By and large, however, all of them have, in one form or another, asked the same questions: What happened in Korea? What will happen in Korea? With invasion and revolution occurring within less than a decade, what has caused such unrest in Korea?

During my recent travels around the world, it was my privilege to meet and converse with hundreds of people of all ranks and from every walk of life. Almost without exception, they expressed great interest in the Korean Military Revolutionary Government and the highest hopes for the New Korea.

In *Korea Tomorrow,* I gave no more than a hint to the answers to the disturbing problems of Korea. It is difficult, even for thoughtful people, to understand the political, economic, and social dilemmas that in our time have confronted the newly independent countries of Asia. Perhaps a key to the riddle lies in sound knowledge and comprehension of the problems of the "New Land of the Morning Calm."

This study of Korea may help us to understand not only Korea but also other newly independent non-Western countries, for although each of the new nations has its own specific problems, all of them also have problems in common. This book is, I hope, a useful answer to questions implied in *Korea Tomorrow,* and will help us to perceive the New Korea as "the beacon of democracy in Asia."

KYUNG CHO CHUNG

Paris

Acknowledgments

WITHOUT THE HELP, direct and indirect, of many people throughout the world, this book could not have been written. This volume is a cooperative effort that has placed me in a position of obligation to more persons that I can list here.

I am greatly indebted to authors, publishers, institutions, universities, press, and governments for permission to quote, and for photographs and a map appearing in their publications. Factual materials in the text were derived from the *New York Times, Newsweek, Time,* the *Voice of Korea, Korean Republic, New Korea,* United Nations, United States, and Republic of Korea publications, as well as books written by specialists on Asia. The numbered footnotes and Bibliography are primarily acknowledgments of sources of matter referred to in the text, and may also serve further research.

I am particularly grateful to Mr. Richard Allen, Mr. John K. Han, Mr. Young Jeung Kim, Dr. Shannon McCune, Professor Robert T. Oliver, the Honorable Edwin Reischauer, Professor Robert A. Scalapino, Mr. Po Sung Kim, and Professor Clarence N. Weems, all of whom allowed me to quote from their valuable publications. I am also deeply indebted to Ambassador Il Kown Chung, General Jae Chun Kim, the Honorable Soo Young Lee, Mr. John F. Orndorff, Mrs. Patty Anderson, Mr. Chae Kyung Oh, Mr. Chun Hong, Mrs.

Y. S. Chung, Miss Pendleton Garrison, and the Reverend Charles C. Song who gave much needed assistance at various stages of the work. Finally I should like to state my profound gratitude to my publisher.

THE AUTHOR

London

Contents

Illustrations

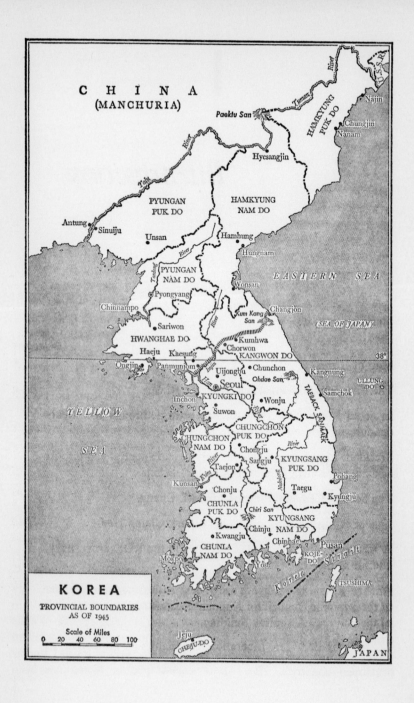

KOREA

PROVINCIAL BOUNDARIES
AS OF 1945

Scale of Miles
0 20 40 60 80 100

I

Introduction

KOREA'S DILEMMA[1]

Today Korea stands as a symbol of global conflict, of cooperation in the free world, and of the new policy of America to help a frontier state of stalwart and courageous people. Korea furnished the world with one of its most dangerous confrontations of Communism and non-Cmmunism, one that could have led to a major international war.

The present situation in South Korea presents both a challenge and a lesson to the United States. The challenge involves not only the democratic progress of one of America's few stanch allies in Asia; it also involves America's chances of winning reliable friends elsewhere in Asia and Africa. And the implications of the lesson extend to the whole pattern of United States policy toward under-developed countries. The risk of catastrophe in Korea has been

1

mounting; the danger of a divided Korea remains; and the threat to world peace grows more serious in the Thermonuclear-Missile Age.

Although Korea was so little known to the world that it was long called the "Hermit Kingdom," its strategically important location on the perimeter of the Asiatic land mass has been thoroughly understood by China, Japan, and Russia. Korea seems destined to become the main field wherein a tug of war for mastery of the Pacific may be contested. Often a target for foreign invasion, Korea is frequently called the "Balkans of the Orient."

The Korean Peninsula resembles a jagged club thrusting southward from Manchuria and the Maritime Province of the Soviet Union; to the east, only 120 miles distant, is Japan. Korea lies in the center of the Far East triangle. As a peninsula, Korea has served as a buffer state between powers in the Pacific and powers on the continent of Asia.

Korea's geographical location places it in a strategic position with regard to Asian affairs, and at the same time presents undeniable problems to powers desirous of controlling its future policies. A strong military power in control of the Korean Peninsula could dominate contiguous states. The country reflects the political, economic, and cultural influence of her powerful neighbors in East Asia.

The fundamental fact underlying Korea's tragedy, like that of ancient Palestine or modern Poland, has been its geographical position, the basic cause for the unfortunate events suffered by Korea throughout history. The peninsula is topographically disadvantageous either for domestic prosperity or for national defense.

Korea has been invaded so often that the brands of ownership of its many masters are clearly visible, and the country's foreign relations have left tangible traces upon it. The only instance in which Korea took the initiative in seeking foreign relations was her entrance into relations with China for the sole purpose of importing China's highly developed cultures of religion, letters, and the arts. The most conspicuous element in Korea's history is the fact that its growth has been constantly affected by foreign influences.

For few nations in modern times has geographical position had more serious results than for the Korean people. Left alone, with no interference from their more powerful neighbors, the peace-loving Korean people might have achieved a unified independence; profiting from contracts with the outside world, they might have developed progressive social and political institutions. The Koreans' intelligence, their historic traditions, their cultural unity, the physical compactness of the country, and the economc interdependence of its parts all favored such a course of development.

Unfortunately, surrounded by her stronger neighbors, Korea's geopolitical location, has forestalled such an outcome. The Korean people have experienced invasions, intervention, foreign military occupations, foreign rule, wars between alien armed forces, and internal struggles stimulated and kept alive by foreign influences, economically and politically. Accordingly, with their desire for peace, the Koreans each day give greetings such as, "May you come in peace," for "Hello"; "May you go in peace," for "Goodbye"; and "May you sleep in peace," for "Good night."

For self-protection, Korea has often been forced to enter into unsought wars, each of which has left the country exhausted and despairing. Its foreign relations have been little more than a struggle for survival. The invasions, devastations, and plunderings of Korea have been written large on the history of Asia. National unity and independence, always dangling just out of reach, have never been grasped. Yet, amid the ruins of their land, the Koreans have maintained an unquenchable aspiration for survival and self-determination.

Despite the invasions of foreign powers, including cultural, economic, and political incursions, the Korean people have maintained their national entity. They never accepted the idea that Korea was an integral part of the Japanese Empire, although Japan attempted to dissipate the identity of Korea; instead, their common struggle for freedom has sealed indissolubly the union of their minds and hearts. They are eager to bear the burdens of the freedom they have sought for so long. Because of their willingness to fight for freedom, the Korean people are called the "Irish of the Orient."

As is characteristic of peninsulas throughout the world, Korea's natural situation has removed it from the main areas of continental migration and war, and has permitted periodic rejuvenation of its civilization. Whereas semi-isolation tends to produce provincialism, periodic cultural invasions have developed in Korea a pattern that incorporates much of its neighbors' ways of life and yet is significantly different from them.

Korea, an ancient and beautiful land aptly named the "Switzer-land of Asia," is also called the "Land of the Morning Calm"; but alas, too few of Korea's mornings are calm, for it is the center of a crossroads. The Korean people have struggled long, and often hope-lessly, to become the masters of their fate, but the status of Korea is an obvious example of the futilities and tensions of the post-Yalta world.

After having ruled Korea for more than thirty-five years, in 1945, at the close of World War II, the Japanese signed surrender documents in the Capitol at Seoul, and withdrew. But the Communists had taken over the largely industrial portion of the country north of the 38th parallel of latitude. The portion to the south, largely agricul-tural, became a republic in 1948.

In June, 1950, Communist forces swept down from the North. During the ensuing three years, South Korea was overrun and devastated. By the time peace was restored through the police action of the United Nations, spearheaded by the United States, most of Korea lay in ruins. Three million people on both sides had lost their lives. The Communists had been driven back above the 38th parallel, but a military line of demarcation across the Korean Peninsula in this area now became an official boundary between the North and the South. One-third of Korea's total population was displaced. In South Korea many found shelter in shacks in the towns and cities. Large numbers were refugees from the Communist North. They had lost their homes, their means of livelihood, and their possessions. There remained the sea and its harvest, available to the coastal dwellers.

There also remained the land, which had been cultivated since time immemorial and which the machinery of modern warfare had passed across but had not blighted. Korean farmers had long ago learned to make use of hillside springs and to build terraces so that they could cultivate every foot of available ground. They worked with primitive tools, using oxen and the power of their own bodies. These rural folk were the backbone of the country. Though they worked their animals hard, they did not spare themselves, either. Lacking sanitary facilities, they nevertheless kept themselves and their clothing as clean as they could. Every community had its market place. Al-though prices were high, the people could purchase the necessities of life, but not much else. More than 80 per cent of the population of South Korea was engaged in agriculture—an ill-balanced economy that would have fared poorly without American aid.

Despite its small area, roughly the size of Great Britain, Korea is a major country with a population of thirty-three million, about the same as that of Spain, and it ranks thirteenth among the nations of the world. The population is divided in the proportion of two to one between agricultural South Korea and industrial North Korea.

Although the Korean people are polite, friendly, patient, artistic, and avidly desire knowledge, economic insecurity and social chaos have instilled in them a strong sense of fear, loneliness, and defeatism. Through it all they maintain their individualism and a good-humored dignity, which are best expressed by their senior citizens in traditional white gown and horsehair hats; but they are extremely skeptical and cynical regarding the existing society and its leaders, and they long for heroic leaders, prophets, and an orderly society.

The Koreans have had no political experience and little administrative knowledge with which to build a stable government. Unfortunately, with the example of a notorious Japanese police force during the long Japanese rule, many Koreans learned to rely upon brute strength to control their fellow men. Consequently, factional groups sprang up among them, intent only on protecting their own selfish interests. Korean stubbornness and inability to compromise or cooperate has its roots in the past; their blind pride, dogmatism, and introversion are part of a deep-rooted national inferiority complex, and the result of long years of domination by hated rulers.

At the foundation of Korean society rests a family system. It is a Korean ideal that every member of the family should do all in his power to ensure the mutual welfare of his kin; from that have emerged favoritism and factionalism, causing corruption. The second Korean social-political unit in importance has been the village, wherein developed an elaborate system of guilds through which local governing principles were evolved to solve cooperatively multiple community problems. Korean national government was organized primarily to ensure a national stability within which local solutions for personal problems could be achieved with maximum justice. Provincial governors were closely controlled by public opinion.

During the centuries of the Korean monarchical system, anony-

mous investigators were sent around the country by the king to re-
dress people's grievances, and the right to direct a petition to the
throne was reserved to the humblest citizen. Because channels were
kept open for continuous reformation, the monarchy was singularly
free from revolutionary outbreaks. Korea had long periods of
brilliant government.

However, when a modernized Western system was thrust upon
Korea in the nineteenth century, the Korean monarchy was in a
serious state of disintegration. The Confucian principles adopted by
the Korean kings centuries earlier had been supplanted by corrupt
and inefficient government. Political-party warfare and factionalism,
which have long been characteristics of Korean political activity,
centered upon the controversy over Westernization, with a conservative group opposing a progressive group.

The long period of their country's history as a Japanese colony had
a profound effect upon Koreans. An almost fanatical desire for
independence and self-government was created among them by the
oppressive treatment they received under Japanese rule. Nationalism
burned all the more fiercely, and a hatred of all governing authority
grew strongly in every Korean heart because of the brutal control of
the Japanese. The violence of their political sentiments toward government is strong, even alarming.

The continued division of Korea and the threat of invasion poised
over it are formidable handicaps. Moreover, Korea has been swept by
battles that have left many deep wounds. Divided into two governments, and confronted with an uncertain future, political leadership
has been subjected to severe restraints and strains. Many Koreans
have opportunistically sought personal advantages, and some have
chosen to cooperate closely and actively with the government. Others
have formed pro-Korean blocs with opposing programs, centering
upon divergent personalities. As was inevitable under such circumstances, recriminations have been bitter, and personal feelings have
been deeply affected.

Owing to despotic rule, no leader could arise from the people, and
the Koreans took no part in a government controlled by a selfish, dishonest, and factional bureaucracy. Whatever diversity and disunity
appear on the Korean political scene are not the result of fundamental
differences in race, religion, or culture within the Korean society. The

Korean people have a long historical continuity and a unique heritage as a nation of one race, one language, one culture, and a proud past. For many centuries, the Japanese called Korea the "Treasure Land of the West."

Historically the Korean people, in their attempts to avoid repeated invasions, withdrew, and became, in fact as well as in name, a Hermit Kingdom. Unfortunately, this was only partially successful. The effects of an earlier Japanese occupation, of Communist control over half of the Korean Peninsula, of industrialization and urbanization and attempted modernization have broken down the Confucian ethical base of their society, and have posed problems to which many Koreans have not been able to adjust.

Like many Asian countries, Korea is a land of conflicts and contrast, of beauty and poverty, of tradition and modernization, of intelligence and inexperience, of personal sacrifice and selfish corruption. South Koreans are very eager to learn, friendly to the United States, and most anxious to develop a modern nation in a free world. Since the Korean people are especially adaptable to the West, South Korea is called the "most Christian land in the Orient." What appeared to be confusion, disorder, uprisings, and revolution in South Korea, is in reality growing pains out of which will come order, stability, and a satisfying way of life.

After a long and unhappy history, the Korean people are now looking impatiently ahead to a new day of progress for a peaceful, democratic nation. At this stage of world development, it must devolve upon mankind as a whole to redeem Korea. Now, with the emergence of international action in support of justice and peace, internationalism —and it alone—can establish Korea as nation, rebuilt and free to live out the destiny of its people. It will be called the New Korea.

II

Old Korea

◆ ◆ ◆ *"There is a history in all
men's lives."*—SHAKESPEARE

KOREA'S HERITAGE[1]

To obtain a rounded picture of the recent political and military
revolutions in Korea, it is essential to glance backward from the
present uncertainty, with its controversies and problems. More than
four thousand years of evolving a way of life together could hardly
be expected to produce less than many common characteristics in all
Koreans, largely because disruptive outside influences were relatively
rare before modern Korea. Because Koreans have never failed to
believe in themselves, it has been possible for them to turn disaster into
a renaissance whenever they had the physical means to do so. The
Korean people have even had the moral stamina and inborn courage
to survive passively when no other means of resistance was possible.

The earliest written records of Korean history begin with establishment of the Silla Kingdom in the south in 57 B.C., the Koguryo

8

Kingdom in the north, twenty years later, and the Paikje Kingdom, in 18 B.C., in the southwest. This period is known in Korean history as the "Era of The Three Kingdoms." Struggles among these three powers for supremacy continued for more than six centuries. Finally, Silla, in alliance with China, crushed Paikje in 600 A.D., and then Koguryo in A.D. 668. The entire Korean Peninsula, unified under the rule of Silla, enjoyed almost three hundred years of peace and prosperity. During this period the level of culture reached one of its highest points in Korea's history.

This era felt the impact of two great influences from the outside world: Buddhism, with its pageantry, and Chinese classical literature, based on Confucianism. The two were deadly rivals, and it was not until about 1392 that the pro-Chinese element became dominant over the Buddhist hierarchy insofar as political influence was concerned. Both are a part of Korean culture today, but neither dominates or controls any phase of Korean life. Finally, Silla fell without significant struggle, and the new Kingdom of Koryo took its place, in 918. This was also a period of continuing progress in all fields of human activity. Korean art began to serve as prototype for Japanese architecture, painting, and ceramics, and Korea was also a channel through which Chinese and Indian cultures flowed to Japan, at the same time diverting much of the best for its own use. However, Korea's utilization of ideas and art forms was its own, and remained distinct.

In 1392 Yi Sung-kei, leader of the army, and a Confucian, founded the third dynasty since Korea's unification as a single nation. This kingdom lasted until 1910, when the Japanese annexed Korea, exploited its resources, and determined its internal progress for the next forty years. Yi and his immediate successors ushered in a flourishing and creative era. All phases of life underwent a renaissance as notable as that of any comparable historical period anywhere. One of the great inventions in the Koryo Dynasty, movable metal printing type, was greatly improved, and scientific instruments, such as the water clock, were invented while Korea was still the Hermit Kingdom and the West was going its own way. The most valuable development was the fifteenth century invention of a phonetic alphabet consisting then of eleven vowels and fourteen consonants, which served to bring education within the reach of everyone in the kingdom.

This was a great achievement, as the nation was surrounded by "character"-using cultures who, for all their brilliance and greater resources, had not taken this remarkable step. Literacy, as a result, became more widespread in Korea, proportionately, than in any other place in Asia. This "Han-gul" alphabet permitted the Bible to be translated and widely read. As a consequence, there is a greater percentage of third- and fourth-generation Christians in Korea than in any other nation in Asia.

Through the eras of Silla, Koryo, and Yi's Chosun Kingdom, the Korean people matured remarkably. The development of their political and social systems, culture, and prosperity was outstanding among Asian nations. Furthermore, at each attempt at foreign invasion, the entire people united in defense of the country, whether they had adequate weapons or not. The simple, loyal, and fiercely patriotic common people of Korea were always masters of the nation's destiny, and their influence was a great factor in bringing about improvements in the social system. Whenever the ruling government deteriorated, they supported a new, healthy movement to overthrow and replace the dying regime.

Of particular significance in this connection is the fact that change of dynasties was always followed by a period of extensive cultural and social progress. The Korean people have never committed an act of aggression against their neighbors, and even when attacked their military action has always been limited to defense. Racial unity was achieved in jointly facing and driving off alien invaders; and as soon as the danger ended, the people returned to their peaceful pursuits. Great advances were made following Silla's unification of the country, Koryo's victory over Silla, and in the periods following Korea's triumph over various foreign invaders. The Asian continental influence that had been strong before the Silla's unification was succeeded by a period of unique growth of the Korean people and by their brilliant cultural achievements.

The wars in which Korea was involved, devastating as they were, nevertheless helped to encourage interchange of different cultures. It is unfortunate that today a unified and prosperous Korea is not being allowed to make its proper contribution to contemporary civilization. Modern Korea has become a geographical stage whereon the interests of major world powers conflict. In the last century of its history, Korea has failed to accomplish two major tasks: its transformation from an isolated feudal society into a modern, strongly centralized nation-state, and the construction of an industrial base for its economy.

Detailed analysis of modern Korea reveals two striking facts: first, broad social and cultural changes were not held to a minimum in the midst of great changes in the material aspects of Korean life: and, second, modernization was not planned by Korean leaders, accepted as desirable by the people, and striven for willingly and whole-heartedly. Korean leaders were not aware that modernization meant national security, not simply abstract political reform and economic and social progress. Industrial and military modernization were the only means by which Korea could defend itself against the threat of invasion. Though in the course of its history, Korea suffered invasions by Mongol, Japanese, Chinese, and Manchu neighbors, the country continuously maintained its national independence until 1910, when it was annexed by Japan, which ruled Korea until the end of the Second World War, in August, 1945.

Japanese policy in Korea was ruthless and oppressive, but the spirit of independence of the Korean people remained alive throughout the four decades of Japanese domination. A great movement by the Korean people to regain their freedom was launched on March 1, 1919. This popular, nonviolent revolution was mercilessly put down by the Japanese Government. However, the torch of independence was carried by patriots in exile abroad, and immediately after the March 1st Independence Movement, a Korean Provisional Government was established in Shanghai. This government-in-exile ceaselessly fought for Korea's independence, and to the people of the homeland it became the symbol of Korean freedom. Throughout the world Koreans worked persistently for liberation, even pleading their case before the League of Nations in 1933, after Japan's seizure of Manchuria. The right of Korea to exist as an independent country was recognized by the statesmen of the Allied Nations of World War II, who declared at Cairo in 1943 that Korea would regain its independence after the war.

The Korean Independence Movement never lost its hold upon the common man in Korea. The overlay of Japanese influence did not radically alter the basic heritage of ancient Korea. Korean nationalism was instead greatly strengthened during the period of Japanese overlordship. A reservoir of patriotism was built up under Japanese rule, and was ready to be tapped at the moment of liberation.

Korea's long, passive resistance to Japan was an incredible psychological achievement for such an outspoken race, and effectively prevented Japan from incorporating Korea into Japanese national life, either culturally or ideologically. Some progress was made in an economic sense, but here the Koreans were not allowed to share except at the lowest level. This in itself stimulated resistance and helped to perpetuate Korea as a nation.

Thwarted in her basic purpose, Japan created a kind of "bamboo curtain" around Korea, and Tokyo became the only generally available source of information for news of Korea. For four decades Japan created the fiction that Koreans were uncultured and incompetent. Few knew that Japan by calculated restrictions had prevented the technical and higher education of all Koreans who had not found asylum in other countries.

As the Second World War progressed, Koreans took hope when liberation appeared to be guaranteed by the Cairo Declaration of December 1, 1943. However, the Potsdam meeting of 1945 confused the issue and delayed Korea's restoration as an independent nation. Then came the expedient of the 38th parallel, originally intended solely to facilitate the surrender of Japanese troops in Korea. This was seized upon by the Russians as a pretext first to occupy and then to take over the northern half of the Korean Peninsula. The belt around Korea's waist was drawn even tighter by the Moscow Agreement of December 7, 1945, whose objectives of "trusteeship" for Korea were anathema to all Koreans. They opposed it, as they had opposed the entire forty years of Japanese rule, by all peaceful means open to them.

The difficulty of molding a strong, independent nation is greatly increased in a war-torn and divided country. Certainly, it is a task worthy of the most experienced to build system out of chaos while giving "on-the-job training" to nearly thirty million independent-minded, harassed, and war-impoverished people.

During the period of the American Military Government, after liberation, few took into account the loyalties of a people whose boundaries had remained unchanged for centuries and whose thirteen provinces were a federated union.

The abysmal failure of the joint United States and Union of Soviet Socialist Republics Conference and the joint U.S.–U.S.S.R. Commission of the winter and spring of 1946 in Seoul foreshadowed the divided state that continues unacceptable to all Koreans to this day; nevertheless, the stigma of trusteeship was prevented. Apart from all else, the Second World War had placed a tremendous burden on the Korean economy, even though its cities and countryside had escaped destruction. Japan had taken everything out and put nothing in. Korea was physically in bad shape. No real maintenance of roads or buildings had been attempted since 1936. Korea's economy suffered from the aftermath of war, liberation, and an unknown future.

From the spring of 1946 to the fall of 1947, when the United States submitted the Korean problem to the United Nations, the two occupation powers were unable to help Korean economic or political readjustment. It was a period of acute distress to the Koreans, for their rehabilitation and independence were being delayed. Naturally, they wanted to get on with the task of reestablishing themselves as a free and responsible nation, under a government of their own choosing, and with the kind of economic assistance that would give them the hope of eventual self-sufficiency. By the nature of Korea's economy, this also meant unification, as no nation is less suited for division, by geographical circumstances and historical economic development, than Korea.

As a result of the decisions of the United Nations General Assembly, on November 14, 1947, as urged by the United States, the liberation of Korea took on reality. Though Korea was still divided at the 38th parallel, South Korea would have to go it alone. A democratically conducted election was held in South Korea on May 10, 1948, under the observation of the United Nations. Thus, on August 15, 1948, Korea became a free nation again. A Korean government was launched, with Syngman Rhee, the acknowledged leader, as first President of Korea. Progress toward an economically improved democratic state in South Korea was well on its way when it was interrupted by the Korean War on June 25, 1950. Refusal of the United Nations to recognize the Soviet-created government in Korea north of the 38th parallel created the excuse for the formal establishment of a "Democratic People's Republic of Korea," on September 9, 1948. On June 27, 1950, two days after the North

Korean Communists crossed the 38th parallel, the Security Council called upon all members of the United Nations to aid in repelling the invasion.

After more than three years of fighting, a miltary armistice was signed on July 27, 1953. The agreed truce line ran generally somewhat above the 38th parallel. The efforts to implement the armistice agreement began at Panmunjom in October, and culminated at Geneva on June 15, 1954. The war failed to settle, and perhaps even aggravated, the problem of Korean unification, which remains as unfinished business of the United Nations. The pledge for peaceful unification of the country through genuinely free elections under United Nations auspices remains. In the meantime, the Korean people remain impounded under the *de facto* control of two regimes, and economic rehabilitation and reconstruction of the country are hampered by its illegal division.

Modern Korea

◆ ◆ ◆*"All governments depend upon the good will of the people."*

—JOHN ADAMS

THE KOREA OF SYNGMAN RHEE[1]

No account of South Korea's situation would be of any worth without a full description of Syngman Rhee, widely praised by many as a great patriot and condemned by many others as a self-seeking tyrant. The Republic of Korea was characterized by a strong head of state, Syngman Rhee, the very embodiment of the nationalist government. He became, for half a century, almost a legend in both East and West, and is considered a symbol of the Korean struggle for freedom and independence.

Lee, Sung-man, as he is called by Koreans, was born on March 26, 1875, in Hwanghae Province, Central Korea, and went to the Methodist Mission Baeje High School in Seoul at twenty. Just before Japan annexed Korea, he came to the United States and enrolled at

George Washington University at the age of thirty as a freshman, and studied at Harvard for a year to get his Master's degree, and for two years at Princeton, where he obtained a Ph.D. in political science. Before and after he came to America, Rhee was the editor of the first daily newspaper published in Korea; he wrote books and delivered many inflammatory addresses against Japan on behalf of the freedom of the Korean people. He lived in Hawaii from 1913 to 1941, and he was once a school principal and President of the Korean provisional Government-in-Exile. He traveled in many parts of the United States and throughout the world, pleading for aid in the cause of Korean independence, and warning in vain of the menace of Japanese military aggression.

After many years' absence, Rhee returned to South Korea as soon as Japan surrendered in 1945. Although the Allied forces liberated Korea from the Japanese rule, Rhee was greeted as a hero by many Koreans. Without any difficulty, he was elected the first President of the Republic of Korea in 1948 and was recognized by the United States.

Owing to his long exile from his native country, he failed to utilize fully the best qualified persons available in his early cabinet appointments. To fortify his own position in the presidency, he used subordinates who did too little, in preference to those who might do too much. He seldom placed full trust in any of his lieutenants; his closest and most trusted advisers were his Austrian-born wife, the former Francesca Douner, and his faithful secretary, Lee Ki Poong, who became Vice President and later committed suicide because of political difficulties caused by his dishonesty.

Rhee, within a few months of his first administration, began the first of the periodic cabinet shake-ups that became a hallmark of his government. His cabinet appointments were based on the criterion of extreme personal devotion rather than on that of specialized qualification. The average life span of his cabinet members and subcabinet members was about a half-year, and as a result the government was unstable. Owing to the absence of capable advisers, although he did not have administrative experience, Rhee himself decided all administrative matters and later became so involved that he was unable to manage the government efficiently.

After the armistice, Rhee's government grew increasingly authoritarian, and the corruption of officials became a national disgrace. Rhee did not accept new ideas, and gradually isolated himself from the people, partly because of the mental and physical infirmities of old age. The Chief Executive was surrounded by a screen of secretaries, guards, and Liberal party officials who utilized his lack of information for their own selfish purposes.

To impose his will on the Legislature, Rhee declared martial law, ostensibly to curb Communist guerrilla activities, and arrested over fifty opposition assemblymen on vague charges of conspiracy. When Rhee's Liberal party was unable to muster sufficient votes to pass Rhee's bills, its members openly purchased the votes of many legislators, occasionally resorting to the use of force. President Rhee's prestige rapidly waned, and he lost popularity even among the conservative rural population, although he was reelected and again reelected to the presidency under his complete control of all government activities and election procedures.

Syngman Rhee's Korea was a mausoleum of civil liberties run by a repressive 300,000-man police apparatus. The stubborn old man at the head of this machine was not easily persuaded to take good advice. He often used harsh tactics, and instituted direct instead of legislative election of the President when he feared loss of control of the Legislature. President Rhee abolished the office of premier to enlarge his own executive power as Chief Executive, and later abolished his own two-term presidential limit.

Rhee's government was often threatened internally by economic weakness and corruption, and externally by the Communist threat posed by riots, and border raids. Owing to growing rivalry between the quick-tempered dictator Rhee and a prerogative-conscious Legislature, political teamwork for efficient government operation became almost non-existent in South Korea. Rhee left a serious vacuum in the internal political situation in South Korea because he did little to develop leaders for the future service of the country.

Throughout Rhee's government, officials reverted to the old practice under Japanese rule of supplementing their meager salaries with bribes. After substantial bribes to officiating bureaucrats, Rhee's government sold to pro-Rhee businessmen factories, homes, and landholdings formerly owned by the Japanese in Korea. Most Koreans were protecting their own interests, and if there was any altruism it was believed to reside in Rhee or Mrs. Rhee, for whatever they did for themselves was believed to be ultimately good for Korea.

Terrorism kept the opposition in line, and the rations system was often used to keep political obstructionism at a minimum. Revocation of deeds to land distributed under Liberal party pressure was threatened if the owner did not support the party or do his part in voting for the members of the Liberal party. Rhee's personal shortcomings during his twelve-year-reign in South Korea were many: his egoism, his unwillingness to accept criticism, his obsession with his own infallibilty, and his advanced age, a condition over which he had no control but which underscored his tendencies toward inflexibility and irresponsibility. Rhee's prejudices made him so susceptible to manipulation by the wrong people around him that it caused his government to become a dictatorship.[2]

Though Syngman Rhee's South Korea made some progress toward a democratic form of government with assistance from the United States, American aid was often misused for political purposes in three ways: (1) loans to farmers against rice crops were manipulated to enrich middlemen and wealthier growers to the detriment of the poorer cultivators; (2) local irrigation projects were awarded in large part for political considerations rather than for purposes of development; (3) dollar awards for industrial development went to favored politicians. Approximately one-fifth of these projects proved unsound for one reason or another, through unexpected market fluctuations and other factors beyond anyone's control. Americans concerned with the aid program were largely thwarted by Liberal party politicians in control of key roles in the administration.[3]

The Rhee government misused aid funds to the amount of $2.2 billion following the Korean armistice. Of the $24 million worth of U.S. fertilizer supplied each year for sale to small farmers at fixed prices, a "sizable" portion actually wound up on the open market at double the fixed price. The fortunate middlemen were Rhee's Liberals. Rural irrigation dams were built, not where United States engineers thought they were needed, but wherever Rhee's party leaders wanted to reward their local henchmen. American surplus cotton always went to the same twelve textile manufacturers, who bought it at unrealistic exchange rates, and made enormous profits selling the finished goods. One cotton-dealing millionaire who built a $100,000 mansion in

Seoul was a brother-in-law of Rhee's influential chief secretary. Five days before the exchange rate was dropped from 500 to 654 hwan per dollar, the government sold five million reserve dollars to a Korean petroleum company controlled by a prominent Liberal. The list could go on and on.[4]

Disregarding the welfare of the people, the government made a political football of the rice-collection program. The shortsighted policy of terminating the grain-collection system allowed rich landlords and profiteers to sell their rice in the black market at prices higher than those the government paid. The fiasco was tantamount to economic and political bankruptcy of the government.

Political Parties[5]

The history of South Korea's political parties is a tangle of complicated intrigue and shifting coalitions, and even includes assassinations of key political leaders such as Kim Koo, Kim Yun Su, Chang Duk Su, and Yu Fun Young. During the last decade before the ROK Army Coup in May, 1961, two major political parties were developed through several national elections. The Liberal and Democratic parties were pronationalist and anti-Communist; there were also uneasy coalitions of rival groups. During Syngman Rhee's tenure, the Liberal party kept absolute control of the national government and a strong majority in the National Assembly, which was however, by no means a rubber stamp for Rhee. During John M. Chang's tenure, the Democratic party had a majority in the National Assembly after the downfall of Syngman Rhee in April, 1960. Because factional disputes to gain the Chief Executive's favor flourished, the Republic of Korea could not be said to have a two-party system.

President Rhee, deposed by a wave of riots, slipped out of Korea on May 28th and flew to his former home in exile—Honolulu. Officials said he went to Hawaii for a rest, but Mr. Rhee's opponents in South Korea were demanding that he be tried for a variety of alleged crimes. Political support for the founder of the Korean Republic rapidly melted away, and in one day 104 of the 138 members of Rhee's Liberal party in the Korean Parliament quit the party, declaring that they were independents.

Both the Liberal and Democratic parties in South Korea were racked with internal strife. The Liberals' split arose over the case of Assemblyman Lee Yong Bom, boss of the Liberals' Kyongsang Namdo provincial chapter. About mid-November, 1957, an unsigned petition from a number of businessmen in Pusan exposing Lee for utilizing his political influence to "monopolize business and lucrative contracts" was circulated among Assembly members. Similar petitions mailed by Pusan Liberals to legislators on December 19th were "lost" by the post office, according to an announcement by Democratic Assemblyman Kim Ton Wuk on December 23rd. Fellow Liberal legislator Chung Hai Yung strongly supported the petition, and charged Lee with seeking graft in the name of the party and Speaker Lee Ki Poong. Chung insisted that Lee Yong Bom "should quit the chairmanship or be ousted from the Liberal party." Instead, Chung himself was ousted for "wantonly accusing" Lee.

A Liberal group headed by Vice Speaker Lee Jae Hak and Representative Kang Song Tae, former Minister of Commerce and Industry, favored Chung, while another Liberal faction, led by Representative Im Chol Ho, organization chief, and Representative Chang Kyung Keun, chief policy maker and former Home Minister, supported Lee. With the "top brass" lined up against the Im-Chang faction, it was only a matter of time until it was defeated. First, Chang was "exiled" to Tokyo on May 22nd, as a member of the Korean delegation negotiating with the Japanese. Later, when the Liberals' powerful party affairs board was reshuffled at the end of June, the dissenters Im and Chang were both dropped.

The Democrats' dissension, which was even more far-reaching than the Liberals', revealed a deep split between the so-called "old faction," led by party chief Chough Pyong Ok, and a "new faction," led by Vice President Chang Myun. The chief argument centered upon charges of fraudulent handling of ballots at the Democratic National Convention in September, 1956. Representative Kim Joon Yun, erstwhile Chough supporter and member of the Democrats' five-man supreme committee until he narrowly missed reelection at the convention, made the charges informally, early in August, 1957. After a Democratic investigation committee failed to verify the charges, Representative Kim reiterated them in a formal statement on August 12, 1957. He said Representative Park Yung Jong told him that Chough Pyong Ok had confided that some 150 fraudulent votes had been cast "without which Kim would easily have been elected to the supreme committee." Kim also said that Cho Si Hwan, a party organization committee member who had recently failed in a suicide attempt, had revealed in his will that 143 fraudulent votes were cast and that Chough's secretary, Lim Keung Jai, had acknowledged reading it in the will.

The Democratic party's central standing committee publicly denied all charges on August 12, 1957, and ousted both Kim and Park for their "antiparty activities by spreading groundless rumors designed to split the party." Kim later founded the Unification party. Chough commented, "I am extremely sorry, but even my personal friendship, as well as ten years' political association with them, cannot but make way for the integration of the party," and offered to resign as party head. The offer was rejected.

On August 16, 1957, a special Democratic investigating committee also denied all charges, and insisted that Cho Si Huan's will, though mentioning his mishandling of party funds, had said nothing about fraudulent votes. Cho countered with the assertion that he had written two wills and that the one addressed to Chough Pyong Ok contained the statement about fraudulent votes. Chough's secretary, Kim Keung Jei, backed Cho, saying he had seen the unpublished will and had heard Chough refer to the fraudulent votes more than ten times.

That this upheaval was causing repercussions in the party rank and file was apparent when Chough warned provincial chapter chairmen and chief inspectors on August 19, 1957, that "those who either defy the decisions of the executive committee or chime in with the antiparty elements shall be subject to disciplinary action." A widespread defection began, however, and by September 24th a total of 1,480 had left the party. Of these, 430 were from Seoul alone. Seoul City Councilor Kim Jin Yong, an intimate friend of the ousted Representative Kim Joon Yun, joined the defectors on September 10th, charging that "the new faction within the party is beset with vicious practices, dictatorship, and undemocratic behavior." However, on September 11th, the party asserted that most of the politicians who left had either been ousted or made the subject of disciplinary action for their antiparty activities.

The Liberals' and Democrats' disagreement on many questions was reflected in their campaign platforms. A surprising Democratic suggestion was made for the unification of Korea through nation-wide elections supervised by the United Nations—but not, they insisted, either by a "neutral" supervisory team, which might include Communist countries, or by an all-Korean commission outside the scope of the present southern and northern regimes. The Liberals viewed this stand as "antistate," and stuck to their insistence on an election in the North alone.

The Liberals called for strengthened defense with modern weapons, preferably atomic, while the Democrats thought arms might appropriately be cut in an economy move. A threefold economic plank in the Liberal platform—which the Democrats labeled a "blank check"—called for canceling usurious debts of farmers and fishermen, doubling the wages to public servants, and abolishing unilateral tax assessment by government officials. The Democrats also favored tax reform, and sought to disband the Home Ministry so as to neutralize the police.

In education, the Democrats wanted to merge the high schools and middle schools, secure sufficient funds for education, and introduce a scholarship system. The Liberals were in favor of strengthening compulsory education, fostering better colleges and universities, and the expansion of atomic-energy research. In social welfare, the Liberals called for increased labor welfare, full employment, and unemployment insurance. The Democrats sought to keep unions from becoming political tools, to better the social-welfare program, and to set up a credit system for a housing program.

President Rhee's Liberal party continued to dominate the political scene, with the Democratic party next in size and prominence. The recent outlawing of the Progressive party left only a few splinter groups.

Parties registered with the Central Election Committee as of January, 1958, aside from the above-mentioned three, were: Korea National party and Labor-Farmer party with some representation in the National Assembly, and the following four with no Assembly representation: Korea Women's National party, led by Louise Yim, president of Chungang University; Independent Labor-Farmer party, led by Yu Lim; Sammin (the People's) party, led by Moon Yong Che; and Korea Democratic party, led by Kim Byung Yun. Two new parties registering later were the Democratic Reformist party and the Unification party. The Democratic Reformist party, inaugurated on

October 15th, 1957, pledged itself to "freedom from terror and poverty" and the "elimination of corrupt conservative forces." Composed chiefly of former Progressives involved in that party's 1956 split over how to unite reformist forces, it was led by Suh Sang Il, former colleague of the Progressive party chief Cho Bong Am.

The Unification party, inaugurated on November 18th, favored "freedom, democracy, and anti-Communism." Led by former Democratic National Assemblyman Kim Joo Yun, it contained many of Kim's protégés from the so-called "old faction" of the Democratic party. Although it hoped to be a "better party than Democrats or Liberals, based on statesmanlike morality and responsibility," it planned to follow the political course of President Rhee. Understandably, the Liberal party was reported backing the new group financially. The overwhelming conservative victory in the May 2nd Assembly election spurred interest in a coalition of smaller parties—particularly those slightly left of center. Charting a mild course differing from that of Cho Bong Am's Progressive party, they hoped to take a liberal position, offer a platform calling for gradual "reform" of capitalism, and choose a name free from "Socialist taint."

On June 9th the Democratic Reformist party, under Suh Sang Il, and the Labor-Farmer party, under Chon Chin Han, agreed on a merger in answer to what they called a "historical demand" of the masses. The two leaders appealed for "a progressive force" to bring "political freedom and economic equality" to the country. Varying interest was also shown by leaders of the Independent Labor-Farmer party, under Yu Lim; the United Socialist party, under Chong Wha Om; and the Korean Nationalist party, led by Yun Chi Yong; as well as by the more conservative Unification party, under Kim Joon Yun, and elements of the now-defunct Korean Independence party of the late Kim Koo, head of the preliberation provisional government in Chungking, China.

Dr. Rhee threw a bombshell onto the political scene on April 15th when he cited the need for a new party. "This country," he said, "needs at least two political parties so that they may help each other to facilitate its development. If they fail to do so, a new political party must be formed with the aid of remarkable personalities." While Rhee's Liberal party made no comment, a Democratic statement charged the President with going too far because the formation of parties should be the people's business, not his personal concern. "Instead of a new party," it asked, "wouldn't people be happy if he saw to it that the Liberal party became a democratic one?"

Democratic leader Chough Pyong Ok recommended a merger of the conservative parties. "Even before the country is reunified," he insisted, "the conservatives must unite." He said the Democrats were ready to discuss this matter if the Liberal party agreed to: disband in the interest of forming a new conservative party, correct administration errors immediately, and purge betrayers of democracy from within its ranks. On April 16th Liberal Assembly Speaker Lee Ki Poong accepted the merger idea in principle, saying it should definitely be carried out, but not for the time being. On April 21st he questioned Chough Pyong Ok's good sense, and said Chough had in effect proposed the dissolution of the Liberal party.

The left wing in South Korea was very weak because of Rhee's strong conservatism and the effect of the Korean War; gradually, however, owing to a return of political freedom and the idea of peaceful unification through neutrality during the Chang government, it became stronger. After the students' uprising in April, 1950, the young generation in Korea grew increasingly powerful, and advocated the unification of South and North Korea by peaceful means, which was Chang's policy.

Under President Rhee the army was more a security force in South Korea than an arm of civilian government, and no army man had great political prestige under the Liberal party. However, the ROK Army was a relatively unknown but potentially powerful organization in the political landscape, and there were many strong, independent-minded military leaders with administrative experience in its ranks.

Rhee's Administration[6]

Under United Nations auspices, the first representative government came into being in South Korea following three years of United States military occupation after the end of the Second World War. In the first year of the Republic, the government took over assets, responsibilities, and functions from the United States Military Government and began functioning truly as a government in its own right. The United Nations General Assembly recognized the Republic of Korea as the only lawful government in Korea.

The second year of the Republic saw steady growth both at internal and international levels. The Republic's position as an independent sovereign member in the community of free nations was recognized by friendly neighbors one after another during that year. On the first day of 1949, President Harry S. Truman of the United States extended formal recognition to the Republic of Korea.

Meanwhile, the young Republic had already begun to feel the acute necessity for a strong Pacific alliance among free democratic nations in order to face the growing threat of Communist expansion in Asia. In June, civic campaigns for the establishment of such a collective defense system spread throughout the country. In July, President Syngman Rhee invited President Chiang Kai-shek of Nationalist China to Korea to discuss the need for and ways to create such an alliance. The conference of the two chiefs of state at the southern port city of Jinhae in July proved to be of historic significance later, when the Asian Peoples' Anti-Communist League was inaugurated at the same city in mid-July, 1954, with eight Asian countries and localities participating. Internally, the government tightened its anti-Communist efforts by outlawing in October about a hundred political and other front organizations that were under the control of the South Korean Labor Communist party.

As one of the fundamental steps toward the build-up of a democratic economy, the government on June 21st declared in force a Land Reform law. In order to carry out the land-distribution program in conformity with the law, the government surveyed all of southern Korea. It then issued distribution notices to 920,000 farmers. As a result, redistributed land amounted to 310,000 chungbo and vested land distributed to 730,000 farmers amounted to 250,000 chungbo. (One chungbo equals 2.45 acres.) The redistribution assured the farmers of titles to their land, and encouraged production. Meanwhile, landlords who sold their land in compliance with the law were encouraged to change their occupations, and many of them were offered the opportunity, under the Vested Property Disposition Law, to participate in vested enterprises.

Another significant step taken in the economic field was the establishment of a banking system. After an extensive study of banking systems of all foreign countries, the government enacted a Bank of Korea Law and a Banking Law on May 5th. On June 12th the Bank of

Korea began its operations as the central bank of the Republic. Despite some achievements, the year was marked by frustration. The blocking of the Republic's ardent desire for membership in the United Nations was a bitter blow. Its application for admission to the world organization was turned down in the United Nations Security Council on April 8th because of the Soviet Union's exercise of the veto.

The year 1950 was marked by the advent of an unprecedented attack on the existence of the fledgling Republic. The North Korean Communist Army, trained and supported by the U.S.S.R., unleashed an unprovoked attack upon the Republic on June 25th. With twenty-seven members of the new National Assembly missing after the Communists invaded the country, the Assembly left Seoul on June 27th, met first at Taejon, and then at Taegu. Subsequently it moved to Pusan, and returned to Seoul in October along with the government. But toward the end of December both again had to leave the capital.

The second year of the Korean War began with the regrouping of the battle-tried United Nations forces for a counterattack that seemed at one stage to be succeeding in driving the Communist invaders back into the North. In the spring of 1951 the Allied troops pushed on through Seoul, and finally smashed the Reds back beyond the 38th parallel late in May.

Meanwhile, the U.S.S.R. delegate to the UN, Jacob Malik, proposed in June that a truce be negotiated in Korea. The proposal was followed by a lull in fighting, and the subsequent arrangements for truce negotiations—as the Communists intended—occasioned a virtual stalemate in the war. The line of division roughly followed the 38th parallel. President Rhee and the entire nation rejected the truce proposal as a Communist machination intended to gain time for the build-up of the splintered Red combat force. Nation-wide campaigns for opposition to the proposal continued in every part of the country virtually throughout the year. The government and the National Assembly repeatedly made clear to friendly nations the Republic's strong opposition to a compromise truce with the Communists, who were formally labeled "aggressors" by the United Nations.

The year 1951 was marked by an important change in relations between Korea and Japan. Through the good offices of the Supreme Commander of the Allied Powers, the first Korean-Japanese conference opened in Tokyo on October 20th with the aim of restoring peaceful relationships between them. But the first preliminary discussion revealed wide differences of opinion about the issues involved. Both sides agreed that the legal status of Korean residents required immediate settlement, but the Japanese wanted to limit the discussion to this subject alone, excluding all others. The Korean delegation, however, took the view that amicable relations between the two nations required full and frank discussion and settlement of all points at issue.

Later, in November, the Japanese side agreed to seek settlement of a variety of problems, including: (1) legal status of Korean residents in Japan; (2) ship ownership; (3) property rights and claims; (4) fisheries agreements; (5) fundamental relationships. Preliminary talks were recessed on November 28th to allow both sides to prepare for the first full session early the following year.

In the same year a change occured in a top government office when the first Vice President of the Republic, Lee Shi Yong, resigned in May, and the National Assembly elected as his successor Kim Sung Soo, once leader of the Democratic Nationalist party, the forerunner of the present Democratic party. From the very beginning of the year 1952, President Rhee continued to demonstrate his absolute opposition to any compromise with the Communist aggressors, while truce talks dragged on without any material progress and a stalemate continued along the 155-mile battle line.

Apart from the various events related to the war, the year was one of development in politics, the economy, and the international relations of the Republic. The Constitution was amended for the first time, on July 4th, to provide for election of the President by universal vote and for creation of an upper house, the House of Councilors, for the Legislature. The constitutional amendments were preceded by controversies between the Legislature and Executive, but a compromise was worked out in the long run. Under the revised Constitution, President Rhee was elected for a second term by direct vote, and Ham Tai Yung was named Vice President in the August 5th elections. They were inaugurated ten days later, on the fourth anniversary of the establishment of the government. Prime Minister John M. Chang resigned in April, and was succeeded by Chang Taek Sang, a member of the House of Representatives. Chang left the office in October, and Paik Too Chin was chosen by President Rhee. Paik was approved by the National Assembly in the same month.

The year also saw a momentous step taken in the progress of

local autonomy in the Republic. Elections were held in April and May to form local legislative bodies and elect administrative heads for the first time, under the constitutional terms providing for local self-government. In January, President Rhee proclaimed a sea-defense zone off the coastline of the peninsula, which established a maritime demarcation line about halfway between Korea and Japan. Called the Peace Line, it had a triple purpose: conservation of valuable marine resources in Korea's coastal waters; elimination of future friction between Korea and Japan; and sea defense against Communist infiltration. The line was based on the preceding MacArthur Line, the purpose of which was to restrict the Japanese fishing fleets to their own waters.

On November 27th-29th, President Rhee visited President Chiang Kai-Shek of China to discuss strengthening of Pacific community relations among anti-Communist friends in Asia, a talk that laid the foundation for the creation of the present Asian Peoples' Anti-Communist League. A significant event in repairing the war-shattered economy was the signing on May 24th of the Agreement of Economic Coordination between the Republic and the United Nations Command. This agreement was a direct outgrowth of the UN Security Council's request that the Unified Command determine requirements for the relief and support of the civilian population of Korea. Born of the agreement was the existing ROK-U.S. Combined Economic Board, which has guided the economic destiny of the Republic in recent times.

The Korean-Japanese conference, opened in April, 1951, resumed its sessions on February 15th, in Tokyo. The conference set up five subcommittees, each charged with a specific issue to study. Both sides agreed to give priority to the five issues agreed upon at the preliminary discussion in the fall of the previous year. But the subcommittees made little progress, and the conference went into an indefinite recess.

Another event of the year that has been deeply engraved in the memory of the nation was the welcome visit by General Dwight D. Eisenhower, then the President-Elect of the United States, in December. The President-Elect visited Korea from December 2nd to 5th, had three conferences with President Rhee, and inspected the various sectors of the battlefront. His visit was for the purpose of surveying

Korea's military and economic situations in order to find a satisfactory solution to the Korean War, as he had pledged to the American people during his election campaign.

Meanwhile, the National Assembly appealed to the President-Elect for increased military and economic aid, recommending at the same time that the Communist invasion forces be driven beyond the Manchurian border. This recommendation was not heeded. Despite Rhee's ardent desire to attain unification by pushing on to the Yalu River, the Korean Armistice Agreement was concluded between the United Nations Command and the North Korean and Chinese Communists on July 27, 1953, after two years of stalemate. Rhee constantly pressed for a denunciation of the armistice.

On November 12th Vice President of the United States Richard Nixon, and Mrs. Nixon, came to Korea on a four-day visit during their goodwill tour of the Far East. During the visit the Vice President assured the Korean people of continued American cooperation with the Republic of Korea in the struggle against aggression.

President and Mrs. Syngman Rhee and an official party went to Washington on July 26, 1954, for an eighteen-day state visit to the United States. President Rhee succeeded in securing solid United States support to strengthen the ROK defense force to cope with the Communist build-up in North Korea. A mutual defense treaty linking the Republic of Korea and the United States came into force on November 18, 1954.

The Asian Peoples' Anti-Communist League was formally organized in a conference held at Jinhae from June 15th to 18th under the initiative of the Republic of Korea. Attending were forty-two delegates from eight countries or localities in the Asian-Pacific region: Nationalist China, Hong Kong, the Republic of Korea, the host country; Macao, the Republic of the Philippines, the Ryukyus, Thailand and Vietnam. The delegates adopted the principles of organization and four resolutions declaring their determination to fight Communism at all levels and in all ways in their respective countries. A Central Liaison Office was set up in Seoul.

The year 1955 marked the laying of the foundation for stability, checking skyrocketing inflation and stabilizing currency values for further implementation of economic reconstruction. After many weeks of conferences, a Korean delegation headed by the ROK

Economic Coordinator Paik Too Chin reached an accord with the United States Government in Washington on August 15th, to set a new exchange rate of 500 hwan to the dollar. Applied to the foreign-exchange transactions of the ROK Government, to the purchase of hwan by American forces in Korea, and with certain limited exceptions regarding American aid furnished in the form of imports into Korea, the new exchange rate played a key role in stabilizing the currency and implementing the economic build-up.

The year was also one of nation-wide patriotic demonstrations by the people to oust the Polish and Czech Communist members of the Neutral Nations Supervisory Commission from South Korea. In the four months ending in December, more than ten million students, laborers, farmers, and other citizens participated in round-the-clock demonstrations to expel the Communists. At the peak of the peaceful demonstrations, the inspection bodies in Gangnung and Taegu were disbanded and the number of inspectors was cut by half at the remaining armistice-stipulated entry ports of Pusan, Goonsan, and Inchun. In June, 1956, all members of the neutral supervisory body who had been operating in the Republic were removed to the Demilitarized Zone, and the operations of the ineffective truce-inspection teams in the Republic were suspended.

On November 28, 1956, the Republic of Korea and the United States signed a Treaty of Friendship, Commerce, and Navigation in a move to strengthen the bonds of friendship and to encourage closer economic and cultural relations between the two countries. Signing for each country were Foreign Minister Cho Chung Whan and American Ambassador Walter C. Dowling. The treaty later was ratified by the legislatures of both countries.

The treaty contained twenty-five articles and a protocol. Under the treaty, each of the two countries, in brief: (1) agreed to accord, within its territories, to citizens and corporations of the other, treatment no less favorable than it accorded to its own citizens and corporations with respect to carrying on commercial and industrial activities; (2) formally endorsed standards regarding the protection of persons, their property, and interests that reflect liberal and enlightened legal and constitutional principles; (3) reasserted adherence to the principles of nondiscriminatory treatment of trade and shipping.

During 1957–1958 the Republic took a dynamic step toward the overdue modernization of the Armed Forces of the Republic and the United Nations in Korea to offset the military imbalance created by the illegal build-up of Communist military strength in the North. This period was marked by a remarkable stride in the government's long-term efforts for the reconstruction of the economy, particularly the development of constructive industries. On June 21st the United Nations Command opened the way to modernization of the United Nations forces in Korea by scrapping Paragraph 13D of the Armistice Agreement, which banned introduction of new weapons. Following this development, modern United States jet planes began touching down on bases in South Korea, and modern arms of atomic capability, including the Honest John rocket, were brought into South Korea. The government hailed the United Nations decision as the first step toward the restoration of South Korean and United Nations forces to defensive parity with the enemy. It also expressed hope that this action would be soon followed by the denunciation of the entire Armistice Agreement.

Outstanding economic achievements during this period began with the signing in January, 1957, of an agreement with the United States for continuation of the 500 to 1 hwan-dollar exchange rate for the remainder of the year. In February another agreement was signed between the two nations, under which the United States Government would sell Korea $18.9 million worth of surplus agricultural products, and would lend most of the proceeds in hwan to Korea for development purposes. In September two huge industrial plants projected by the United Nations Korean Reconstruction Agency were put into operation—a cement plant at Moongyung with an annual production capacity of 200,000 metric tons, and a flat-glass plant at Inchun, with a capacity of 12 million square feet of glass a year.

On September 18th to 21st, Ngo-dinh-Diem, President of the Republic of Vietnam, officially visited Korea on the invitation of President Rhee. Through a series of conferences, the two Presidents reaffirmed their common determination to fight Communist activities, and emphasized the necessity of cooperation in the cultural field in order to safeguard the true values of Asian civilization as the basis of democracy in their two nations.

From April 25th to 28th the Prime Minister of Turkey, Adnan

Menderes, visited the Republic upon the invitation of the government. He held talks with the President and Foreign Minister of Korea, in which they reviewed the international situation and in particular discussed problems of common interest. They shared the belief that none of the free nations can coexist with the enemies of freedom.

At the end of 1957, the Republic and Japan reached agreement for the resumption of their long-suspended negotiations. Under the agreement, Japan officially withdrew the controversial Kubota statement and its claim to 85 per cent of the property in Korea, the two conditions the government had demanded as the prerequisite to resumption of talks. At the same time the two governments agreed to mutual release of detainees.

Negotiations were opened on April 15, 1958, one and a half months behind schedule, in Tokyo, and both sides agreed soon afterward on an agenda, which included: (1) fundamental relations; (2) fisheries and the Peace Line; (3) Korea's property rights and claims; and (4) the legal status of Korean residents in Japan. The conference set up four subcommittees to deal with each item of the agenda, and all of them, except the one on fisheries and the Peace Line, went into session. The Republic had also exchanged legations with Germany, and embassies with four friendly nations. Four of them, namely, those in London, Manila, Saigon, and Bonn, were elevated from the status of legation. On May 2, 1958, general elections were held to elect 233 representatives to the fourth House of Representatives. The new House went into session on June 7th with Lee Ki Poong elected as Speaker and Lee Jae Hak and Han Hi Suk as Vice Speakers, all of whom were from the Liberal party.

South Korea's first government had similarities to both the American presidential system and the British parliamentary system. The President had strong executive powers. He nominated a prime minister, who had to be approved by the National Assembly but who was not required to be a member of the Assembly. Under certain conditions a vote of nonconfidence could be cast by the Assembly against the prime minister, but this in no way affected the President's position. On the other hand, the President on his own initiative could arbitrarily force the resignation of the prime minister.

The country's first Constitution, promulgated on July 17, 1948, provided for election of the President by the National Assembly. The term was four years. As the time for the second election neared, in 1952, it appeared doubtful that incumbent President Syngman Rhee would be reelected. Strong pressures were then brought to bear on the National Assembly by the executive branch, using methods of a very questionable nature, which resulted in the passage of a constitutional amendment on July 4, 1952, changing the method of choosing the President to election by direct popular vote. The amendment also added a House of Councilors to the National Assembly, with the original Assembly becoming the House of Representatives. A month later, in August, Dr. Rhee was reelected President.

A second constitutional change occurred in November 1954. The government Liberal-party-dominated House of Representatives voted on November 27th on a bill to amend twenty-eight articles of the Constitution. It was generally assumed that under the law 136 votes in favor were required for passage. Only 135 were cast for the bill, and the presiding vice chairman, a member of the Liberal party, declared it rejected. However, the next day an official government spokesman stated that according to the government's interpretation the measure had passed, and announced its immediate promulgation.

Three important points in the amendment were: (1) the abolition of the office of prime minister and authorization for the President to preside directly over the State Council and appoint its members; (2) the then incumbent President Rhee was exempted from the constitutional limitation of two consecutive four-year terms; (3) provision was made for the Vice President to succeed the President should the latter die in office.

The internal political situation in South Korea was confused and fraught with strife and unrest in 1956. The key factor in South Korea's presidential election on May 15th was the power held by President Syngman Rhee. He had the power to force the National Assembly to make an exception to the Constitution enabling him to run for office for life; he had the power to secure his party's unanimous nomination for third-term candidacy; he had the power to make the people draft him as a candidate; and he had the power to elect himself. His supporters and his English-language newspaper, the *Korean Republic,* boasted that "his victory in the election is a foregone conclusion." Of course, with his vast force of agents, he did not have to canvass for votes personally. In other words, Koreans were resigned to the fact that the election would be a mockery of democracy. Opposition parties had been made so impotent during Rhee's eight years of rule that they could not contest the presidential elections with any measure of effectiveness. The all-powerful incumbent not only controlled the military and police forces, but the nation's finances as well. Other candidates were subjected to political pressures and financial hardship in their campaigns, since businessmen were afraid to make any contribution to the opposition lest they incur Rhee's wrath.

In 1956 a major new party, the Democratic party, was founded by opposition leaders. It nominated P. S. Shinicky and John M. Chang, as presidential and vice-presidential candidates respectively, to run in the coming national election of 1956. The Liberal party nominated incumbent Syngman Rhee as presidential candidate for a third term, and selected Lee Ki Poong as its vice presidential candidate. A third party, the Progressive party, nominated Cho Bong Am and Pak Ki Chool as its candidates. Shinicky died suddenly just a few days before the election. He was not replaced, since the Korean election law made no provision for a new nomination.

The death of Shinicky, former National Assembly chairman, resulted in political confusion, although Rhee's ultimate reelection was generally conceded; the main question was the size of his majority. Shinicky's death did not, as was supposed, open a new way for a "united front" of the Democratic and Progressive parties to unseat the Rhee administration.

Rhee, named by the Assembly in 1948 and elected under martial law in 1952, was reelected without opposition on May 15, 1956, polling 54 per cent of the presidential vote. The only real race was for the Vice Presidency, with seven candidates contesting for the role of the man who would become heir apparent to the Presidency before 1960, as Rhee was then eighty-one years of age. The 3,500,000 votes of the independents decided this battle. The death of Shinicky and the withdrawal of the Progressive candidate gave John Chang a good chance to edge out Rhee's running mate, Lee Ki Poong.

Syngman Rhee was elected, obtaining 5,000,000 votes. Cast for Cho were 2,100,000 votes, while 1.8 million votes were declared invalid, most of which were presumably cast for the deceased Democratic party candidate, whose name remained on the ballot. John M. Chang won the vice presidential race, receiving 4,000,000 votes to 3.8 million for Lee Ki Poong.

In countries where free and democratic elections are held, a change in the party in power occurs from time to time. The election of the Democratic party's vice presidential candidate and the large vote cast for the Progressive party presidential candidate, as well as for the deceased Shinicky, gave every indication that the Korean people also wanted a change. Two years later, in the general elections of May, 1958, for the House of Representatives, the indication became more pronounced when the Democratic party increased its seats from 48 to 79.

Rhee's government charged the *Kyung-hyung Press,* one of three leading newspapers in South Korea who supported Chang, and its editorial writer with instigation and propagation of a rebellion against Syngman Rhee's administration. This Catholic-backed newspaper was closed down on April 30th by Information Director Chun Sung Chun, an American-educated Protestant.

Rhee's Korean Supreme Court upheld the death sentence imposed on Cho Bong Am, a reformed Communist who served as Minister of Agriculture and Forestry in President Rhee's first cabinet in 1948. He was arrested in January, 1958, and was sentenced by the Seoul District Court to five years' imprisonment, but was sentenced to death by the Rhee government's appeal to the Seoul Appellate Court. The head of the outlawed Progressive party, and twice an unsuccessful candidate for the presidency against Syngman Rhee, Cho was said to have made contact with the Communist North to overthrow Rhee's government.

As the election date approached, it became obvious that further unusual measures were being taken by the Liberal party to ensure election of its candidates. Presidential candidates from three minor parties were forcefully prevented from registering; the registration of many voters was disallowed in the cities, where Democratic Party sentiment was particularly strong; and widespread police intimidation was reported in rural areas.

On election day many registered voters in Seoul and other cities were openly denied the right to cast their ballots. In the armed forces the marked ballot had to be shown to unit officers before being cast, and in the country voters were required to enter polling booths in groups, so that secrecy was impossible.

There were even divisions within divisions. Intraparty bickering, heightened by the National Assembly elections, was almost matched by a major tug of war among different branches of government—in some cases within the same branch. The issues frequently touched the Constitution itself. A major political problem in the executive branch was how to handle John Chang who, though a member of the opposition Democratic party, was elected Vice President in 1956. There was a tendency to play down or ignore the Vice President's role, and there was also a concerted attempt to change the Constitution, thus erasing Chang's succession to the presidency in the event of President Syngman Rhee's disability or death. Rhee's Liberal party played an important role in blocking the creation of a House of Councilors, the National Assembly's upper house, which the Vice President was supposed to head.

The election resulted in the new Republic's electing a President from one party and a Vice President from another, with different parties' interests conflicting in the executive body, although the Vice President's only duty under the ROK Government structure was to administer such tasks as the President assigned to him. To secure the full cooperation of the opposition party, the ROK Government was faced with the problem of changing its cabinet members.

The consequences of this election pointed up the fact that time was needed to develop the people's understanding of what constitutes a democratic election and effective administration, based on the democratic principle of separation of power.

Korea's Security Law[7]

The steady loss of ground by President Rhee and his Liberal party in the presidential election of 1956 and the legislative election of 1958 brought in its wake panicky attempts to control every phase of South Korea's life. Despite Rhee's protestations, to him there was no law but his rule, and his will was the will of the people.

The Taegu mayoralty won by the Democratic candidate marked the end of the era of government-appointed mayors, because the Local Autonomy Law, promulgated in 1956, called for the people thereafter to elect their own civic administrators. The nation-wide implications of the Taegu election proved the unpopularity of Rhee's government and his Liberal party. On November 30th Rhee's party sanctioned the abolition of both direct and indirect elections and submitted a revised Local Autonomy bill to the Assembly on December 11th. This bill was killed by the Home Affairs Committee on December 23rd.

The bill that caused the greatest national consternation was the one amending the National Security Law and submitted to the Assembly on November 18th. From the outset the Rhee government insisted that the new bill was designed only to combat Communist infiltration, but to many it appeared designed to squelch all political opposition, as well as individual liberties. The provisions of the law were too broad and so vague that the Rhee government's dragnet could catch any "fish" it desired.

Legislative feelings on the National Security bill had been intense for months, but what really ignited them was the Liberals' unilateral passage of the bill in the Legislative and Judiciary Committee on December 19th. The committee, composed of ten Liberals and six Democrats, began its meeting at 3:00 P.M. The six Democrats, tied up at a parley of their own, showed up exactly three minutes later. In the intervening time the Liberals had seen fit to pass the controversial bill and report it out. Angry and stunned Democrats throughout the Assembly, insisting vainly that the action be nullified, began a sitdown strike in the main Assembly hall to forestall the bill's passage there in a similar surprise move.

When Liberal legislators entered the hall on December 20th and security officers tried to clear it of mattresses and other articles the strikers had used the night before, there was a fight in which two Democratic legislators, Kim Chae Kon and Kim Eung Ju, were injured and sent to the hospital in an ambulance. But the strike continued.

Liberal leaders insisted that the committee's passage of the bill had been legal, and urged the strikers to leave the hall unconditionally and apologize for their "illegal acts." The Democrats demanded that the bill be nullified, and pledged a fight to the finish for its revision or withdrawal. All negotiations broke down on December 21st with a joint statement that "no solution could be found despite the

efforts of both parties to solve the extraordinary political situation."
Vice President Chang briefly visited the strikers on December 21st for
a round of encouragement and handshaking.

Seoul police cordoned off the National Assembly Building area
on December 22nd and rerouted traffic from nearby streets, while
policemen assigned to the scene carefully checked pedestrians who
wanted to pass the building during rush hours. On Christmas Eve
some three hundred "security guards" entered the Assembly chamber
at 9:40 A.M. and dragged out the strikers bodily, taking them to a
restaurant in the basement and a club office on the first floor where
they were kept under guard for the rest of that day's session. At the
end of the hour-long struggle—with eighty-five strikers (seventy-nine
Democrats and six independents) fighting three hundred "guards"—
many legislators were injured, three were knocked unconscious, and
eight were hospitalized.

Later, Democratic legislators charged that the "guards" were
actually policemen whose wages for the "extracurricular" duty were
illegally obtained. The National Assembly Law requires consultation
with the Steering Committee on any change in the number of security
guards and on any appropriation of over 1,000,000 hwan from the
Assembly budget. The three hundred "security guards" hired from
December 23rd to 31st involved an estimated 15,000,000 hwan for
new uniforms and salaries, yet the Steering Committee had not
authorized a cent of the expenditure. Metropolitan Police Director
Lee Kang Hak denied the guards were policemen, but the Democrats
remained unconvinced.

When the session officially opened at 10:43 A.M., not a single
opposition legislator was present. On hand were 128 Liberal legislators and a number of high-ranking government officials. The chairman
of the Legislation and Judiciary Committee broke the record his
committee had set a few days earlier with a two-minute report on
that committee's action. Justice Minister Hong Chin Ki then gave
the administration's view of the bill. When the Liberals passed the
bill by a vote of 128-0, it was exactly 13 minutes after the session
had opened. Within the next 42 minutes, or by 11:38 A.M., two more
vitally important bills were passed—those revising the Local Autonomy Law and the House of Councilors Election Law. Eighteen minutes after the afternoon session began, the 1959 budget bill was

passed with no discussion. By the time the session recessed at 4:22 P.M., the total number of bills passed that day had reached 22. At the close, Speaker Lee Ki Poong expressed "regret" at the opposition's "absence" from the voting.

The National Security Law, the Local Autonomy Law, and the House of Councilors Election Law were promulgated on December 26th and went into effect on January 15th. The main agency to enforce the National Security Law was to be an anti-Communist intelligence bureau, to be set up in the attorney general's office in accord with an amendment to the Prosecutor's Office Law. An election for the House of Councilors was to be held not later than January 24, 1959. However, Rhee's Liberal party long avoided creation of an upper house for the National Assembly because they feared the loss of their seats to the opposition Democratic party. An amendment to the Election Law for the House of Councilors was passed, together with twenty-one other bills, without discussion on December 24, 1958, leaving the date for the formation of the upper house to the discretion of the President.

The press was up in arms over provisions of the National Security bill relating to freedom of speech. A group of editors issued a statement on November 21st declaring that the bill was designed not only to infringe on freedom of the press but also to crush fundamental human rights. They said they would work to defeat the bill and would "spare no efforts to accomplish our object." The statement was signed by editors in chief and editors of the *Kyung-hyang Shinmun, Chosun Ilbo* and *Hankook Ilbo,* and editors of the Donghwa News Agency, *Orient Press, Hankook Kyungjai* (Economic) *Shinmun, Dong-A Ilbo,* the *Korea Times, Yunhap Shinmun,* Hapdong News Agency, and *Jayu Shinmun.* Four official and semiofficial publications that did not sign the statement were the *Seoul Shinmun, Seige Ilbo,* Segye News Service, *Sanup Kyungjai Shinmun* and the *Korean Republic.*

Strong reaction to the legislative railroading came from all levels. Vice President Chang and former Chief Justice Kim Byung Ro flatly called the bill's passage illegal. A ground swell of resistance against the bill began some time before its actual passage. Genuinely spontaneous demonstrations sprang up all over South Korea. On November 28th Metropolitan Police Director Lee Kang Hak announced that, effective immediately, no outdoor assemblies would be permitted for an unspecified period of time. He said information had been obtained of a major Communist plot to subvert the country, and denied that there were political motivations for the restriction. He said the measure would affect even religious gatherings, student meetings, and annual public events. The basis for this ruling, said Lee, was Ordinance 55 of the United States Military Government, which he considered still existent despite Article 100 of the Constitution, which says, "Existing laws and ordinances shall be in effect to the extent that they do not conflict with this Constitution." The ruling would certainly appear to conflict with Article 13 of the Constitution, which says, "Citizens shall not be subjected to any restrictions on the freedom of speech, press, assembly and association except as specified by law." The Democratic legislator Yun Hyon Nam and thirteen colleagues proposed a resolution on December 1st to rescind the ban on these grounds, but no action was taken.

There were scores of demonstrations that were invariably suppressed by the police. Though leaflets were scattered, signs carried, and slogans shouted, the only demonstrations that managed to get under way before being dispersed occurred on Christmas Day in Pusan and Taegu. After these two rallies took place, Seoul police set up a mobile patrol team of some hundred policemen to remain at headquarters, and another hundred were under orders to stand by.

The best organized protest came from a group of politicians (chiefly of the Democratic, Democratic Reformist and Labor-Farmer parties), journalists, writers, lawyers, and other figures from all over South Korea who gathered at the Taesung Building in Seoul on December 23rd to form an opposition. On December 24th the group denounced the forced passage of the twenty-two bills as "shameless and illegal," and declared: "Fellow countrymen and youths! Will you stand by and watch the gallant representatives of the opposition fall in the fight for democracy and freedom in this country? Or will you join in our holy crusade to save our ailing country? You have to make a choice—life or death!" They also said: "All is not over yet. Despite lamentation and shock at this hour, we will fight for democracy and freedom in this country to the last."

The Rhee government was not idle while this opposition movement was forming. On December 2nd the Liberal party formally inaugurated the Anti-Communist Combat Committee to back the National Security bill. It embraced the Liberal party and Liberal-affiliated groups, such as the Federation of Korean Trade Unions, the National Society, and the Korean Women's, Farmers' and Fisherman's associations, as well as the Anti-Communist Youth Corps composed of former prisoners of war.

Another Liberal-backed organization was the Anti-Communist Youth League, formed on January 22nd to help work out Dr. Rhee's plans. With members of the Kookminhoe's (National Association) Youth Construction Corps forming the main nucleus, the other merging groups were the Anti-Communist Unification Youth Association, the Korean Anti-Communist Youth Group, the Student Volunteer Corps, the Korean Youth Affairs Institute, and the Young Workers' Association. Three days after this group was formed, the Democrats announced plans to form their own youth group. Although this Anti-Communist Youth League was organized at a large indoor rally in Seoul's Municipal Theater on January 22nd, it was not until January 25th that the police announced permission for indoor gatherings.

The tremendous political upheaval in Korea naturally caused comment from other nations. The United States Government, which on December 22nd said through spokesman Lincoln White, "This is an internal matter of Korea on which we have no comment," on December 24th indicated in a prepared statement: "We are disappointed to note that the majority Liberal Party and the opposition Democratic Party did not reach a settlement of this issue in the Assembly. We hope that this legislation will be implemented so as to counter the threat of Communist subversion and that it will not hinder the continual development of democratic institutions and processes in the Republic of Korea." While many observers considered the American statement remarkably restrained, this view was apparently not shared by the backers of Rhee.

President Rhee announced that he was a candidate for a fourth term. City mayors and village heads were appointed, not elected, and President Rhee increased the number of Supreme Court judges. At the end of their ten-year terms, he might either retain them or deny them reappointment. The independence of the judiciary was called into question. Though the government assured the public that the new security law would be administered with meticulous concern for popular rights, many Koreans disputed the abolition of local elections. The reason given for the abolition was that during the past ten years rural Koreans had shown their inability to choose capable city and county officials. An effective system of checks and balances had not yet been implemented, and fear prevailed that President Rhee could, under an omnibus security law, silence all political protests.

Basic democratic principle—government by the full and free consent of the governed—has rarely been challenged in Korea. The test of a new young nation must be how well that ideal is kept alive. It was therefore hoped that the omnibus security law would be implemented in such a way as to counter the threat of enemy subversions without hindering the continued development of democratic institutions and processes in a free Korea. However, peacemaking efforts were set back when President Rhee of the Liberal party met with Vice President Chang, a Democrat. This rebuff caused more difficulty in making a compromise. The ensuing nation-wide political crisis in South Korea deeply disturbed the United States as the main sponsor of the fledgling democracy.[8]

The 1960 Election[9]

Although his Liberal government lost face when 50,000 Koreans in Japan chose repatriation to North Korea, and although it had grown unpopular owing to President Rhee's autocratic methods, Rhee acquired, not unjustly, the title of "Father of the Country," and became the embodiment of the nationalistic Government of South Korea. Though Rhee was eighty-five year old, he was to seek reelection for an unprecedented fourth term. Since President Rhee was the only figure nationally known among Korea's illiterate people, he was practically impossible to beat at the polls, although he was the oldest man among the chief executives of the world.

President Rhee's major opponent, the sixty-five-year-old Democrat Chough Pyung Ok, fell ill, and died, virtually assuring Rhee of a fourth four-year term. Without a change in the election laws, the opposition Democratic party was not able to renominate another presidential candidate. The presidential election date was changed to March 15th from May for the purpose of avoiding interference with spring planting. Without an opponent, President Rhee undoubtedly would poll one-third of the total of 10,400,000 eligible voters. For the third time in three campaigns, death erased President Rhee's major opponent in the presidential election. One by one, Dr. Rhee's most redoubtable opponents for the position of Chief Executive had been struck down by death. In 1952 the Progressive party leader Cho Bong Am became the candidate for the presidency, but he was convicted of having plotted with Communist North Korea and was hanged on July 31, 1959. The Democratic party's popular P. H. Shinicky died of a heart attack ten days before the presidential election in 1956.

With President Rhee's age as a factor, the vice presidential race became much more important, since the President and Vice President were not elected on a single ticket in South Korea. Actually, the Vice President emerges with only two duties: to preside over an upper house when and if it is created and to carry out tasks that may be assigned by the President. The real race for the Vice Presidency was between Korea's leading Roman Catholic layman, John Myun Chang, and Rhee's running mate, Lee Ki Poong, Speaker of the National Assembly.

A dramatic exposé of alleged irregular election plans of Rhee's Liberal party was made by the opposition Democratic party twelve days before the March 15th presidential and vice presidential election. A seventy-one-page letter to the Central Election Committee outlined the facts that had been "ascertained" through the help of conscientious police and other public officials.

Reported Liberal plans for the campaign period included the maintenance of a close watch on the movements of regular voters as well as of Democratic sympathizers, and on those of foreign diplomats, reporters, and merchants in Korea; the uncovering of past and present misdeeds of Democratic followers and their families, and encouragement of Democratic factional feuds; the restriction of opposition campaigners' activities and the buying off of opposition election committeemen with money or promised offices.

Alleged plans for voting day included: assurance of an 85 per cent vote for the Liberals by (*a*) prior stuffing of one-third of the total ballots—marked for the Liberal ticket—into polling boxes, and (*b*) by forcing voters to cast their ballots in the presence of others, ensuring a two-thirds majority; mobilization of Anti-Communist Youth League members and other action groups, provided with Liberal armbands and green uniforms, to keep people one hundred meters from the polling booths while waiting to vote; and restriction on activities of opposition election committeemen and ballot checkers.

The Democrats urged the Central Election Committee to take the following measures to curb election irregularities: recognition of the right of an opposition committeeman to put his seal on ballots and on polling boxes after the voting was over; installation of a single polling box at each polling booth to prevent voting in so-called three- or nine-man groups; the right to vote privately; guarantee of freedom to remain inside the hundred-meter-limit line from the polling booths; restriction on entry into polling booths of plain-clothes men and uniformed policemen to times when they were requested by the relevant election committees.

The Liberal party, of course, strenuously denounced these charges on the same day they were made, on March 3rd. One spokesman called the exposé "unfounded drama, full of unimaginable falsification," and the then Home Minister Choi In Kyu labeled it "fantastic fiction."

The semimobilization of all segments of society into the Liberal campaign was apparent throughout the period. On March 4th the Democrats protested to the CEC against numerous newspaper advertisements and leaflets put out by various social and trade associations in support of the Liberal party. Such activity, they charged, violated Article 26 of the presidential and vice-presidential election law, which provides that no one but heads of candidates' election offices and their prescribed campaigners should work for any candidate. The Democrats also complained that the assumption of posts on the Liberals' central electioneering committee by some presidents and university deans violated articles 24 and 27, which state that teachers should not take part in political movements or influence students to support or oppose certain political parties.

The Liberals countered that the activities of various associations were not "electioneering movements" but part of the Liberal party's natural efforts to expand its membership, while the election activities of presidents of private universities were not unlawful since such men were not civil servants. However, Article 41 of the law on educational civil servants says the provisions should apply to directors and teachers of pivate schools. Although the armed forces were supposed to have nothing to do with active campaigning, this was not always the case. On March 10th the Democrats' Cholla Namdo chapter accused the four army commanders of violating the election laws.

The Democrats charged that Colonel Kim mobilized soldiers and used military equipment in favor of the Liberal party during the campaign and that General Kim, of the 31st Division and the Infantry School, respectively, formed three- and five-man teams of soldiers and allowed their men to paste campaign posters inside the military compound.

The police were blamed by Democrats and other opposition groups for interference during the campaign period, the election itself, and afterward. Their influence was apparent in the opposition's attempts to acquire suitable places for public gatherings. The vice-presidential candidate John Chang commented on March 5th, after a campaign tour, that "in every city wherein I spoke, the local administration was very careful not to let me use a large area. It is a mean and base strategy, degrading Liberal prestige and helping to draw popular sympathy to the opposition side." Other spokesmen scored the "deliberate sabotage" obvious in such cases as the then Home Minister Choi In Kyu's March 2nd ban against use of the Han River banks because such places were "unsuitable for maintaining public order." Candidates from splinter parties had even worse luck. Legislator Kim Chun Yon and Miss Yim Yung Shin—running for Vice President on the Unification and Korean National Women's Party tickets, respectively—were refused the use of public sites throughout their "whistle-stop" tours.

On March 1st, "Samil Day" or the forty-first anniversary of the 1919 independence movement, strange posters appeared in the major cities under the name of the nonregistered "Save the Country Iron-Blood Society." They showed Democratic candidate Chang, in Japanese wartime national uniform, posing with Japanese officials, and referred to his Japanese name—Tsutomu Tamaoka—and outlined Chang's alleged association with Japanese authorities and activities during World War II. Although President Rhee, conveniently vacationing at Chinhae, reportedly said, "We should not treat the Vice President in such a way," and asked the Home Minister on March 2nd to have the posters removed, the Democrats felt they could never have been placed so extensively—and during curfew at that—without the help of the police. Significantly, the Kyongsang Namdo police chief praised the posters on March 3rd as an "expression of patriotism."

Other Liberal campaign and election practices were deplored by the opposition. One was the printing and use of bogus ballots to "instruct" the populace on how they should vote on election day. What brought on the criticism was the discovery that 80,000 voting slips had been printed by the Liberal party's Kyongju branch in six local printing houses. On March 10th Democrats demanded that the Liberals be prohibited from using sham voting slips on the ground that Paragraph 2, Article 82, of the presidential and vice-presidential election law restricts the issuance of ballots to nonelection supervisory organizations. The Kyongsang Pukto provincial election committee ruled on March 11th that sham votes could be used if the size and type of print differed from that of the regular ballot slips issued by the election supervisory commission. On March 11th President Rhee ordered Home Minister Choi In Kyu to put an end to such "disturbing" election campaign methods as "practical voting with imitation ballots," but by then the ballots had done their damage.

A practice the Liberals had used earlier in National Assembly by-elections, and which the Democrats rightly guessed would be used again, was "group voting," where individuals entered the polls in groups of three or nine. On March 8th Liberal legislator Cho Sun insisted that "the group action will end when the members of the group are inside the polls," but admitted that the units were designed to "secure internal consolidation among the Liberal membership on the voting day." Democratic spokesmen Cho Chae Chun, of the National Assembly, and Hyun Suk Ho, organization chief, insisted on March 9th that the units resembled the "cell units in Communist societies, having been organized through coercion," and urged the Liberals to disband them "because their formation is against constitutional provisions on freedom of association."

Another bone of contention was the voters' lists. On February 27th—three days after a "confirmation period" for the lists closed—a total of 52,874 persons objected to the exclusion of their names from voters' lists compiled by town ward offices. The Democrats charged that the lists might have been tampered with so as to include "ghost voters," and Assemblyman Cho Chae Chun demanded that they be reexamined in the presence of representatives from both parties. But on March 4th Liberal legislator Han Hui Suk called the Democratic charges "nonsense," and said, "We do not intend to disturb their [the Liberal party's] examination of the list of voters within the legal provisions."

Still another unhappy factor was the handling of registration of Democratic voting witnesses. By the March 11th deadline, only about half the Democratic checkers had been able to register because of what Democratic organization chief Hyun Suk Ho called "deliberate sabotage by officials" who absented themselves from their offices during office hours. He said a number of registrants had withdrawn or "had disappeared, having been threatened if they did not do so." The CEC instructed its lower echelons on March 11th to "recognize as legally registered checkers those who have not been formally registered but who have evidence that they did report to the relevant committee for the purpose of registration." Hyun advised such individuals "to appear at relevant polls, and attempt to enter them." Getting past guards at the polls, however, was another matter.

Some checkers who did manage to register still had problems. As of the day before the election, March 14th, in different parts of South Korea seven poll observers had been assaulted. Near the Kimpo International Airport, one was stabbed ten times by unidentified youths only two minutes after the chief of the Yanksuh-myon police was reported to have been at the scene. Other violent incidents occurred up to, during, and after election day. On March 7th a busload of Democratic campaigners was held up in broad daylight on the Wulsan-Unyang road in Kyong-sang Namdo by a group of unidentified masked men. They forced all passengers to get out, searched their baggage, destroyed all loudspeaker equipment they found, and left in two trucks immediately afterward. A "shortage of manpower" kept nearby policemen from inspecting the scene. Wulsan police said on March 9th that the violence had not been planned but had occurred "coincidentally" and that the mobsters who attacked a passenger did not know he was a Democratic campaigner. One wonders how the absent police were so clairvoyant on these men's motives!

Death also figured in the picture. Kim Myong Ho, treasurer of the Democratic chapter at Yosu, Cholla Namdo, was beaten to death with iron rods and wooden sticks on March 9th by seven or eight mobsters who also injured Kim Bong Chae, managing director of *Yosu Ilbo*. The mobsters attacked them at about 7:30 P.M. as they were installing loudspeaker equipment at the office of the Democratic Yosu city chapter. The wounded men said two plain-clothes men were present during the assault but disappeared. National Police announced on March 11th that they had caught the principal offender— one Chung In Suk, twenty-two and unemployed—who allegedly told them he had assaulted Kim because of Kim's personal hatred for him. A Liberal electioneering committee said police findings showed the party had nothing to do with the case.

As election day approached, the atmosphere grew more tense. Opposition forces, feeling the need of group cooperation in urging a free election, formed the Committee for Fair Election on February 28th. Its aim was to propagate, through nation-wide publicity media, the people's "constitutionally provided right to vote for their own choice and to refuse interference in their choice." Chang Lee Wook, a leader of Heungsa-dan, was named chairman. Almost all opposition leaders of minority parties—even the two unwanted running mates of President Rhee—were included, as were many lawyers, journalists, and writers.

The government promised that everything possible would be done to assure a free election and that violators would be prosecuted. Then Home Minister Choi In Kyu announced on March 10th that a special police force, including traffic police, would be deployed around the polls and ballot-counting offices to guard against possible terrorism. (This was not necessarily helpful, however, since the police often either instigated or passively observed incidents of terrorism.) Choi said the next day that the Ministry of Commerce and Industry would instruct electric-distributing companies to ensure a continuing supply of current to the counting offices, where in past elections sudden blackouts had facilitated ballot switching and other misdeeds.

When the election finally took place on March 15th, 97 per cent of the nation's 11,196,490 eligible voters cast their ballots at 8,108 polling places throughout the country. The island province of Cheju Do had the highest voting rate, 97 per cent. Returns complete except for one of South Korea's electoral districts gave Syngman Rhee 9,512,793 votes as unopposed candidate for President. Vice-presidential candidates came out as follows: Lee Ki Poong, Liberal party, 8,220,587; John M. Chang, incumbent, Democratic party, 1,844,257; Kim Chun Yon, Unification party, 245,526; and Yim Yung Shin, Korean National Women's Party, 99,090.

Lee Ki Poong, who had lost out to Chang in 1956, received nearly four times what Chang polled this time. Chang did not win over Lee in a single district, even in Seoul where he had scored a 4.5 to 1 victory over Lee in 1956. Chang received 378,399 votes this time compared with 509,693 for Lee. In Kosung, Kangwon Do, a former Communist area north of the 38th parallel, Chang received only 37 compared with Lee's 15,518. President Rhee, in Seoul, where he did poorly in 1956, received 72.2 per cent of the total of 948,245 votes cast, or 673,796.

The number of invalid votes totaled 1,228,896, or about 11.3 per cent of the total of 10,862,272. The CEC did not specify for whom the invalid votes were cast, but it was apparent that they went for the dead Democratic candidate Chough Pyong Ok. The UN Commission for the Unification and Rehabilitation of Korea (UNCURK) made a token observation. It sent out five teams, each headed by one of the five resident representatives to the UNCURK committee, and including two or three Korean assistants. Eight teams from the American Embassy made their own observation.

Vice President John Chang charged on March 14th that the "people have been completely deprived of their sovereign rights," and on March 16th that the election had been held in the grip of "illegality, terrorism and murder." Democratic spokesman Cho Chae Chun, in a dramatic gesture thirty minutes before the voting booths closed on March 15th, called the election "illegal, null and void" and said the Democrats would seek a court injunction to invalidate it. Just before the official announcement of the Liberal victory was made in the National Assembly on March 18th, Democratic legislators pointedly walked out in protest. Before they did so, they observed a brief silence for those "who died for the cause of a fair election," and shouted three slogans: "The March 15th election is illegal, null and void!" "Out with Syngman Rhee's administration!" and "Hold another presidential and vice-presidential election!"

The Democratic party filed a suit in the Supreme Court on April 11th against Kim Doo Il, a justice of the Supreme Court who was also the CEC chairman, to invalidate the election. The brief listed the following grounds: (1) the CEC mishandled elections by tolerating an "early election," which deprived about 400,000 eligible voters of the right to cast their ballots; (2) the CEC "assisted" Liberals and police in election frauds and irregularities, and election workers helped the Liberal party by stuffing about 40 per cent of the total votes in bundles in ballot boxes in advance of or during balloting; (3) the registration of Chang Taek Sang and Park Ki Chul as presidential and vice-presidential candidates was obstructed by "terroristic forces" on February 13th, the deadline for registration.

In the National Assembly on April 11th—the same day the Democrats filed the nullification suit—Democratic legislator Lee Chong Nam called the March 15th election "unacceptable in a legal as well as in an ethical sense," and gave the following points: (1) Opposition checkers were almost entirely deprived of the right to inspect ballot boxes, having been obstructed by police, men of the Anti-Communist Youth League, and unidentified gangsters. (2) Five methods of election rigging were employed—(*a*) open voting; (*b*) voting by timing organized groups of voters; (*c*) voting in teams of three or nine men each; (*d*) double balloting (approximately 50 per cent of eligible voters were deprived of the right to vote); and (*e*) voting in bundles. (3) Administration branches on the whole were involved in the election rigging—the police being under secret instruction to cast 80 per cent of ballots either before or after the start of voting, all marked in advance for the Liberal party. The CEC, when asked to correct these irregularities, had refused to take up the request. While the CEC chairman had earlier promised to guarantee free access to polling booths, this applied only to Liberals with armbands, men of the Anti-Communist Youth League, public servants, and police. (4) The police, Anti-Communist Youth League members, public servants, and other unidentified gangsters committed acts of terrorism and created more than a hundred casualties, including nine deaths.

The first successful antigovernment parade since the Republic of Korea was founded was held in Seoul on April 6th. Rhee had ruled against such demonstrations but did not try to stop it, most probably to convince foreign visitors from the International Press Institute of South Korea's "freedom"—press and otherwise. Police kept bystand-

The First Republic President Syngman Rhee.

In Seoul Korea University students swarm through the streets denouncing "rigged" March elections. (*ROK, Korea Today 1961*)

ers from joining the original two thousand in the parade, but thousands kept abreast of it and shouted the slogans "Out with Syngman Rhee's administration!" "The March 15th election was illegal; we want a reelection!" and "Don't disturb the freedom of peaceful assembly and demonstration!" There was some clubbing of youths and other violence at the close, but this was not part of the main demonstration.

The Democratic party was not the only one to file an election-nullification suit. Independent legislator Chang Taek Sang urged the Supreme Court on April 2nd to nullify the March 15th election on the following grounds: (1) the registration of Chang and of Park Ki Chul, former Progressive party vice chairman, for presidential and vice-presidential candidates, was blocked; (2) the CEC erred in turning down their registration documents, submitted at 7:00 P.M. on February 13th, without sufficiently checking as the law stipulates; (3) the "early election"—four months ahead of the legal deadline of July 15th—deprived about 400,000 voters of the right to cast their ballots (about 1,000,000 eligible voters are added every year); (4) the election should be nullified because of the widespread evidence of fraud and irregularities.

Student demonstrations were held in Seoul, Taejon, Suwon, Pusan, Osan, and Chinhae before and after the election. Despite National Police Director Lee Kang Hak's warning on March 11th that participants "will be punished severely by law after the election," and despite the often brutal police retaliation on the scene—there was frequent evidence of personal courage. Placards and handbills were carried or scattered by students' at their risk.

The Rhee government relied on the handy alibi of "Communist infiltration" when internal disorders arose. This time was no exception, but the charge was made belatedly. Vice Attorney General So Chin Sup said on March 30th and again on April 13th that the Masan riots, at least, showed no evidence of instigation by Communist espionage agents. Even Rhee urged on April 13th that the people not participate in any riot that would "eventually provide Communists with good opportunities." However, on April 19th Ambassador Yang You Chan insisted that his government strongly suspected Communist influence. He said that the Pyongyang radio had broadcast hourly exhortations to the rioters, that Communist leaflets had been passed out during the demonstrations calling for overthrow of the government and for the withdrawal of United Nations and United States troops, and that the buildings of the ROK Army counterintelligence group and the Anti-Communist Youth League—which he insisted had nothing to do with domestic politics—were among those burned.

The United States Government, however, believed "the demonstrations in Korea were a reflection of popular dissatisfaction over the conduct of the recent elections and repressive measures unsuited to a free democracy." An earlier American Embassy statement pointedly referred to "the justifiable grievances toward which the demonstrations were directed." The text of the statement given in Washington on April 19th by Lincoln White follows:

The Secretary called in the Korean Ambassador this afternoon to impress upon him the profound and growing concern of this government over the serious continuing public unrest and acts of violence in Korea. Although these matters are admittedly the responsibility of the Republic of Korea, this government—that is to say the United States—has been obliged to take cognizance of them. This is because the United States, as the principal sponsor of the Republic of Korea as an applicant for United Nations membership, has in the eyes of the world always been closely associated with Korea as a friend, supporter and ally.

Korean Ambassador Yang was informed that this government believes that the demonstrations in Korea are a reflection of popular dissatisfaction over the conduct of the recent elections and repressive measures unsuited to a free democracy. The Secretary asked Ambassador Yang to draw to the attention of his government the seriousness of the repercussions abroad which are likely to result in a marked weakening of the Republic of Korea's international position and prestige. The Secretary suggested that the Korean government should, in its own best interest, and in order to restore public confidence, take necessary and effective action aimed at protecting democratic rights of freedom of speech, of assembly, and of the press, as well as preserving the secrecy of the ballot and preventing unfair discrimination against political opponents of a party in power.

A phenomenon of the election year had been the prevalence of student demonstrations. For the first time there seemed to be a concerted ground swell of feeling throughout South Korea that even the familiar threats of reprisal and cries of "Communist infiltration" could not stem. The consequences of this election in Korea pointed up the fact that time was needed for a young nation to learn the peaceful, orderly political behavior so essential to a two-party system and to develop the people's understanding of what constitutes a Democratic election.

THE KOREA OF THE STUDENTS[10]

The spirit of freedom triumphed over tyranny in Korea. The despotism of twelve years finally fell before the wrath of the Korean people. Fortunately, the April revolution was carried out with a minimum of bloodshed and destruction. The glory belongs chiefly to the Korean students, in the vanguard of freedom, who behaved magnificently in fighting and in maintaining law and order. Credit should also go to the ROK Army, which scrupulously saw to it that those who demand their legitimate rights were protected. They, together with the students, were truly soldiers of freedom.

If the Korean student had not been willing to die at the barricades before the Kyung-Mu-Dae, then justice would have perished throughout Korea. This was increasingly the belief of many people, irrespective of political affiliations, as day by day the magnitude of the evils fostered by the Rhee regime was disclosed.

Before examining the grievances that finally provoked the students to revolt, two important facts must be mentioned. First, Communist agents had nothing to do with the revolt. Communists, as always, may have tried to take advantage of the situation, but they had no part in instigating the demonstrations. While political corruption was undoubtedly the chief agent in precipitating the uprising, the students were not motivated by political considerations. The issues were moral and spiritual, not political. Evils of every kind were steadily encroaching upon the supreme human values of liberty and justice. Without these precious possessions, life would be empty and meaningless. Cynicism was increasing, pessimism was the prevailing mood, and no one had a word of hope or salvation.

The Korean student, influenced by tradition and custom, is often shy and reticent in the presence of foreigners, but the stranger, if tactful, will soon discover that the educated Korean has an unusually active and keen mind, alive to the importance of the problems that confront Korea today. They are aware that the very survival of South Korea as a free and independent state is uncertain. It is surrounded by enemies, and suffers from severe economic difficulties greatly aggravated by the Korean War and the subsequent division of the country. The Republic supports a large army at great cost; it is plagued by an enormous "black market"; and it receives foreign aid in amounts that easily lead to corruption. In such critical times many people realized the importance of a strong, honest, intelligent, and democratic government devoted to the service of the people and welfare of the state. Only a small group of Liberal party stalwarts, and an even smaller group of uninformed people, believed that the government was sincere in its oft-repeated declarations of concern for democracy and integrity. Most people believed that the government had become corrupt and hypocritical.

Everyone knew that Communism was a serious threat to South Korea, but thoughtful people rightly suspected that the Security Law was being used more to protect the ruling party from its political enemies than to secure the country against the dangers of Communism. The students, as well as other people, saw in the Anti-Communist Youth League another dishonest trick by which "hoodlums" or "gangsters" could be recruited to defend the government by assisting the politically conditioned police in ugly situations. It was quite obvious that some of the worst evils of Communism were being employed under the guise of anti-Communism.

Students were also disgusted with compulsory parades and organized enthusiasm. For the government to proclaim a holiday or organize a parade to celebrate "Human Rights Day" seemed ironical and hypocritical. Possibly one of the most blatant acts of hyprocrisy was the decision to fix the date of the election on March 15th for the "benefit of the farmers,"—in reality, for the benefit of Syngman Rhee. Stories of corruption may have been exaggerated, but everyone knew that the friends of the government were a highly privileged class, especially in the matter of obtaining loans from banks. If prosperity followed the loan, and frequently it did, the Liberal party expected a thank offering.

The love of money had corrupted even more people than had the love of power. One was often shocked to see such luxury in a city of great poverty. Even schools and colleges, established by Christian missions, and possessing great prestige in America, might be crowded with the children of the rich, and have few or no scholarships to offer the children of the poor.

For some time evil of every kind had been employed with remarkable success, and there seemed no reason why hyprocrisy, deception, and corruption should not be continued as the strategic policy for the approaching presidential elections. But evil has a habit of getting out of control. As the campaign got under way, one or two Democrats were killed; photographers were beaten by thugs; open voting for members of the "one happy family" was practiced either by advice or by coercion; ballot boxes were "stuffed"; and corrupt police and hoodlums played their part effectively. As anticipated, there was a tremendous victory for the Liberal party candidates. Though the aged President was shielded by his efficient bodyguards and secretaries, he knew what was happening. Big celebrations with parades and fireworks, to commemorate the victory, were canceled, owing to reports of growing unrest and widespread indignation against the shockingly corrupt methods employed by the government party to win the elections.

Men intoxicated by power are unreliable judges of their own behavior, and insensitive to the feelings and opinions of others. At Masan, evil got completely out of control, and police fired into a crowd of indignant and outraged students and citizens who were protesting against the election campaign. Investigation showed that most were shot in the back while fleeing from the police who had protected the friends of the government during the campaign. Within a few days the great political victory was being recognized for what it was: an overwhelming moral disaster. Though a small group of Liberal party members were among the first to denounce the evil strategy employed by their own party, they were immediately warned to obey party bosses or expect punishment.

The citizens of Masan and Pusan refused to be bullied or intimidated by the police, or deceived by the official lies of "Communist instigation." In spite of warnings, demonstrations continued both in these and in other cities. Opposition members denounced the elections as fraudulent and invalid. The situation was rapidly worsening for the government. The United States informed the Rhee government of its great concern, and warned against the continued use of severe repressive measures.

Ever since the illegal passage of the Security Laws and Local Autonomy Act with the help of hoodlums and under the threat of armed police, many students had been desperate to find means of dealing effectively with the two major contemporary evils: the slow but sure death of democracy and liberty and the increasing vitality and spread of corruption. Suddenly faith triumphed over despair, paralyzing perplexities and problems vanished overnight, and the students, joyfully and courageously, accepted their task of restoring democracy and of shattering the monstrous evil that had come to believe in its own omnipotence. The shocking scandals of the election, the ever-threatening police, the brutal attack at Masan, the courage and defiance of the people—seemed to act like a moral catalyst, and the Student Revolution was born. The students of Seoul, which is the scholastic as well as the political center of Korea, were on the march, chanting their slogans: "New and honest elections," "Return to democracy," "Neutrality of students," "Freedom of the campus," "Our demonstrations are peaceful, not political."

The story of the Student Revolution will be recorded in the annals of Korean history as a great and memorable event. Though it is not within the scope of this book to deal with the details of the demonstrations, the final tragic events that terminated the presidency of Syngman Rhee, the unknown power and influence of Park Maria, and the delegated authority of her weak and ailing husband, Lee Ki Poong, it is necessary to speak of some of the many important events that followed rapidly one after the other during the fateful week of April 18th to 24th. First, the sudden and brutal attack upon the dispersing students of Korea University.

There had been no clash between students and police on Monday. The behavior of each had been exemplary. Following the advice of their president, Yu Chin Oh, the students were returning to the university campus, when, in the dusk, agents of the police suddenly attacked them with clubs, stones, and heavy pieces of chains. In Seoul alone there were approximately seven hundred hoodlums at the disposal of the police.

The brutal attack aroused the anger and intensified the courage of every student. One could not help admiring their spirit when, on the following day, with arms linked and chanting their slogans, they marched down University Road, Chong Ro, to the barricades erected at the Kyung-Mu-Dae, and to their death.

Provoked to anger by police brutalities and by their disappointment at not seeing the President, to whom they wished to relate their grievances, they exhibited remarkable restraint. To see them driving fire engines, trucks, jeeps, and taxis they had captured or commandeered, and celebrating the victory they anticipated, was an unexpected termination to a day that might easily have ended in serious rioting.

During several fateful weeks, events followed rapidly one after another, marking the beginning of the end. On February 28, 1960, the Democratic party launched its presidential campaign at Taegu, a liberal stronghold. The Democratic party's Vice-President-elect arrived for the rally that began the dramatic Taegu incident. On Sunday students were unexpectedly ordered to attend school. Realizing the true nature of this order, which had been planned to keep the students away from the Democratic rally and the opportunity of hearing Dr. Chang's speech, the students gathered in groups of thirty and forty, and began to march toward the banks of the Susong River, where the Democratic rally was to be held. At 1:30 P.M. students gathered in front of the government's offices and called for their academic freedom. Suddenly police swooped down and dispersed most of them, arresting about thirty students who had led the demonstration. Police tried to attribute the student demonstration to a political party's plot. But in the end they released the students after finding out that they were demonstrating for liberal action solely on their own initiative.

Under the Constitution, the right to vote by secret ballot in a free election is guaranteed. Nevertheless, this right had been abused by the police measures implemented by the Liberal party. Home Minister Choi In Kyu assured Dr. Rhee of his reelection—even if he had to use strong-arm tactics. On election day the Democratic party issued a statement revealing the fraud involved in the election and demanded that the elections be nullified. At the same time the Democratic party headquarters in Seoul telegraphed instructions to their provincial branches, ordering their voting observers to withdraw from the polls. Upon receiving the message, the Democrats of the Masan branch thronged the streets and began demonstrating anew, shouting, "We oppose the unfair elections!" During the election, police surrounded ballot booths, interfered with the voters' secret ballots, and committed other election irregularities. By 7:30 P. M., on March 15th, the Liberal party announced its victory by claiming 80 per cent of the votes cast.

The angry citizens of Masan began to demonstrate throughout the city. Police suppressed the demonstrators by firing upon the citizens, causing many deaths and hundreds of injuries. Though the government authorities called this tragic incident "a Communist-inspired movement," news of the brutal police action at Masan spread throughout the country, and the issue became a national one.

On April 11th a fisherman of Masan drew up the mutilated body of Kim Chu Yol, seventeen, missing since the March 15th election-day demonstration. It was here that the national explosion began. Public sentiment against the police and the elite of the Liberal party began to boil. About twenty girls from Masan Occupational Girl's School, standing at the head of the crowd, shouted, "Let's wage a demonstration!" They left the Masan Provincial Hospital and headed for Old Masan at 6:05 P. M. As the demonstrators marched through the streets, spectators joined their ranks. Upon reaching the Nam Sung Police barrack, the demonstrators, now numbering nearly five hundred, shouted out to the police officer on duty, "Give us the one that committed the murder!" A number of students stoned the police barrack. All the windows were broken, and the astonished police officers within sought to escape. Demonstrators dashed inside and destroyed and burned all the documents.

The next targets attacked were the Masan City Hall and the Masan Police Station, both of which served as the bastions of the Liberal party in its implementation of rigged elections on March 15th. The two buildings were battered with rocks. Rioters went on to attack the house of an assemblyman who had betrayed the Democratic party, then the party out of power. They continued on to numerous other public buildings and to firms, factories, and the homes of those who were known as the chief supporters of the Liberal party.

With table legs, signboards, and stones in their hands, demonstrators again marched on the Masan Police Station. Upon reaching the station, they pulled the police chief's jeep out of an alley and set it on fire. They broke into the ammunition storeroom at the police station and took some grenades, wounding the security section chief and twelve other police officers. The chief, bleeding from serious wounds, was dragged in front of the crowd by some demonstrators.

At the height of the demonstration, the police force became confused under the vigorous hail of stones and clubs, but they later regrouped in preparation for a counterattack. They were issued rifles with which to crush the will of the citizens who dared wage battle against authority. Several demonstrators were shot to death. Under the rain of bullets, demonstrators scattered throughout the city, in numerous streets and alleys, still stoning public buildings and carrying clubs. Their destructive demonstration did not subside until after midnight.

The following morning, April 12, 1960, the demonstrations continued. A raging crowd headed by high-school students demonstrated continuously from ten that morning. The anger and excitement of the citizenry erupted in fury, and they joined the students. The number of demonstrators had reached nearly three thousand when they were again met with police bullets, and again they had to yield to superior force.

On April 16th a group of students who had not participated in the previous demonstrations marched peacefully, with flowers, in the memory of Kim Chu Yol. When they shouted at a police squad, they were met with tear gas and water from fire hoses. As the result of the clashes between the demonstrators and the police, one boy was shot to death and seven other people were injured, some of them seriously.

Because the force of the police could not be matched by that of barehanded demonstrators, the Second Masan Incident, which ultimately led to the Korea-wide April Revolution, subsided. Nevertheless, this incident incited uprisings in major cities throughout the country as the freedom-loving people protested against the unfair treatment of students, political interference in schools, and rigged elections.

The April 18th demonstration by the students of Korea University followed. Police vainly tried to hold back and disperse the overwhelming flow of students as they forced their way through the police barricades and headed for downtown Seoul along Chong Ro Street to Capital Avenue.

Around two o'clock in the afternoon, the students, shouting their slogans and singing, began a sitdown demonstration in front of the National Assembly Hall, completely blocking traffic in the area. After hours of protest, the students finally began to disperse in compliance with a request by Representative Lee Chul Soung, a member of the Democratic party. Lee persuaded them to return to their schools and homes, saying any complaints about the government should be resolved by the politicians. He also promised that he would take steps to act upon their complaints and would attempt to give them satisfactory answers.

While the students were returning to their schools, they were attacked by the police-controlled political hoodlums. The incident took place near the Chon-Il motion-picture house, not far from the East Gate Police Station, and there were dozens of casualties on both sides.

College-student demonstrations were first undertaken by members of the College of Liberal Arts and Sciences of Seoul National University. At 9:30 A.M., on April 19th, about two thousand students marched in the streets with placards reading, "No one can be trusted" and "The people lament bitterly."

The demonstrators were met by the police force, which had been alerted for any mob action. About fifty armed policemen launched an attack upon the demonstrators, and they were dispersed in about five minutes. Despite the tear-gas bombs, the students' will to fight was unrelenting. They re-formed, and marched through a smoke screen toward the National Assembly Building. This time they were met by a police force of nearly two hundred. The brutal attempt of the police to quell the demonstrators was followed by mass arrests.

By 10:40 A. M. the number of demonstrators had increased to nearly a hundred thousand. The spontaneous response to the call to join the students in the fight added enormous strength to the masses of demonstrators, and most colleges and universities in the city were represented. Around 11:50 A.M., the police attempted to repel three thousand student demonstrators whose target was the presidential mansion. At the sight of the students swarming toward their barricade, the police opened fire on the marchers. The students continued to march forward. When the distance between the mob and the first barricade, fortified by barbed wire, was only forty yards, rifle fire and tear-gas explosions became heavier.

Unable to repel the wave of violent demonstrators remorselessly approaching them, the police force behind the first barricade began to pull back. Their preplanned tactic was to meet the demonstrators behind a second barricade at the entrance to Kyong-Mu-Dae, the presidential mansion, where they had concentrated all their attacking force.

Having seen the blood of their comrades shed, the students cried out, "Let's take the lives of the murderers!" and "Freedom and democracy belong to us!" Overcoming their fear of rifle fire, they kept marching, and the street became a bloody battleground. When demonstrators reached a point about fifty yards from the last fortress, the entire police force opened fire. Phalanx leaders began falling to the ground as rice plants yield to the scythe at harvesttime.

The rioters managed to push two streetcars toward the barbed wire in an attempt to break through the barricade. Another attempt at breaking the barricade with a jeep failed. Finally, their desperate struggle succeeded when they used wire clippers. With a fire truck in front of them as a shield, demonstrators tried to get near enough to break into the presidential mansion. They demanded punishment for the hoodlums who had attacked the Korea University students, and the immediate dissolution of the Liberal party's government.

The frightened police were now firing indiscriminately into the crowd, causing numerous casualties. The demonstrators began to throw stones at the police, destroyed police boxes, set fire to the Anti-Communist Center Building, the *Seoul Shinmun,* a government-controlled daily paper, and other buildings. Law and order in the capital city had become a thing of the past.

Emergency Martial Law was proclaimed throughout all major cities in an effort to restore law and order. At the same time, many allied countries, including the United States, expressed deep regret over the brutal police tactics used in dispersing unarmed demonstrators who were fighting to establish democratic principles.

The government, however, disregarding the opinions of friendly countries, refused to take the request for granting fundamental rights of the people into immediate consideration, and ignored these honest demands.

By nightfall, from the hilltops outside Seoul, searchlights played across the empty city. The dark bulks of army tanks stood at the main intersections, and troops with fixed bayonets guarded government

buildings. Smoke from still-smoldering ruins hung over Seoul as it
had over the war-wrecked capital ten years earlier.

On April 24th Dr. Rhee announced his "divorce" from the
Liberal party, and promised to "seek to serve the nation solely as its
Chief Executive at the head of its administration." Following is the
text of his statement:

The terrible tragedy of April 19th has left a deep scar upon Korea
and the hearts of our people. Our beloved nation has been shaken and
our prestige in the free world has been grievously damaged. I have no
words to express the depth of my sorrow for the shocking loss of life.
All who died are members of our ancient Korean family, and our grief
is that of close relatives mourning the loss of their loved ones.

Especially our boundless sympathies go out to the fathers and mothers
and the brothers and sisters of those young people who laid down their
lives so prematurely. We pray to God that the wounded will be healed
quickly and that never gain shall we suffer such pain and such disgrace.

In examining my own conscience I have carefully considered my
thoughts and actions as the nation's Chief Executive for almost twelve
years.

I believed it was essential to establish strong political parties in order
to have a democratic nation and to help bring about liberation of the
northern half of our country from the Communists. It seemed that par-
tisanship would permit moderate differences and lead to a national
policy reflecting various points of view.

Political parties would eliminate excesses of factionalism, I thought,
and strengthen the application of democratic principles. As in other
free nations, this should have led to free and strongly constructive
government—or so I hoped. Consequently, I not only founded the Liberal party but sought to encourage a sound opposition. Right or wrong,
for better or worse, parties are now established. They cannot be wished
out of existence—only made better.

But I have come to think that it will be better for me—as the President—to divorce myself from the party and seek to serve the nation
solely as its Chief Executive at the head of its administration. From
such a position, and without partisan interest or inclination, I can join
our people in encouraging political parties to purify themselves and serve
the interests of the nation unselfishly.

All our parties should stand for freedom and for democratic practice
in all things. When they do, the liberties and the safety of the people
will be augmented and our parliamentary representatives will be able to

enact sound laws and develop healthy and honest institutions to serve nation and people. Additionally, and to encourage the implementation of these changes, I hope that our government adminstration will be taken completely out of politics. Public servants then will be able to carry out their duties with honesty and complete fairness. Thus can we correct the mistakes of the past and assure Korea of efficient and incorrupt administration.

At the same time, such a fresh, objective approach to government will assure impartial justice in punishing those whose guilt is connected with the recent civil disturbances. We want no retribution, but we do want the punishment of any who murdered and destroyed, and we must have a government trusted by all who make certain that such is the case.

These are fundamental changes, and they will be made as rapidly as possible. Members of the cabinet have already tendered their resignations in order to accept the responsibility for what has happened. These resignations will be accepted. I am now trying to find new and able men to head the various departments of the government. Only those who command the trust and respect of the people will be considered. In order to obtain such persons, I am consulting with elder statesmen and leaders from various walks of Korean life, and this without regard to their former political interest or lack of it.

Any delay will be solely because it is difficult to find men who are sufficiently outstanding, and also because I want to be absolutely sure that they measure up to the expectations of the people. Government work is now piling up, and the appointments will be made and announced publicly at the earliest possible moment.

After that, I know that the people will support the new ministers in their efforts to bring order and public service into the government, to enhance morale, to develop the nation's strength and to lay a sound strong groundwork for the unification of Korea under freedom and democracy.

I am personally confident that Korea will emerge from this time of trouble stronger and more united than ever before. As always, I pledge my own best endeavors and my very life to this cause. The sorrow that has afflicted us strengthens my own determination to serve the nation and people selflessly and with greater success for all the days that may be left to me.

Dr. Rhee's statement, however, did not seem to satisfy anyone. The newly resigned Vice President John Chang commented on April

24th that Rhee was dodging "the fundamental issue of a new election," and said the nation was awaiting "deeds, not words."

Student agitation—which had come to be known as the "4/19 Movement" in honor of the tragic April 19th incident—boiled over again on April 25th, the day after Dr. Rhee's "divorce" statement. Two hundred university professors drew up a fifteen-point declaration, supporting the students' fight, at a meeting in the faculty building of Seoul National University Medical College. They then marched three miles to the National Assembly building—gathering a crowd of around ten thousand en route—and an elderly professor read the declaration aloud point by point as bystanders cheered. It demanded that the president and other high administrative officials, legislators, and Supreme Court justices step down and that the National Police be neutralized, urged the dismissal of politically appointed professors, and praised the students' demonstrations as a "genuine expression of popular grievances against injustice and corruption" but advised them to stay out of politics.

The professor met no police resistance such as had crippled the valor of the student demonstrators. They were reinforced and joined by about two thousand students and other supporters of their cause. After nightfall, the steel-helmeted troops enforcing martial law were moved to assist the demonstrators by guiding them in the dark streets. Under the protection of the soldiers, who came to sympathize with the demonstrators, the spirit to fight against authority flamed even higher. The shouts of the people echoed through Seoul.

On April 26th demonstrations began at five o'clock in the morning. Not fearing the armed troops at various spots in the city, the people of Seoul became excited enough to resist any force that might be sent against them. About sixty students commandeered a passenger bus and several taxis and drove them through the streets. Crowds along the way shouted encouragement, and soldiers merely watched them pass by.

The ROK Army troops posted in Seoul showed almost complete indifference to their assigned tasks of keeping the crowds dispersed. By their indifference they gave the impression of siding with the people. Their sympathetic attitude toward the common cause gave heart to the demonstrators, who carried on unhindered by authorities. The soldiers restrained some of the more violent demonstrators, not to put the demonstrations to an end but to keep some semblance of order in the city. The soldiers were keenly responsive to the shouting of the crowd, which was chanting, "Set them free!" ROK troops were fully aware of the injustice done the people and of the unbearable conditions under which they lived. Although tanks and squads of soldiers were in evidence, aside from throwing over a hundred tear-gas shells into the throng and urging it to disperse over loudspeakers, the army did nothing. Students surrounded the soldiers, occasionally roughing them up but avowing their friendship. Troops sometimes explained to bystanders, "We are soldiers, but we are Koreans too, and these are our people."

On April 26th the tempo accelerated. Some 100,000 persons demonstrated near Dr. Rhee's mansion, shouting, "Get out, Syngman Rhee!" They took over at least six army tanks and ten army trucks. Junior high school students toppled Rhee's statue in downtown Pagoda Park. The next day they were chased by collegians who, though demanding Rhee's resignation, realized his role in Korean history and were determined to put "the President" back in his place. They recovered the body but not the head. Police fired on demonstrators at Dongdaemun Police Station near the Seoul East Gate, killing or wounding at least thirty. The police station was set aflame.

On April 26th the National Assembly, in an unprecedented move, unanimously demanded Rhee's resignation. Only a quorum, or 136 out of 233 members, was present. The resolution also called for nullification of the March 15th elections, creation of a "perfect" parliamentary system of government with a prime minister elected by the Assembly, dissolution of the present National Assembly after it altered the government structure, and holding of new elections for the President, Vice President, and a new National Assembly.

Dr. Rhee issued a statement, also on April 26th, in which he made a few concessions:

Since I returned home after the liberation, I have lived in amity with all patriotic people, and I have no regrets. I have always wanted to do, and will continue to do, whatever the people desire and follow.

I received the report that our beloved young students and other patriots are demanding several things of me. I will follow their wishes in my judgment. One thing I request is that our brethren keep in mind the Communist forces above the 38th parallel, who at this moment are seeking every chance to invade us; we should do our best not to give the Communists any such chance.

1. I will resign from the presidency if the people so desire.

2. Since there are reports of many unfair practices in the March 15th presidential and vice-presidential elections. I have instructed that new elections be held.

3. In order to eliminate all frauds in connection with the last elections, I have told Speaker Lee Ki Poong to resign from every public position he holds.

4. As I have already stated, I will agree with the constitutional amendment for a parliamentary system.

The United States Embassy in Seoul made the following comment on April 26th, the same day Rhee issued his statement:

The United States Embassy is watching with deepening concern the anguish of this nation. We fully support the effort being made to maintain law and order in Seoul and other cities. There is an obligation on the part of the Korean population to support the authorities in maintaining order. There is an equally deep obligation on the part of the authorities to understand the sentiment of the people and to take immediate adequate action to meet justifiable grievances. All measures by demonstrators and authorities alike must be adequate to maintain law and order as well as to provide justice and to produce real forthright solutions. This is no time for temporizing.

In Washington, on April 26th, the Department of State called a meeting of representatives of the sixteen nations that had fought in Korea. All but South Africa and Ethiopia attended. Lincoln White, as spokesman, told reporters that Assistant Secretary of State for Far Eastern Affairs J. Graham Parsons had reviewed the situation, and said, "Those present joined in expressing the hope that there would be an early resolution of the situation in a manner which would permit the orderly functioning of democratic government in the Republic of Korea."

Also in Washington, Ambassador Yang You Chan resigned on April 26th because of "mistakes" in assuming "Communist influence in the rioting in Korea." He noted that "a diplomat is an honest man sent out to lie for his country." On April 27th Ambassador Walter

P. McConaughy returned from a visit to Dr. Rhee "convinced that the authorities are earnestly working toward redressing the justifiable grievances of the people." He called this "a day that will long be remembered by the Republic of Korea and its many friends abroad."

President Rhee was informed that public sentiment was running against his government. His adviser was Commander in Chief of Martial Law General Song Yo Chan. He conferred with Dr. Rhee for about fifty minutes, finally persuading the President to consent to meet with representatives of the demonstrators. The representatives consisted of three ordinary citizens, a college student, and a high school student. When they met Dr. Rhee face to face to submit the letter of declaration, they burst into tears.

The letter delivered by the spokesmen contained the following conditions: resignation of the President; reelection of a President and Vice President; deprivation of Vice President Elect Lee Ki Poong of all public offices; and establishment of a cabinet system of government. Stubborn and obstinate though he may have been throughout the twelve long years of his reign, President Rhee had no alternative but to gratify their demands by making it known to the people that he would resign as President. He also agreed to fulfill the other conditions that the latter demanded.

At 10:30 A.M., on April 27th, a new era began when President Syngman Rhee released a message stating that he was willing to resign from the presidency. The President's four-point statement follows:

1. If the people so desire, I will resign the post of President.

2. Since it is reported that there were many irregularities in the March 15th elections, I have already ordered new elections, for the posts of President and Vice President.

3. I have already advised Speaker Lee Ki Poong to completely withdraw from all official positions.

4. If the people so desire, efforts will be directed to amend the Constitution and adopt a cabinet system, as I have already agreed.

President Rhee bowed to the inevitable. In a one-sentence announcement, issued through the Office of Public Information, he said, "I, Syngman Rhee, honoring the resolution of the National Assembly, resign as President, and wish to devote the rest of my life to the nation and people as a citizen."

The Assembly accepted his resignation on May 3rd, and the government was turned over temporarily to the new Foreign Minister, Huh Chung, who had been named to that post on April 25th. Also named on the same day were Lee Ho as Home Minister and Kwon Seung Yul as Minister of Justice. The cabinet had resigned en bloc on April 21st. The National Assembly, of which Lee was speaker, passed a resolution on April 27th urging Lee's resignation and that of six other Liberals. The prevailing mood of the population was one of near delirium. One correspondent wrote that "the reaction and emotion were the greatest since the liberation from Japanese rule in 1945."

On May 9th, eleven days after ex-President Rhee had moved out of the presidential palace and into Pear Blossom Villa as a private citizen, President Eisenhower sent him the following letter:

The vastness of the events which have taken place in Korea has claimed the attention of the entire world. I can assure you that no one has followed them with more anxious sympathy than I.

With your voluntary withdrawal from political life, I am reminded ever more strongly of how much your country will remain in your debt. The rebirth of Korea in 1945 was the fruition of your long years of patient and arduous labor. Your tenacity and indomitable courage at a time when the Republic was the prey of Communist armies won the admiration of the entire Free World as well as the gratitude of all Koreans. Since then, under your guidance, Korea has recovered from the deepest wounds of that conflict and is today a monument to your life-long work.

I cannot but feel that your decision, momentous as it is, is yet another example of wisdom as well as selfless service. I assure you that the United States will continue to feel itself bound by strong ties of sympathy to Korea under your successors.

My best wishes for many years of health and happiness in the honored retirement which you have done so much to earn.

Dr. Rhee issued the following comment on the President's letter on May 9th:

President Eisenhower's letter moves me deeply—not because of personal sentiment addressed to me, but because of the pledge of continued American friendship and support for Korea. If my own resignation has contributed to safeguarding Korean security and independence, then it is worth while on that ground alone, and without regard to domestic political considerations involved.

The Korean position of President Eisenhower and the American people is vitally important to this country, and I am confident all Koreans will rejoice at renewed evidence of U.S. dedication to the free, democratic, prosperous, and united Korea we all want. This is another reason, I believe, why the Korean people will give President Eisenhower one of history's greatest welcomes when he comes here in June. Speaking from my retirement, and having renounced all political considerations for the rest of my life, I urge my fellow citizens to express their respect and admiration for President Eisenhower and the great American nation.

My own role in Korea will be judged by history, and all facts are in the record. But President Eisenhower and the American government will continue to be our first line of reliance for free survival itself. His letter to me is not a personal letter—however warmly courteous it may be—but an expression of the common cause between the United States and the Republic of Korea.

As tension began to ease, college students organized teams to help restore law and order in Seoul. The day after the declaration of resignation by the President, students, riding together with soldiers, gave orders to their colleagues to stay at home. Later, when the victory over the government was complete, the students assumed the traffic duties of the police, who had wisely stayed at home or had taken refuge in the large police stations.

Early on April 28th, Rhee's hand-picked running mate, and Speaker of the House of Representatives, Lee Ki Poong, and his whole family carried out a suicide pact because of their involvement in great financial and political corruption. Lee, a confidential secretary and protégé of President Rhee who had been blamed for conditions leading to the bloody revolution, and his family had gone into hiding in small quarters in the annex to the presidential mansion.

Lee, his wife Maria Park, and younger son Kang Wook sat together on a couch. Across from them stood Lee's eldest son—whom Rhee had adopted as his own son—ROK Second Lieutenant Kang Suk. At the agreed moment, Kang Suk raised his .45 army pistol and killed his father with one shot. He then killed his mother and his younger brother. Finally, after making sure they were dead, he turned the gun on himself, shot twice, and fell dead.[11]

On the afternoon of the same day, Dr. Syngman Rhee left his beloved presidential mansion for his old private house, the Eiwha-chang, and the Rhee regime came to an end.

Suppression had been no more acceptable from a home-grown government than from foreign rule. By ignoring this simple truth, President Rhee had turned the clock back more than forty years. The war cry of thousands who braved the fire of Rhee's police was "Remember the spirit of 1919!" The tragic irony of the situation probably was not lost on Rhee, for he had been a leader of the Korean revolt of 1919 against Japanese rule, which the Japanese had suppressed with a ruthlessness that served him as a model.

The April Revolution required the courage of the students to risk their lives in protest against the bankruptcy and corruption of Rhee's government. The forbearance and secret support, respectively, of the United States and the ROK Army assisted the success of the revolution. The attitude of the army was a crucial factor, as was that of America. The publication of the Conlon Report of the United States Senate Foreign Relations Committee exposed the corruption of the Rhee government and contributed to the uprising of the students and of the college professors. The Conlon Report, Section on Korea, by Professor Robert A. Scalapino of the University of California, was severely critical of President Rhee's misrule, and urgently demanded reform. The success of the April Revolution was assured when the United States released ROK Army troops from the United Nations command to enforce martial law in an effort to restore order.

Behind the scenes, United States Ambassador Walter P. McConaughy had got in touch with President Syngman Rhee, notifying him of the United States' concern at the turn of events, and delivered a demand from the United States Government that Dr. Rhee "take immediate and adequate action to meet justifiable grievances, since the Republic of Korea is still to a great extent a United Nations responsibility, and many Americans have been shouldering the United Nations' burden in South Korea." Many Koreans applauded the key role played by the United States in events accompanying the downfall of Rhee's government. The only criticism heard among Koreans was implied in the frequently raised question, "Why didn't the United States act sooner?"

The United States Department of State conducted itself properly during the revolution. It was clearly on the side of freedom. Had it done otherwise, the United States would have discredited itself not only in Korea but also in other parts of Asia as a supporter of tyranny. No one can fight Communism by destroying freedom and democracy. The United States did not make South Korea a democratic show window, but it did sow seeds of democracy there that will grow under proper guidance. The downfall of Syngman Rhee was, of course, a blow to the prestige of both the United States and the United Nations, which participated in the defense of South Korea in 1950.

Although Rhee called in the ROK Army Chief of Staff, Lieutenant General Song Yo Chan, and placed Seoul under martial law, and though South Korea's able and hard-driving General Song was firm, his sympathies clearly lay with the Korean students. He was convinced, along with Ambassador McConaughy, that the only way the ROK Army could save Rhee's government would be by shooting down students in droves, unless President Rhee gave way. To avoid such a blood bath, General Song deliberately set out to dislodge Dr. Rhee from the presidency, and permitted the student leaders to form a delegation to see President Rhee and demand that new elections be held and that he resign.

During the uprisings the police fired on nearly 100,000 demonstrators, killing 183 and wounding 6,259 throughout South Korea. The following note was a young Korean student's letter to her mother, just before she joined the demonstration:

"DEAR MOTHER, I am sorry that I have left you to join the demonstration without saying goodby. I will fight to the last against the fraudulent election. All my high school friends, together with the students of the Republic of Korea, are participating in the bloody street demonstrations for the cause of democracy.

Mother, please do not scold me for taking part in the demonstrations: Who will demonstrate if we don't? I know I am still an unthinking child, but I also know how to show my love for my country and my people. All my schoolmates are ready to lay down their lives for our country, and so am I. I do not mind even if I should die during the demonstrations.

Mother, I know you will feel grieved about my decision because you love me so much; but you should be cheerful when you think of the freedom of the people and the bright future of our country. It would seem that in my mind I have already joined the demonstration crowd. Since I am writing this note very hurriedly, my hand is shaking. I pray that you keep in good health. Let me say again, I made up my mind to lay down my life for the cause of democracy. I have to close; time is short.

The *Yunhap Shinmun,* on April 30, 1960, reported that the writer of this note, Miss Chin Young Suk, a fifteen-year-old high school girl, died from a Seoul police bullet during the April 19th student demonstration. Miss Chin died shouting, "Minjujui-Mansei!" (Long live democracy!)

The press commented that the entire world admired her deed, which will be remembered down the centuries as an example of courage, gallantry, and heroism in the name of service to mankind. The remarkable restraint of the Korean students deserves special commendation, and the April Revolution will go down in Korean history, along with the revolution of March, 1919, as one of the notable chapters in the Korean struggle for freedom.

Korean Students[12]

Korean university students are in the midst of an unstable society, taking part in its political life and helping to change its course. The universities of modern Asia are agencies for social change instead of mere repositories of knowledge and communities of scholars. This is how the revolutionary movements of South Korea and other Asian countries conceive of their universities, and much of the leadership and political strategy for national independence and rebellion against oppressive governments in those countries is developed in the universities.

The Korean student is in a vicious circle. He goes to a university because his country badly needs the services he can give it once he is trained. At the same time, his country is not yet ready to train him and to accept him.

As Asian students, Koreans have come of age in unstable societies whose aims and structure are still in the process of formation, where political forces push and pull them in many directions at once, and where they are called upon for a degree of political, economic, and social maturity they have not yet acquired.

Though tuition and resident fees are low, the general poverty of the Korean population puts insurmountable obstacles in the way of thousands of able prospective students. Except for a few students in a very few adequate universities, the conditions of education are almost impossibly difficult for the young Korean of college caliber. The universities are neither sufficient in number nor appropriate in structure for the needs of the new societies they serve.

The curriculum is still largely shaped by Continental or British patterns. It is a bookish program, with little personal relation between the faculty and the students, with no sense of identity between the student and his university, and with a perennial shortage of translated textbooks. Since the most modern knowledge in the fields taught is contained in texts printed in Western languages, the student must learn a Western language before coming to the university. This is not easy, considering the present state of secondary education. The only alternative is to try to learn a Western language and at the same time learn the content of the knowledge written in that language.

The image of a dynamic and progressive America still exists in Korea, especially among the young. Korean students judge the United States with pro-Korean concern. They weigh American actions and policies by their results and intentions rather than on ideological or historical grounds. Their relations with Americans are cordial and cooperative. They are anxious to go to America, to read American books, to meet American people. They are hungry for Western knowledge and American education.

Korean students have demonstrated their readiness to assume responsibility for building a new society with American assistance; they are progressive in spirit, and they reject any attempt to encourage dictatorial government or political movements whose aim is to control them. The new Korean generation is the first to grow up in the era of national independence. The West is not doctrinally rejected so much as the West thinks, nor is it prejudged in the eyes of Korean students.

There are considerable American aid programs already, both public and private, and the extent of this aid to Korean students and institutions over the past decade represents no small amount of materials, scholarships, and teaching hours. Yet the United States has not begun to think in the large concepts demanded by the size of the problem. American foreign policy has concentrated on winning mili-

tary and political allies rather than on making common cause with
the Asian students who are now creating new societies.

The United States must develop a bold national program of educational aid to Korean students. Government funds should be transferred from foreign military aid to the cultural budget. The major
foundations, universities, and many other organizations, some of them
affiliated with church groups, possess the experience and are in touch
with the administrative personnel to make such a wide educational
program possible, once the necessary funds are available. Korean
students are the ones on whom will depend the future relations of
Korea with the rest of the world, including the United States. The
Korean student is the key man in Korea.

THE KOREA OF HUH CHUNG[13]

The Republic of South Korea, created under United Nations
auspices as a free and democratic state, was of vital concern to the
United States and much of the West. From 1950 to 1953, the United
States and fifteen other United Nations members helped the Republic
of Korea to repel a Communist invasion, at a cost of 33,629 American
and about 2,000,000 South Korean lives. Since the Korean War,
which ended in a truce that left Korea still divided, the United States
has spent more than $2,500,000,000 in aid for the Republic of
Korea.

Because South Korea is a vital link in the chain of Western defenses rimming the East Asia mainland, the United States retains air
bases and two army divisions on the Republic of Korea's soil. The
United States supported Dr. Rhee's government after the Second
World War solely because Korea is the last outpost of the West on
the mainland of East Asia. American aid was given to the Rhee
government because of Korea's strategic importance, and not because
Rhee's Korea was a democratic government.

Many critically examined United States policy in Korea from 1945
onward, stating that Rhee might have been pressured into reforms that
would have made the revolution of 1960 unnecessary, if Rhee had
been less exalted by his allies during the Korean War and if American aid had been made conditional on certain standards of behavior.
They failed to realize that the United States did not want to intervene
in South Korea's internal political affairs.

Before his resignation, President Rhee appointed three ministers to the cabinet. The new Foreign Minister, Huh Chung, an ex-journalist and independent former premier once dismissed by President Rhee but recalled by him as a senior member of the cabinet, formed an interim government pursuant to the existing Constitution, and held office pending the adoption of constitutional changes and the holding of new elections for the National Assembly. The interim government undertook a series of immediate reforms, and brought to trial those considered responsible for violations of the election and other laws.

The government's probe of fraud in the March 15th presidential elections affected three members of the fallen Rhee cabinet: former Home Minister Choi In Kyu, former Finance Minister Song In Sang, and former Justice Minister Hong Chin Ki. Mr. Hong told prosecutors that a six-man special committee composed of cabinet ministers had drafted the elaborate plans for rigging the elections and had forced government employees to help, according to sources in the prosecutor's office. The ex-ministers who were involved with those already arrested were former Defense Minister Kim Chung Yul, former Communications Minister Kwak Wi Yung, and ex-Transportation Minister Kim Il Hwan.

Huh Chung, a soft-spoken man with a scholarly air, was handed the task of rebuilding the wreckage of Rhee's shattered government. Mr. Huh continued to rule under martial law, pending establishment of a caretaker cabinet. In his first pronouncement after taking power, he gave promise of a better day by pledging himself to enact reforms that would take the police out of politics and stop waste in American aid; he said he would call new elections within the constitutional limit of three months and would seek to improve relations with the United States and with Japan.[14]

The Huh government abolished the militant Student Defense Corps in another move to end the regimentation built up under former President Rhee. The action ended a powerful propaganda organization that had enrolled the entire student body of the country's universities, colleges, and high schools. It was established on September 28, 1949, by presidential order. The corps' commander in chief was the Minister of Education. Rhee used the Student Defense Corps to dramatize his various causes. Huge turnouts of students under orders bolstered his stand against the 1953 Korean war armistic and his anti-Japanese policies.[15]

The secret departure of former President Rhee and his wife for Hawaii in a chartered plane, which was permitted by Acting President Huh and American Ambassador McConaughy, became an important issue in the National Assembly. Former President Rhee was mentioned in connection with numerous charges concerning the alleged transfer of foreign-exchange funds abroad. Dr. Rhee's Austrian-born wife, Francesca, denied in Hawaii that the former President was implicated in any illegal dealings.

Members of the Democratic party bitterly criticized the secrecy of Dr. Rhee's departure. Some members felt that the development was a desirable one in view of the uncertain political atmosphere in South Korea. In Taegu, where the opposition to Dr. Rhee's rule was particularly strong, about fifteen hundred college students demonstrated in the street against the government's permitting the former President to leave the country, with signs carried by the students demanding an end of the Huh government, the expulsion of Ambassador McConaughy, and the recall of Dr. Rhee.

On April 26, 1960, the House of Representatives unanimously adopted a motion to establish an *ad hoc* committee to draft constitutional amendments. Upon completion of the drafting of the amendments, this committee held a public hearing on May 5th with the participation of prominent legal experts. The draft amendments, signed by 175 members of the House, were submitted to that body on May 11th. The acting President announced the proposed amendments to the public on the same day.

The House of Representatives adopted the constitutional amendments on June 15th by 208 votes to 3. On the same day, the government formally promulgated the amendments to the Constitution. These amendments were of outstanding importance in the relationship between the organs of government. They led to a change in the pattern of government from a "presidential system" to a "parliamentary system," with a cabinet responsible to the legislature. Within the framework of the Constitution, as amended, the policies of the Executive no longer emanated from the President but from the State Council headed by the prime minister.

These changes, making the Chief Executive directly responsible to the National Assembly, were influenced not only by the events of March 15, 1960, but also by a desire to resolve certain practical difficulties that have existed since the beginnings of the Republic in reconciling the respective roles of the President, the prime minister (when this office existed), and the National Assembly under a Constitution containing elements of both a presidential system and a parliamentary system. Thus the net effect of these constitutional changes was to make the National Assembly the main repository of power.

Under this Constitution, legislative power was exercised by the National Assembly, which was composed of two houses—the House of Representatives and the House of Councilors. The members of both houses are elected by "universal, equal, direct and secret vote." The members of the House of Representatives hold office for a term of four years, and those of the House of Councilors for a term of six years. Elections for half of the membership of the House of Councilors are to be held every three years. The House of Representatives elects a speaker and two vice speakers, and the House of Councilors a president and a vice president. Bills pertaining to legislative and budgetary matters are first presented to the House of Representatives.

If the House of Councilors disagrees with the House of Representatives, it can either pass a resolution different from the one adopted by the House of Representatives or refrain from adopting a resolution within certain specified time limits. The House of Representatives in either case can override the action of the House of Councilors by adopting budget bills by a simple majority and other bills by a two-thirds majority. The number and election of the members of the House of Representatives is determined by law, while the members of the House of Councilors are elected by districts composed of special cities and provinces, and their number is not to exceed one-fourth of the fixed number of the members of the House of Representatives.

Under the Constitution, as amended, the President, who is elected by the members of both Houses of the National Assembly at a joint session, is the head of the state and represents the state, but his powers were curtailed. He confirms the appointment and dismissal of public officials, including members of the State Council. Executive powers are vested in the State Council, composed of the prime minister and members whose total number is not to be more than fifteen nor less than eight. The majority, including the prime minister, must be members of the National Assembly, except when the House of Representatives has been dissolved. The prime minister is to be nominated by the President and approved by the House of Representatives. In case the President's nominations have been twice rejected by the House of Representatives, or no nomination has been made within five days after the President has failed to obtain the consent of the House of Representatives for his first nomination, the prime minister is to be elected by the House of Representatives.

The heads of ministries are to be appointed by the prime minister from among the members of the State Council. The members of the State Council are appointed and dismissed by the prime minister, subject to confirmation by the President. The State Council is jointly responsible to the House of Representatives. It must resign as a whole when the House of Representatives had adopted a no-confidence resolution, unless the Council decides to dissolve the House of Representatives within ten days.

The Constitution vests judicial power in the courts, which include a Supreme Court. The organization of the courts is determined by law. As amended, the Constitution provides that the Chief Justice and Justices of the Supreme Court are elected by an "electors group" organized by those qualified as judges, and are confirmed by the President. Other judges are appointed by the Chief Justice upon the decision of the Congress of Justices. The tenure of judges remains fixed at ten years, subject to reappointment. There is now also a separate Constitutional Court, whose members are appointed by the President, the Supreme Court, and the House of Councilors. Each of these appoints three of the total of nine members.

The general election for the new House of Representatives was to be held late in July, 1960. The present National Assembly, whose members were elected for a four-year term in 1958, was dissolved one day before the general election. The new government was to be formed on August 15th, Korea's Liberation Day. Elections for the Upper House were to be held within six months after the promulgation of the new Constitution. The proceedings in the Assembly and the new Constitution were welcomed by hundreds of impatient college students.

The Acting President asked the United States, in effect, to pay the costs of the overthrow of the Syngman Rhee government. The amount was $20,000,000, which would enable the "caretaker" cabinet under

Foreign Minister Huh Chung to cover extraordinary deficits incurred in the confused aftermath of the recent civil upheaval. The new elections of the National Assembly cost the Korean government the equivalent of about $1,000,000. In addition, the government was confronted with demands by thousands of workers in state enterprises for back pay amounting to about $5,000,000. The new cabinet faced an expected deficit in tax collections equivalent to about $10,000,000.

The cost of administering martial law in Seoul and other major cities, and of repairing numerous public buildings burned by anti-government rioters, was close to $20,000,000. Local tax collections had almost ceased after the election of March 15th. Employees in the government-operated coal mines, shipping companies, and numerous other state-controlled enterprises received no wages for weeks. These economics effects were traced to the disruption accompanying the resignation of Dr. Rhee, which was followed by the departure of officials in charge of a wide range of government activities. With a trade deficit in 1959 amounting to $219,000,000, South Korea was admittedly dependent on United States assistance for her economic life. Korean and American officials charged with administering the aid program were engaged in a searching investigation of corruption and mismanagement that had drained American-sponsored projects of huge sums. The caretaker government headed by Foreign Minister Huh Chung promised to weed political influences out of the United States aid program.[16]

The Huh government announced a six-point program of major measures to stablize South Korea's economy. The provisions were: (1) stabilization of prices for farm products and other commodities, and provision of the "maximum available" funds to aid medium and small enterprises, export industries, and farming; (2) extension and liberalization of foreign trade and normalization of trade with Japan; (3) freeing of farm cooperatives from political influence; (4) development of government enterprises on a self-sustaining basis, and their gradual transfer to private ownership; (5) revision of the tax system, with the adoption of "reasonable and fair" taxation to ensure the accumulation of private capital; (6) continuation of the Rhee three-year economic development program through the most effective allocation of limited resources.

The Liberal party collapsed when 104 of the 138 party members in the South Korean National Assembly announced that they had become independents desirous of complying "with the spirit of the democratic revolution" that toppled the Rhee government. With the collapse of the Liberals, the Democrats, headed by former Vice President John M. Chang, became the strongest party in the Assembly, with a total of seventy seats. A total of 114 members of the Assembly were independents. Some of the remaining thirty-four Liberals were expected to join the independent ranks in the hope of improving their chances of being reelected. The three smaller groups seeking congressional posts were the Popular Socialists, the Liberal party (formerly the ruling Rhee party), and the Korean Socialist party.

South Korea's National Assembly approved a revised National Security Law eliminating press restrictions and other disputed features of the measure adopted late in 1958 during the regime of the former President.

The Acting President removed the provincial governors and leaders of the police in an attempt to weed out the former totalitarian regime, and accepted resignations from all nine governors who had been appointed, and from twenty-one high officers of Rhee's discredited national police force.

Huh continued as head of an interim government until the end of July, 1960. He maintained the independence of the judiciary, neutralized the police, and preserved local autonomy. In rewriting fifty-five provisions of the existing Constitution, the bill dropped most of the provisions in the old charter that empowered the government to restrict basic liberties and rights.[17]

South Koreans of all ranks took President Eisenhower to their hearts during his two-day visit to the Republic, a visit that demonstrated America's sympathetic concern for South Korea and its courageous citizens. Two million South Koreans in their Sunday best, some of them walking ten miles from the provinces, turned out to greet the American President on June 19th and 20th. What mattered most was not the size of the crowd but its spontaneous warmth, expressing thanks for American aid. Coinciding with the tenth anniversary of the Korean War, on June 25th, President Eisenhower's visit to the front, though short, reemphasized the United Nations effort that first stopped and then rolled back the Communist invaders to the present truce line. As President Eisenhower said in his speech to the Korean National Assembly, the Republic of Korea was a proving ground for democracy.

Owing to their unfortunate experience of excessive one-man rule under Rhee, the Huh government proposed to strip the President of his vast powers, making him in effect a figurehead, and to entrust most executive power to a prime minister and a cabinet wholly dependent on what promised to be a parliament of many parties. The amended Constitution, promulgated on June 16, 1960, by South Koreans as the Second Republic Constitution, moved not so much toward the British parliamentary system as toward the ill-fated method of the Fourth French Republic, a system that led to political instability. The parliamentary system may work under the British two-party method, but it has brought only instability to nations with less-developed party traditions or a multiplicity of parties, such as Korea has. The care-taker government in South Korea left room for the same error, with the result that it may be replaced by military dictatorship or by a presidential regime, as in France. The primary function of government is to govern, and any regime incapable of doing so will not long endure.

THE KOREA OF JOHN M. CHANG[18]

Stable progress of democracy may not be feasible in a society faced with such internal economical problems and external military threats as those of the Republic of Korea. However, slow headway was made in young South Korea during the last turbulent decade of political instability and war. South Koreans have recently been practicing public politics on a larger scale, and with more vigor and intelligence, than at any other time in Korean history. Their participation was marked by the growing exercise of individual free will, the hallmark of a democratic society. There was no blind worship of a national hero on the one hand, or meek obedience to the orders of village headmen on the other. Increasingly, even the rural electorate appeared to consult "self-interest" when they cast their ballot.

The Chang government consciously realized the necessity for improvement in their political ideas and national aims. From the time of the April Revolution, a government by the people was founded on solid democratic principles; and the Koreans are now making great efforts to achieve a government for the people to complete the democratic process.

The year 1960 saw a major change in the government structure of the Republic of Korea, when on June 15th a new parliamentary system was adopted to replace the strong President-centered system that had been in existence for the twelve years since the formal establishment of the Republic on August 15, 1948. On June 15th the House of Representatives adopted a new Constitution, introducing a major change in the government's executive structure, and substituting a straight parliamentary system for the previous presidential system. The post of President, as head of state, was continued, but it was transformed into a largely ceremonial position without executive authority. The executive power was placed in the hands of a State Council headed by a prime minister. The latter and a majority of the cabinet ministers are required to be members of the National Assembly. The prime minister appoints his own cabinet, and is required to resign if he receives a vote of nonconfidence in the House of Representatives on a major issue. In this case, however, he has authority to dissolve the House and order new elections.

Following adoption of the new Constitution, the old Assembly dissolved itself, designating July 29th as the date for a new general election. Provisions were also made, for the first time since the passage of the 1952 constitutional amendment, to elect the House of Councilors. In this election, whose conduct was called "very satisfactory" by UNCURK, the Democratic party won a majority of seats in the House of Representatives. The second largest group was composed of independents, with the remaining members divided among splinter parties. After some intraparty bickering, the new Assembly on August 12th elected Yun Posun, British-educated archaeologist, as President for a five-year term. President Yun first nominated Mr. Kim Do Yun for the position of prime minister. Mr. Kim was turned down by the Assembly, and Dr. John Myun Chang, head of the Democratic party and the first Korean Ambassador to Washington, was then designated. He was elected prime minister on August 19th, by only two votes and against half of his own divided party. The nomination was approved.

Attempts to form a government consisting of equal numbers of

President Eisenhower reads his arrival statement at the airport as acting President Chung Huh (*right*) listens. (*ROK, Korea Today 1961*)

The Second Republic Premier John M. Chang. (*ROK, Korea Today, 1961*)

cabinet members from the "new" and from the "old" factions of the Democratic party, along with independents, were at first unsuccessful, and on August 23rd Dr. Chang formed a Cabinet that consisted, in addition to the prime minister, of eleven members of the "new" faction, two independents, and one member from the "old" faction who accepted the post without the endorsement of his faction.

In announcing the formation of this cabinet, the prime minister expressed his intention to continue efforts to organize a government consisting of "old" and "new" faction members as well as of independents. On September 7th four key members from the "new" faction of the cabinet resigned, reportedly in order to provide an opportunity for the establishment of such a government. Finally, on September 12th, Dr. Chang announced the formation of a new government that included four additional "old" faction members. A fifth member of the "old" faction was appointed to the Cabinet on September 15th.

This endeavor to form a stable government representative of the popular will as expressed in the national elections of July 29, 1960, demonstrated a significant continuation of the spirit of restraint and moderation on the part of the Korean people and its leaders. In a policy statement before the National Assembly on August 27th, the prime minister said that his government would lay stress on unification through free elections throughout Korea under the supervision of the United Nations. He reiterated the desire of his country to secure admission to membership in the United Nations.

On September 6th the Foreign Minister of the Republic of Korea officially transmitted to the Committee of UNCURK the text of a seven-point foreign-policy statement that had been made public on August 24th. In this statement, *inter alia,* the Government of the Republic of Korea held that the unification of Korea should be achieved through United Nations supervised free elections throughout Korea pursuant to the United Nations resolutions. The reckless policy of unification by force advocated by the past Rhee's government, it was declared, should be discarded. The statement also emphasized the desire of the Korean Government to achieve admission to membership in the United Nations and also indicated that the government would seek further to extend its diplomatic relationships. Foreign Minister Chung stressed that diplomatic relations between the Republic of Korea and Japan should be made normal as soon as possible on the principle of mutual respect and reciprocity.

The change in government brought about a major shift in foreign policy. The new government had given its backing to a general election throughout Korea, under the supervision of the United Nations, in order to reunite the two parts of the nation. A new attitude had also been taken toward Korean-Japanese relations. On September 6th Japanese Foreign Minister Zentaro Kosaka made an unofficial visit to Seoul, and on October 25th negotiations were begun in Tokyo to settle the long-standing problems between the two countries. The new administration also announced plans to widen the country's diplomatic relations, including the establishment of ties with various new Afro-Asian states, and with additional countries of the free world.

The fall of the Rhee government disclosed a chaotic economic picture. New economic plans included the establishment of a National Construction Service that would absorb large numbers of the presently unemployed labor force into such projects as road building, land reformation, water-resources development, and reforestation. A new Rural Development Authority was to be entrusted with community development projects, agricultural extension services, and cottage industries. Plans also called for the intensive development of sources of electric power to meet additional immediate needs and anticipated future demands. Major emphasis was also being placed on the promotion of small industries, especially those oriented toward export, to help improve Korea's imbalance of trade and alleviate unemployment.

The course of events of 1960 is a testimonial to the general acceptance by the Korean people of the concept of democratic government. The mass demonstrations popularly designated as the April Revolution was described by UNCURK as "a spontaneous expression of resentment against the previous government for its failure to observe democratic processes to the satisfaction of the people." The constitutional changes of June were effected by the National Assembly —the regularly established legislative body—and the elections at the end of July and the subsequent selection of the President and prime minister by the new National Assembly were in accordance with constitutional processes. Korea's democracy was less than twelve years old, and this election was only the third time that the Korean people had elected their Chief Executive by direct vote.

Unfortunately, the election did bring about the unusual situation of Chang's Korea electing a President from one party faction, "Old Guard" Democrat, and a prime minister from another party faction, called "New" Democrat. Owing to the parliamentary system, the dilemma of two different factions having an interest in the same executive body arose immediately. Intraparty bickering in the Democratic party arose between "new" and "old" Democratic factions. The majority party in the South Korea National Assembly was a new form of arbitrary control.

There was little real difference between the party platforms of the "old" and "new" Democrats; both were nationalistic and anti-Communist. Neither was distinguished for the exercise of the rare political virtues of tolerance and compromise. They were motivated by a crass desire for power. The legislative work of the National Assembly was very limited, although some important measures were taken and considerable time was spent in unfruitful general debate. Sessions were also often hampered by failure to muster a quorum of members. The Democratic party, which split into a number of feuding factions, demonstrated the absence of a foundation for any effective two-party system in Korea.

With unprecedented speed and efficiency, the legislature passed bills providing for large salary and allowance increases for members, but did nothing for the pitifully underpaid civil servants, police, teachers, and other government employees. The executive branch of the government was appallingly weak. Cabinet change followed cabinet change, destroying continuity in administration. Nepotism was the order of the day; competent, experienced government employees were abruptly dismissed to make way for friends and relatives of government officials and legislators. Corruption continued, and was at least as widespread as during the Rhee administration.

The massive corruption stemmed from the embezzlement and misappropriation of Korean Government funds, bribes extracted from citizens by government employees and police, and the evasion, through bribery, of many millions of dollars in income and other taxes. In sharp contrast, aid provided and partly administered by the United States and the United Nations was, in general, wisely and efficiently expended on thousands of reconstruction projects of great and permanent value to the nation. The reasons for this peculiar double standard in government operations are too obvious to require explanation.

Public dissatisfaction increased as the incapability of the Chang government became obvious. The administration was unable to secure the cooperation of its huge majority in the legislature; it was unable to cope with mounting unrest and dissatisfaction; it was unable to control the increasing waves of riotous daily demonstrations; it was unable or unwilling to stop corruption; it was unable to combat the hitherto unheard-of anti-American, "neutralist," and openly pro-Communist policies advocated by opportunist politicians and newspapers. The Communists in the North were quick to take advantage of the political and ideological vacuum. Increasing numbers of Communist agents and saboteurs filtered down from the North, taking advantage of Korea's long and tortuous coast line. Others were smuggled in from Japan. Some of the so-called "newspapers" which sprang up by the hundreds during the Chang regime were actually financed by Communist groups among the Korean residents in Japan and by the Japanese Communist party.

Meanwhile business and industry stagnated. Millions of unemployed were without relief. The farmers were desperate—caught between crop failures and usurious interest rates on loans frequently as high as 80 per cent per year. Actual starvation occurred in some parts of the country. In the cities, organized gangsters and hoodlums made life miserable and unsafe for small businessmen and citizens, often with police connivance. Crying mothers and crippled student heroes of the April Revolution demonstrated in downtown Seoul, shouting demands for the resignation of John M. Chang, his cabinet, and the National Assembly. This was the first major outbreak of antigovernment sentiment since the July 29th national elections, when South Koreans burned ballot boxes and assaulted government officials and former members of Rhee's Liberal party who ran for reelection.

Policemen were issued weapons for the first time since the government of former President Syngman Rhee fell. Army commanders were alerted to stand by in case the uprisings spread. The demonstrators charged that Chang's government and the National Assembly had failed to accomplish the revolutionary tasks of the April uprising. They protested a ruling of the Seoul District Court that ignored demands of the prosecution for death sentences for nine of forty-eight former Rhee officials. Former Seoul Police Chief Yoo Choong Yul was condemned to death, but Judge Chang Joon Taek ignored demands for death penalties for the other defendants.

The student demonstrators invaded the Assembly, ousted the Speaker, and demanded that the Assembly and government resign because the punishments were "too lenient." President Yun Posun asked the National Assembly to enact a law to punish the former Rhee collaborators. He said that the court decisions "ignored the righteous sentiment of the people and their revolutionary spirit." Yun's demands, issued in a special statement, followed charges by the demonstrators that Chang's government was an extension of the Rhee regime. Savage postelection rioting that brought out police to restore order forced postponement of the first session of the new Assembly set for August 15th. The riots broke out in three areas of South Central Korea, and spread to Seoul. The student-led demonstrations flared when a handful of pro-Rhee legislators were returned to office. Students said the elections were "rigged," and rose up in violent opposition.

The secretariat of the new bicameral Assembly agreed with the decision of the winning Democratic party to wait until new elections could be held in a dozen constituencies. That meant a delay of at least two weeks in setting up a new government. The rioters and demonstrators were protesting the handful of members of Rhee's Liberal-Democratic party who were elected to the new National Assembly.

There were some charges of election rigging, particularly in cases where Liberal-Democratic candidates ran for office successfully despite the fact hat they were in jail. There was no question, however, of Rhee's old party controlling the new government. Official returns from 219 districts gave the Democratic party of former Vice President John M. Chang 167 seats, more than the two-thirds required to control the 233-seat lower chamber of the National Assembly which elected a President and approved a prime minister.

Dr. Robert Scalapino, author of the Korea Section of the Conlon Report, summarized the task of Chang's government:

In the aftermath of the April Uprising, some degree of disillusionment was inevitable. To recede from heroism is always difficult. In the stark, cold after-dawn of an intoxicating strike for liberty, one sees again the never-ending, never-totally-solved problems implicit in human society. After having risked so much, it is difficult to avoid impatience. Thus every revolution is followed by some degree of disillusionment. But surely it is incumbent upon any government holding power in Korea at this point in history to bend every effort to meet problems upon which progress is long overdue. There are two immediate issues that demand full and urgent attention. The first of these relates to economic development. All Koreans who wish to work should have that opportunity; the problem of unemployment must be given top priority. The modernization of the Korean economy must also be pushed with all possible speed. Corruption should be punished ruthlessly; it is equivalent to espionage in its effect upon the nation. The tax reforms recently introduced should be enforced. Success in these respects is vital.

Today, the Republic of Korea has only a few years to prove that it can hold or acquire the full support of the Korean people. Its advantages of the past have been mainly negative: the cruelty, the grimness of life, and the totalitarianism of the Communist North. But at some point, negative advantages will not be enough. The people, and particularly the young people of the Republic want action. What are their aspirations? First, they want a state that feels deeply the responsibility to enable its citizens to enjoy a decent standard of living. There is a strong desire for a welfare state with political freedom. The Chang government is aware of this desire and is striving in some measure to meet it. Whether that government has a sufficient sense of urgency, a sufficient commitment and drive to be successful, only history will determine.[19]

Unfortunately, a basic difficulty was the failure of democratic parliamentary processes in the National Assembly. Where the responsibility was placed for these failures depended upon the party faction: Premier Chang's ruling Democratic party or the minority Democratic party, both of which included equally patriotic anti-Communist Koreans. Korean politicians revealed lamentable inexperience with democracy. The contest being waged in South Korea was an intramural struggle that found Chang's strong-handed government contending against a growing opposition that threatened to unseat it. The difficulties were formidable, and the task of developing the institutions of representative government in a country that had limited tradition or experience of such government was challenging.

Rhee's successor worried over the prospect of nation-wide demonstrations against his government on the anniversary of the April Revolution. As a preventive, the Chang cabinet submitted two bills to control street demonstrations and give the government more effective means of cracking down on South Korea's illegal—but active—Communist party. Left-wing organizers, capitalizing on widespread distrust of the two proposed bills, staged on antigovernment rally in Seoul's City Hall Plaza.

As *Time* reported the situation in South Korea:

Taking up torches and banners, the crowd surged through Seoul's main streets chanting, "Overthrow the Chang regime." Cops in combat dress moved in and tried to seize the torches. An agitator yelled, "Kill the police," and sticks and stones started to fly. Before the dust had settled, the mob had destroyed two police Jeeps and stormed to within 200 yards of Chang's residence; 40 policemen and six demonstrators were injured, and 119 rioters were arrested. The following day there was another demonstration. More than 2,000 of South Korea's 2,500,000 unemployed, many of them women with babies strapped to their backs, marched through the streets bearing banners: "Anti-Communism is fine, but we need three meals a day, too."[20]

As antigovernment rallies mushroomed throughout South Korea, President Yun summoned Chang and the leader of the opposition New Democratic party to a midnight meeting at the presidential palace, and asked them to agree to a "political cease-fire" until such time as the government was free of danger of being overthrown from the extreme left—a far-off day in a war-weary nation where at least 25 per cent of the labor force is out of work and where low wages, an inadequate food supply, and a high birth rate compound years of economic mismanagement.

In the heady days after Rhee's regime was overthrown, hopes had been high that stability and prosperity lay just ahead under the Democratic party leadership of Dr. John Chang. But reform-minded young Koreans were soon disillusioned. Inheriting a virtually empty treasury, Chang has barely been able to avert his country's economic collapse. Production was lagging badly, and unemployment was growing. Official corruption seemed as rampant as ever; influence peddling by officials on behalf of their rich friends was hardly concealed. In the National Assembly high-living deputies stalled off wage increases for civil servants, but did not hesitate to vote themselves a handsome pay boost to $700 monthly.

The dreary outlook for Chang's Korea was described by the *New York Times* correspondent, A. M. Rosenthal as follows:

The Republic of Korea is in a time of trouble and want and no one can see its end. The most moving thing about this country is that after more than half a century of travail, it suffers not so much from despair as from expectations that are unfulfilled but still alive. Seoul is a ramshackle city, and the only touches of beauty are in the surrounding mountains and the hidden gardens where the old kings of Korea strolled, in remote contemplation. But it is a city of life. Its streets are loud with the sounds of commerce, a hand-to-mouth commerce typical of those Asian cities where the people are grimly poor but energetic enough to keep fighting. Jitney drivers shout for a full passenger load, hundreds of curbside peddlers scream the special quality of their trays of pens, belts, wallets and pins, a junkman clangs his bell through the market and marketmen chant the virtues of their onions and tomatoes.

Politically there is unhappiness and a continuous murmur of complaint. Yet, at least as far as the younger people are concerned, the attitude, despite the cynicism, is not of lethargy but of demand. But in Government offices, foreign embassies and the restaurants where opposition leaders complain to foreigners, the talk almost always runs up against the terrible reality that South Korea is a country where too many are sharing too little. No one knows an answer except the one answer that always presents itself and which no one likes—a Korea dependent for the foreseeable future, perhaps for decades, upon the self-interest and charity of another land—the United States.

There is an economic crisis at the moment, but it is not so much a separate crisis as part of an unending series of crises. The crisis of the spring of 1961 is an outgrowth of the crisis of the spring of 1960. Last year the Government of Dr. Syngman Rhee was overthrown by a student street rebellion. The new Government of Premier John M. Chang is still caught in the backwash of that revolution. One of the first and still unsatisfied demands of the revolution was for the punishment of businessmen who had made fortunes by evading taxes or bribing tax collectors or paying politicians for import and export licenses or greasing the right Korean palm to be recommended to United States officials for plantbuilding funds.

But the lists, published and unpublished, of the men who are to be charged reads like a Who's Who of Korean business. To have taken drastic steps against these men immediately would have been to paralyze the

South Korean economy. The volume of industrial production went up during 1960 by about 9 per cent, but this was largely because of the coming into operation of new United States-built projects and increased coal mining. Even this curve dipped in December when, according to past trends, it should have been going up. At the same time, investments declined, the growth rate slowed and unemployment increased.

No one is sure how many unemployed there are because of the lack of reliable statistics. The total is usually estimated at 2,500,000, or about 25 per cent of the labor force and it probably is much higher. The price of food in Seoul has risen sharply. In the first two months of this year the price of such essentials as rice, barley, and other grains went up 50 per cent. The wage and price structure is a built-in invitation to corruption. Few men earn enough to be able to afford the luxury of honesty. A medium-rank government official may earn the equivalent of about $40 a month. The Bank of Korea estimates that it costs twice that much for a family of six to live. The wife may work and the children peddle, but the total income is almost never enough to made do.

When it comes to the future everyone just shakes his head at the thought of what South Korean will be like in ten years with 5,000,000 more people. Reunification with the richer and manpower-hungry Communist state to the north would theoretically solve many problems. But it is difficult to find any responsible leader here who believes that the Communists would ever accept anything but total domination, however it may be disguised temporarily.

Everybody talks about the problems. They are a heritage of decades and built so deeply into the cement of society that nobody really knows how to dig them out. Everybody simply lists them, in frustration—a divided country, wars, devastation, too many people on too little land, not enough jobs and not enough resources to create enough industry to sop up the unemployed, inefficiency and graft as traditions and the "spring hunger," those lean months before the June crop can be harvested. But the social discontent of this spring is an offshoot of last year's revolution. Last spring, for the first time in the memory of most men, the Koreans found themselves free from dictatorship, foreign or domestic, free to talk and shout and hope and say what they hoped for.

Their hopes of sudden, blessed change have not come true and they search for scapegoats. There are men who work hard and plan, but there are others to whom cynicism has become the answer. Ideas that were once forbidden fruit—neutralism, economic democracy, the right to march and protest and hang up signs saying down with this or that—were plucked and tasted. Sometimes in Seoul men say things loudly just because they have the right to say them and want to remind the people they have the right. Opposition leaders complain that the new Government is just as bad as the old. But when they are asked what they would do if they were in power, they do not have much to say.

Newspaper writers and students talk about the need for increasing ties with neutral nations—partly because they believe it and partly because this was a swiftly punished heresy in Dr. Rhee's time. They snap angrily at the United States out of their own sense of humiliation for national dependence on the American dollar, but then demand that the United States contribute more and more. There is an education fever in the city. An elevator boy keeps a hand on the controls and an eye on an English-Korean dictionary. Older people act a bit frightened of the students who led the rioting of 1960 and tasted the power of rule by agitation. The students are not always sure of what they want, but they want it quickly.[21]

Since Dr. Chang, a teacher turned politician, took office as prime minister, after sending Dr. Rhee into exile in Honolulu, he had no way to cure his painful problems—a divided country, a staggering economy, unemployment, an exploding population, and an unrealistic expectation of better times—although he faced the first anniversary of the outbreak of rioting against the rigged elections of 1960. Because the Chang government, burdened by economic realities, had no way of meeting such problems, it was concerned that the student would riot again. Dr. Chang's Korea was still burdened with partition and the heritages of the Korean War and maladministration, but he did not produce any miracles, and often moved too slowly.

While corruption was no longer openly tolerated by the government, it still existed; consequently, the Chang regime was not widely popular. Approximately 500,000 new mouths are being added yearly to South Korea's population of 23,000,000, putting a greater premium on arable land and forcing many farmers into an insecure city existence. Chang, a Roman Catholic, opposed any kind of artificial birth control or legalized abortion. His political opposition had done little more than complain, and had neither real strength nor a party platform. The farmers suffered from regular periods of hunger, and many left to live uncertainly in the cities. Though South Koreans were discontent and cynical, their mood was not revolutionary. The demonstrators carried torchlights, and shouted, "Give us jobs and bread!"

Economic distress was the largest contributor to the dissatisfaction of Koreans with the Chang government. Between the end of December, 1960, and the beginning of April, 1961, the price of grain went up 23.7 per cent. One of the reasons for this sharp rise was the 4.4 per cent drop in grain output in 1960. The basic reason, however, was the fact that 43 per cent of the farms in South Korea are little more than an acre (or less) in size, and seldom provide their tillers with enough food to last them from the autumn rice harvest to the summer barley harvest. In 1961 the term "spring hunger" was even more applicable than usual; the government provided relief grain to some 20 per cent of Korea's farm families. Domestic production had been hard hit by the high cost of rice and the resulting decrease in consumer purchasing power. The government instituted an increase in the foreign-exchange rate from 650 hwan to 1,300 hwan to the U.S. dollar in January and February, 1961, as well as a 60 per cent increase in freight rates. The cost of production rose as a result. Both factors together led to a marked decline in domestic production of such items as cotton and woolen yarn, newsprint, soap, and plastic goods in February, 1961.[22]

The problem of the "ex post facto" laws of the previous November, permitting a special court to punish those responsible for the rigged election, police shootings, and "grave antidemocratic acts" of the Rhee regime, was not solved by the government. A new bill to punish persons who acquired "illegal wealth" through political connections was revised in favor of various business groups. The amended bill affected only a hundred businessmen, instead of the forty thousand who were originally to be punished. The student-initiated austerity drive, as well as the New Democratic party's "Fresh Tide Society" campaign for the same object, lost impetus, making the Chang Government the chief exponent of austerity.

During the course of the year, the younger members of the Democratic party often defied the party leadership. A "Junior Democrats Fraternity" was formed at one time, and tried, by joining with younger members of the New Democratic party, to form a "third political force" within the lower house. However, many left the fraternity on the grounds that it was fermenting dissension within the party, and in January, 1961, even the most defiant were placated by a cabinet reshuffle in which two posts were given to members of their own group. Yet in February, another of the group charged a cabinet minister with involvement in an alleged scandal concerning the export of tungsten ore; the opposition New Democratic party took the opportunity to propose an investigation. Democratic party leaders denounced the resulting report as "grossly distorted and too subjective."

A peaceful unification of the country is the primary objective of the Korean people, both in the North and in the South, at the moment. The American resolution to invite a representative from North Korea and South Korea to debate the unification question under the competence and authority of the United Nations was accepted by the Political Commitee of the General Assembly on April 12th, but so far the South Koreans refuse to sit down to debate until North Korea specifically admits United Nations authority. Meanwhile, the students in South Korea are calling for cultural exchanges between the two sections of the country, which, in their belief, could lead to a popular movement toward unification that would transcend ideological differences and by-pass what they term the lack of sincerity of the South Korean Government, on the one hand, and the puppet character of the North Korean Government, on the other. Younger members of the New Democratic party also favored an exchange program. Some politicians, college professors, and students advocated a neutral Korea as the way out of the unification impasse. Practically no one, however, proposed political negotiations with the Communists.[23]

Chang's new, all-Democratic cabinet was announced on January 30th. Five ministers, four of whose offices had been held by former "Old Guard" Democrats, together with three parliamentary vice ministers, were replaced by members of the National Assembly. As a single-party cabinet is a prerequisite to the normal functioning of the cabinet system, the reshuffle was desirable though belated. With a belief that the new cabinet represented the best the Democrats could offer, the highest expectations were that it would take an epoch-making turn toward better and stronger government.[24]

The vital tasks of the Democratic administration were two: first, to settle the problems left by the April Revolution; second, to build up a free welfare society. The first included punishment of the Liberal masterminds of the rigged March presidential election, antidemocratic elements, and illicit profiteers. The second called for unemployment relief, and safeguarding public peace and economic stability through anti-inflationary policies and extensive development projects. Such domestic undertakings had to move forward with a dynamic foreign policy based on the normalization of Korean-Japanese relations, and foreign aid, as well as the territorial reunification of Korea.

To complete the yet unfinished revolution and carry out the mammoth job of putting the national economy on its own feet required assiduous labor and dedication on the part of the government. The Chang government had to halt the rocketing price index and provide jobs for the unemployed. But Chang, an American-educated school teacher, had little chance of carrying his program through unless the Republic of Korea could shake off the addiction to anarchy displayed by politicians and ordinary students alike in the revolution against Rhee, or by the ROK Army leaders. Though Chang very sensibly wanted to cut at least 100,000 men from the ROK Army's 500,000, Asia's largest military force outside Red China, to restore the nation's derelict budget, Korea's *Hankuk Daily News,* pondering on Chang's Korea, said, "We cannot help worrying about the future of the parliamentary system in this country."

Newsweek reported on Chang's Korea, on April 3rd, 1961, just a little over a month before the ROK Army coup:

> Chang's efforts at reform have so far failed to clear up the mess left by Rhee's graft-ridden regime. Indeed, the 22 million South Koreans are now worse off economically than at any time since the war that cost the United States 157,530 lives and $5 billion. Thirty-two factories are idle, 2 million peasants are officially classified as "suffering from hunger," tens of thousands of jobless are living in slums. Korea has moved into the time of chungung (the annual "spring hunger") which lasts until June crops are harvested, and Chang is none too certain that he will still be in power at harvest time.[25]

In fairness to Dr. John Chang, it should be noted that his government used the bulk of United States aid to rehabilitate the war-ravaged Korean economy. He also had to appropriate more than a third of each year's budget to maintain the more than 500,000-man ROK Army. But corruption was still prevalent in government, and Chang should have acted fast to weed out abuses.

THE KOREA OF THE ROK ARMY[26]

The ROK Army has always been the basis of South Korea's strength, and it still is so today. The United States Army's assistance in the development of South Korea's defense force began shortly after the end of the Second World War in 1945, when the first American soldiers arrived to assist South Koreans to attain a free and independent status after nearly half a century of Japanese rule. The establishment of the Republic of Korea in 1948 deployed American troops on occupation duty in South Korea, with five hundred highly trained and professionally qualified American officers and men, known as the Korean Military Advisory Group, providing advice and assistance in the development of internal security forces for the Republic.

Through the United States Military Advisory Group, much has been accomplished toward the goal of a well-trained, self-reliant ROK Army. Soldiers transferred from the South Korean Army are serving under the United States flag in their own country, and are known as "Katusans," meaning Koreans attached to the United States Army. They have responsibilities equal to those of the United States troops, and are serving in corps artillery units in a missile command that is armed with Honest John rockets.

South Koreans have demanded an early conclusion of a status of forces agreement, between the Republic of Korea and the United States, governing the legal jurisdiction of American forces in Korea. Pressure by legislators, the press, and labor unionists was applied at about the same time as the long-delayed negotiations for such an agreement. The National Union of Korean Employees of the American Forces launched a determined movement to collect one million signatures on a petition calling for a status of forces agreement, saying its members were deprived of the rights of collective bargaining because there was no such agreement between Korea and the United States.

Some members of the National Assembly urged the Chang government to expedite negotiations. It was in 1954 that the Seoul government made its first proposals concerning the legal jurisdiction of American servicemen in Korea, and other administrative matters such as customs, immigration, and use of land and facilities. The United States, however, shrugged its shoulders to the proposal on the grounds that Korea was still technically at war with the Communists. Under an agreement signed immediately following the start of the Korean War in 1950, the Seoul government had waived all administrative and legal jurisdiction over American troops, and had offered whatever facilities were needed for the United States forces to fight Communist aggression.

Shortly after the armistice was signed in 1953, the ROK Government, then led by Syngman Rhee, asked that the Taejon agreement be reviewed. Korean demands for a status of forces agreement, under which Korean courts could try American soldiers for crimes against Koreans, increased when several incidents involving the shooting of Koreans by GI's occurred in the fall of 1957.

The American Government signed an agreement to pay utility charges. Then the Democratic party, during the July 29th general elections, pledged itself to press for the early conclusion of a status of forces agreement, and the new government then resumed discussions with the American Embassy. Koreans hoped that the United States would make an arrangement governing payment of land and building rentals and customs and immigration procedures, even if it continued to refuse to turn over the legal jurisdiction of its servicemen to Korean courts.

In November, 1959, many South Korean army officers were removed from service by Lieutenant General You Chan Song, Army Chief of Staff, because they were found guilty of taking bribes from contract-hungry businessmen. Before and after the April Revolution that ousted the Rhee government, many of Korea's most experienced military commanders were being forced into retirement because of political pressure.

General Carter B. Magruder, former United Nations Commander in Korea, warned the ROK Army to refrain from accusing its seniors of irregularities committed in the past. In October, 1960, General Magruder urged an end to military dissension and disputes within the ROK forces, in order to maintain the confidence of South Korea's allies and of her own people in the Armed Forces.

Most leaders of the young ROK Army returned home from exile in China and other countries, or were liberated from forced service in the Japanese Army at the end of the Second World War. ROK Army officers are not only young and aggressive, but also have combat experience as a result of service in the Korean War. Serving in the largest organization in South Korea, they have had more administrative training and management experience than some businessmen or civilians in the government. ROK Army soldiers have undergone hardships and privations, developing a strong capacity for physical endurance, and they perform better on the offensive than on the defensive, being combative by nature.

Owing to vastly increased artillery firepower, a constantly improving troop-training program, and the existence of a battle-trained ready reserve in the ROK Army, Chang's government discussed with the United Nations Command in November, 1960, the possibility of reducing by at least 100,000 the strength of its armed forces. The reason for such a reduction is the financial strain imposed on South Korea's budget.

Though the North Korean Communist Army has 150,000 fewer men than the ROK Army, they are stronger in military potential. They are known to have 1,000 fighter planes in combat readiness, of which 700 are MIG 15's or more advanced Russian fighter planes; but they are less well equipped as regards their navy. The Chinese Communist Army, of unknown size, stands behind the North Korean Army across the Yalu River in Manchuria, and is presumably ready to go to the aid of the North Korean Communists.

The Republic of Korea Army is supported by an air force of two wings, each with about seventy-five F-86 jet fighters in operation. The United States Fifth Air Force and air arm of the Seventh Fleet, with its carrier-based fighter bombers, are available as an air umbrella for South Korea. The coast lines of South Korea are protected by the United States Navy with heavy destroyers and an undisclosed number of other vessels. The half-million South Korean Army troops have been welded into a tough fighting machine, working in concert with the United Nations forces, composed of two United States divisions, plus an infantry company each from Thai and Turkey. The introduction of modern weapons into Korea has directly affected the ROK Army. Korean troops have been trained in atomic warfare and the use of other modern weapons. The ROK Army continues its training program, and is the strongest anti-Communist force in Asia.[27]

General Guy S. Meloy, Commander in Chief of the United Nations Command, summed up the combat readiness of the ROK and United Nations troops: "The danger of attack is ever with us. The United Nations Command is constantly on the alert to thwart any such sudden move."

The Republic of Korea's Army[28]

The Republic of Korea's Armed Forces consist of the army, the navy, which includes a marine corps, and the air force. Its organization is similar to that of the World War II United States Army, and its ranks generally correspond closely to those in the United States Army; also, the Army Chief of Staff commands all components. The ROK Army, the fourth largest in the world, has an estimated strength of approximately 567,000 officers and men. It is probably topped only by the armies of Communist China, the Soviet Union, and the United States.

Operational control of the field army is exercised by the commander in chief of the United Nations Command. Before the ROK Army military revolution in May, 1961, the Republic of Korea designated the prime minister as commander in chief of the national defense forces, and gave him authority to declare war, with the consent of the National Assembly. Directly subordinate to a civilian minister are the military chiefs of the three services. The ROK Joint Chiefs of Staff have not attained comparable influence and authority to, while it resembles, its United States counterpart.

The ROK Army uses the general staff system of the United States Army field armies, corps, and divisions, namely, G-1, personnel; G-2, intelligence; G-3, plans and operations; and G-4, logistics. ROK Army Headquarters has the responsibility for organizing, training, and equipping ROK ground forces for the conduct of sustained combat operations. The First ROK Army is a field army, assigned the mission of defending a large portion of the main battle positions along the Demilitarized Zone. The First Army also is responsible for security of the area within its boundaries, and for the training of all troops assigned.

The Second ROK Army has been shifted from its logistics support mission to manpower mobilization and veterans' training. Logistics is under the direct control of the Army Chief of Staff. Under the plan of operation, the Second Army handles many projects under the United States Armed Forces Assistance to Korea Program. The ROK Army Training Command is responsible for direction, supervision, coordination, and inspection of the army, and the development of tactics, techniques, and matériel for use by the army. It includes the service schools, except the Korean Military Academy and the Korean Command and General Staff College, which are directly under the Army Chief of Staff.

Major units of the army are twenty active divisions of about 13,000 officers and men each, organized into five corps. Ten reserve divisions are partly equipped, and engage in regular scheduled training under the direction of the Second Army. Active army divisions generally are similar to World War II triangular United States divisions, but have no organic tank or AAA-AW battalions. Although the infantry regiments do include a reconnaissance company in addition to the one found at division level, no heavy mortar company is authorized for the regiment.

The nucleus of the modern ROK Navy was the 2,000-man Coast Guard, organized by the United States Military Government in Korea, which was converted into the navy in 1948. During the Korean War, it gained considerable experience, under the United Nations Command, in patrolling and mine sweeping. Its small size makes its capability limited. It has a strength of about 16,880, and one fleet. Almost all vessels were formerly United States ships. The ROK Marine Corps consists of one division, similar in size and organization to a World War II United States Marine Corps division. The navy is relatively behind other service branches in its modernization program, except for the addition of a rocket-firing vessel to its fleet this year. The navy has worked to bolster its strength with destroyer-type craft. ROK Marines have continued to receive modern equipment, including amphibious armored vehicles.

The ROK Air Force possessed twenty operational aircraft, all trainers, at the outbreak of the Korean War. It has an extremely limited capability, having only two fighter wings with eighty F-86 aircraft, and a transport squadron with World War II C-46 aircraft. Total personnel strength is approximately 23,000 officers and men. The ROK Air Force includes a number of F-86 jets capable of all-weather combat missions. Most of the air-defense networks are manned by ROK Air Force personnel.

The modern Republic of Korea Army dates back to the time when the United States forces entered South Korea on September 13, 1945, and disarmed the Japanese military. The United States Military Government established the National Defense Command to foster and develop the Korean Constabulary and Coast Guard. The United States Military Government recognized that United States aid was indispensable for the establishment of a Korean army. The Military English Language Institute was founded on December 5, 1945, under the jurisdiction of the National Defense Command, to train military staff members in the English language. About two hundred students were selected from among those who had experienced military life in Japan, China, and Manchuria, and they received the fundamental English training needed for military affairs.

The Military English Language Institute moved to Taenung in the suburbs of Seoul on February 27, 1946. The two hundred students who entered the institute when it was founded graduated on December 15, 1946. Many officials of the Military Government completed their courses at the institute on March 30, 1947, and upon their graduation the institute was dissolved.

The United States Military Government formed a regiment on January 15, 1946, setting up a provisional office of the South Korea National Defense Constabulary in the Department of National Defense. On February 7th, the General Headquarters of the South Korea National Defense Constabulary was officially founded at he Headquarters of the First Regiment in Taenung, and rank and insignia were designated. Later, the Japanese "orderly" system was abolished on March 6th and the United States system was adopted.

The first regiments were small in size, not exceeding a battalion or a company. However, the organization of eight regiments was carried out without delay. Because of the armed-forces expansion, it became vitally important to train officers. Thus, following the dossolution of the Military English Language Institute, the South Korea National Defense Military Academy was established on May 1st, and the training of officers was launched, using United States methods.

When the Joint Conference of the United States and the Soviet Union was opened in Seoul, and the decisions made at the Moscow Foreign Ministers' Conference were under discussion, the Soviet delegation protested the use of the term Department of National Defense as "unsuitable." The United States delegation then made the concessions of changing the names of the Department of National Defense to that of the Department of National Security, the South Korea National Defense Constabulary to that of the Korean Constabulary, and the South Korea National Defense Constabulary Military Academy to that of the Korea Constabulary Military Academy.

After the United States Military Government was transferred to the South Korea Interim Government, the Chief of the Department of National Security was replaced by a Korean. Yu Dong Yul was installed as the first Chief of the Department of National Security on September 12, 1946, and Colonel Kim Sang Kyun later was installed as General Chief of Staff and Commander in Chief of the Department. The Armed Forces established in March, 1946, were gradually expanded, and the formation was almost completed by May, 1948. A recruiting campaign later was launched for eight more regiments. At this time ranks were changed, and Japanese military terms were replaced. On September 1, 1947, troops were reequipped with new weapons and uniforms supplied by the United States. As a result of the increase in the number of regiments, organization of brigades composed of three regiments each was needed for the purpose of easing command. Thus, the 1st, 2nd, and the 3rd brigades were established on December 1, 1947, and the 4th and 5th on April 29, 1948.

When the Government of the Republic of Korea was established on August 15, 1948, the great importance of a defense force was increased. On August 16th ceremonies were held installing the Minister of National Defense and relieving the Chief of the Department of National Security. After the transfer of administrative duties from the United States Military Government to the Republic of Korea Government, the Korea Constabulary of the South Korea Interim Government was reorganized as the Republic of Korea Army. The Coast Guard became the ROK Navy.

Following formal activation of the Republic of Korea Army, the army promptly began a build-up. Defense Minister General Lee Bum Suk, the first man to assume the post, began by strengthening the internal mechanism of the new Armed Forces. The firm foundations of a sound military development emerged as a number of capable men with military background were brought in.

On November 30, 1948, the national assembly passed the Law for the Organization of the National Army. In accordance with this provision, the Ministry of National Defense was created to supplant the Department of National Security. Army and Navy headquarters were put under the Defense Ministry. Brigadier General Lee Ung Joon and Colonel Chung Il Kwon were appointed the first Army Chief of Staff and Chief of the General Staff respectively.

On December 15th of the same year, various service branches were established in accordance with the Law for the Organization of the National Army. These are: cavalry, artillery, engineer, signal corps, commissary, accounting, ordnance, aide, inspection, medical corps, military police, aviation corps, and general staff. Shortly before —on December 1st—the three-point Pledge of the National Army and the Doctrine for the Enlisted Men were distributed.

The Republic, striving for the rapid upbuilding of the army in the face of growing Communist aggression, developed it into an organization of six new regiments and two brigades during the first five months after the army was created. Additional army build-ups include the 17th, 18th, 19th, 21st, 23rd, and 25th regiments and the 7th and 8th brigades. By May 12, 1949, all brigades in existence were expanded in strength to a division each.

The growing National Army was able completely to subdue the Communist conspiracy of the North Korean puppet clique which had become more and more active in the Republic as a source of confusion and disunity. Communist subversives had taken sides with guerrillas in a series of murders and other crimes. The army completed the mop-up of all armed Communist guerrillas on Cheju-do Island by March, 1949. The 9th ROK Regiment took part in the anti-Red operations, which lasted for more than thirteen months, beginning April 3, 1948.

While the Cheju-do campaign was still going on, an army rebellion took place in Yosu on October 19, 1948. The revolt was actually plotted by some Communist-tainted members of the 14th Regiment. It spread quickly as it gained the support of local Red elements. It was brought under control, however, on November 27th of the same year. Similar incidents on a minor scale broke out in Taegu and Pohang. With the rebellion over, the army conducted a campaign to eradicate a number of Communist elements within its ranks, and thus achieved maximum security.

Beginning early in May, 1949, the North Korean Communist puppet clique made armed incursions from time to time against our security forces along the 38th parallel. These were designed to test our defenses and to stir up unrest in the Republic. About four hundred Red troops, on May 3, 1949, deployed in the Kaesung area across the line, and seized Songaksan Mountain by force. The 1st ROK Division, garrisoned in the area, promptly rolled into action, and repelled the Red troops.

The heroic action of ROK soldiers led the Republic's garrisons to victory over the Communist troops. Two weeks later, another Red assault came in the U-po area, and again it was met by a strong and successful ROK counterattack. The U-po battle of May 16th and 17th was won after two days' intensive fighting. On May 19th, two days after the U-po battle, another wave of Red troops attempted to capture the town of Paikchon. Our troops from the Kaesung area moved into action swiftly, and repelled the enemy.

On July 23, 1949, the Red Army threw heavy artillery fire into Kaesum City without warning. It was another attempt to invade the city after the Reds' defeat in May. On August 3rd the Red assault was driven back swiftly by our determined defense forces. Meanwhile, in the Central Sector, near the Chunchon area, enemy troops launched an onslaught from Kwandae-ri onto our defense positions in the Shinnam area in an attempt to capture Hill 681 and Hill 233 northwest of Kuman-ni. The enemy forces were repulsed by the 7th ROK Regiment elements in this sector on August 20th. In the Uijongbu area, ROK forces killed 120 enemy troops in a battle in which the Reds had essayed a thrust deep into the south.

Meanwhile, in the Ongjin Peninsula on the west coast, the 12th ROK Regiment smashed strong Red assaulting forces and killed two hundred Communist invaders on August 4th. Another Red attempt to break through our defense positions in the area failed. It came on October 15th, when a strong enemy force surged into our lines under heavy and widespread artillery support. This attempt was again defeated by ROK counterattackers. Three days later, on October 20th, another group of some hundred Red troops was completely shattered by our garrison troops. After failing in a series of armed actions against the Republic, the enemy shifted its futile offensives to a "peace offensive" for the next move.

At the time the Communist North Korean puppet army launched its treacherous invasion of the Republic of Korea in June, 1950, the enemy had more than 200,000 men. The North Korean Army was made up of ten infantry divisions, and soon after the outbreak of the Korean War the Reds organized two more divisions, the 16th and 17th, plus the 2nd, 3rd, 4th, 5th, 6th, 10th, 12th, and 13th, already in existence. Enemy infantry strength was 154,000. The two divisions organized soon after the war broke out were combined into the so-called 105th Field Combat Division. Enemy ground troops had supporting units, including field artillery regiments and antiaircraft regiments. The 1st, 3rd, and 7th divisions became the so-called 38th Line Security Guard. Other units were a home security unit, a railroad security division, and Korea-Manchuria boundary security units. The enemy was equipped with heavy tanks and artillery, as well as fighter planes.

Compared to this enemy strength, our Armed Forces were deficient. The backbone of our ground troops was a force of only 100,000 men, eight divisions of about 80,000 men with about 17,000 men in a few supporting units. The ROK Army had only 27 armored vehicles, 140 guns of .105 caliber, 1900 bazookas, but no tanks. ROK naval forces had 30 vessels, and our air power consisted of but 10 training planes. It was with such deficient armament that the Republic of Korea Army had to fight the well-equipped Communist aggressors.

The enemy bluntly declared they would bring all of South Korea under their control by the anniversary of Liberation Day on August 15th. But the gallant ROK Army fought the Communist onslaught in bloody battles day after day and upset the enemy schedule by "delaying actions." United Nations forces, meanwhile, were called into action in compliance with the resolution adopted by the United Nations Security Council.

In preparation for last-ditch enemy attacks, the ROK Army set up powerful defensive lines, along with the UN Forces, which were being continuously reinforced. The United States 25th, 2nd, 27th, and 1st Cavalry divisions and the ROK 1st Division manned the defense lines. The ROK 2nd Corps was deployed along the central sector, and the ROK 1st Corps along the eastern sector. The delaying action was ended. The Eight United States Army announced that it would not retreat.

The enemy, failing in attacks against defense positions at Naktong launched attacks on September 4th against the northern sector in a final desperate effort. Enemy troops crossed Yongchon-Pohang Highway and moved south. They reached Yongchon on September 9th, but the ROK 2nd Corps repulsed the enemy. On September 10th, UN units outflanked the enemy 15th Division, along with its artillery units around Yongchon, and annihilated them. The enemy offensive ended. UN forces were ready to commence over-all counterattacks, thus ending the delaying actions.

The UN air force began heavy bombing of coastal areas on September 12th. On September 13th the naval bombardment of Inchon began. When the 7th United States Division landed at Inchon, half of its members were Koreans who had been trained in Japan. The United States 1st Marine Division, the ROK 17th Infantry Regiment, ROK Marine Corps, and British Marines also took part in the amphibious operation. Kim Il Sung, North Korean premier, named Minister of Defense Choi Yong Gun as commander of the Communist Seoul Garrison following the invasion of Inchon. Choi resisted desperately with the 20,000 Red troops under his command.

The ROK and United States Marines reached Seoul on September 23rd. The United States 1st Marine Division crossed the Han River at Mapo on September 25th. The United States 7th Division and the ROK 17th Regiment, after crossing the Han in force, entered Seoul from the southeast. Seoul was completely restored to Allied control on September 26th, after fierce street fighting. The Eighth United States Army, deployed along the Naktong defense line, launched an offensive on September 16th, in an operation coordinated with the Inchon invasion. The ROK Army, meanwhile, began an advance from its central and eastern sectors. The Communists began retreating all along the front in the face of determined counterattacks by UN units. Red troops, who fought stubbornly along the East Coast, began to retreat on September 17th. The ROK 3rd Division pursued them rapidly, and arrived at the 38th parallel on September 30th. The division then waited for an order to march across the parallel.

The 2nd Corps arrived in Seoul on October 3rd. The United States 1st Cavalry, United States 24th Infantry, ROK 1st Division, and the British 27th Brigade marched north along the Seoul-Pusan Railroad and arrived at the 38th Parallel on October 5th. The 25th Division advanced north through Chinju, Hadong, Namwon, and Kwangju, and the 2nd Division moved through Chogye, Chinan, and Chonju. At the same time, ROK Marines landed at Yosu and Mokpo, and engaged straggling Red troops. The mop-up operation was completed early in October.

The ROK 3rd Division reached the southern outskirts of Wonsan on September 9th, after crossing the 38th parallel and fighting through Yangyang, Kansong, Kosong, and Changjon. The Communist 5th Division was cut off from its route of escape, and its deputy commander was captured by UN units. The Capital Division and the 3rd Division marched through Inje, Kojo, and Sinkosan. The two divisions occupied Wonsan on October 10th.

On the Central Front, the ROK 8th Division reached Tokchon after marching through Chorwon, Kumhwa, Pyongyang, and Inchon. The 6th Division marched through Chunchon, Hwachon, Wonsan, Yangdok, and Sungchon to Sunchon. Along the West Coast, the United States 9th Division kept marching north. The United States 1st Corps, with the 1st Cavalry Division, marched along the Kyongbu Railroad. UN Forces, with the 1st ROK Division in the vanguard, occupied Pyongyang at 1:00 P.M. October 19th.

The enemy moved their high command to Hichon and Kanggye after losing Pyongyang. Their line of defense was moved gradually back to the Manchurian border. Their troops were routed. The ROK 6th Division advanced on the eastern wing, and occupied Hichon on October 24th. It later changed its direction of march to move along the Hoemoktong-Chosan route. The 7th Regiment of the 6th Division occupied Chosan on October 26th and arrived at the Yalu.

Supported by elements of the United States Navy and Air Force, the ROK Capital Division marched on Songjin after passing through Myongchon. While the ROK Army was advancing, the United States 10th Corps, comprising the United States 1st Marines and United States 7th Division, which had just arrived in Korea, landed at Wonsan and began a drive toward the Tuman River, which flows along the Korea-Manchuria border. The United States 10th Corps, which had successfully landed at Inchon, drove into Kote-ri on November 10th, along the Hamhung and Chongjin Reservoir. The units continued to advance toward Hesanjin, on the Korean-Manchurian border, and finally occupied it on November 21st.

When the 7th Regiment of the 6th ROK Division arrived at the banks of the Yalu River, north of Chosan, the 2nd Regiment of the 6th Division, located at Onjong-ni, and one regiment of the 1st ROK Division, at Unsan, were attacked by a huge force of Chinese Communists who swarmed across the Yalu. Chinese Communist intervention in the Korean War had been predicted. The Chinese had prepared themselves for intervention, and after the collapse of the North Korean puppet forces, which were on the verge of complete defeat, the Chinese intervened.

The Chinese Communist forces consisted of four armies of about 120,000 men. With their great superiority in manpower, the Chinese inflicted heavy losses upon UN forces. On December 5th the Reds succeeded in infiltrating Chongju, Pakchon, and Yongbyon, and subsequently managed to dent the UN lines linking Chongju, Yongbyon, Kaechon, and Tokchon. The enemy 1st Corps, attacking from north of Kaesong, crossed the Imjin River and occupied Seoul on January 4th. Elements of the corps started to advance toward Inchon after crossing the Han River. The main Red forces, however, were diverted toward Suwon and Osan. The Red 2nd Corps, heading south from Inje, occupied Pyongchang and Yongwol on January 15th. By occupying these towns the Reds cut off the Chungang rail line, and continued to advance south. Chinese Communists invading from north of Chunchon then occupied Hongchon and Wonju. These forces were followed by the Reds' 5th Division, and UN Forces were forced to give up Wonju on January 8th.

In a new operation to bleed the enemy, UN Forces launched a counterattack, and regained Osan on January 15th. On January 17th our reconnaissance units, supported by tanks, battled into Suwon. In the Wonju area, meanwhile, the 2nd United States Division continued to battle the enemy. UN Forces drove the Reds from the Pyongchang and Chipyong areas on June 3rd. Paratroops were dropped at Kimpo Airfield. Simultaneously, the 25th United States Division and the British Brigade recaptured Yongdungpo and Inchon.

On March 2nd, elements of United States forces succeeded in crossing the Han River at several points, and on March 7th the United States 25th Division crossed the river in force at Yangsu-ri, and launched a drive north. The Reds holding in Seoul, threatened with being outflanked, retreated from the city. The 3rd ROK and United States 3rd divisions entered Seoul without resistence. On

January 23rd the United States 187th Airborne Regiment dropped near Munsan-ni and joined forces with the 1st United States Cavalry Division, which was rushed there from Uijongbu.

The ROK Army, undergoing all these trials, crushed the Communist foe internationally and domestically. The army was expanded in quantity and improved in quality. Firepower and airpower were greatly increased. One field army and one corps were organized, and the total number of divisions and regiments was increased. Facilities in field surgical hospitals, field artillery groups, field engineer groups, and field ordnance groups were increased. A ROK Army small-arms and artillery-rebuilding factory, printing factory, and chemical-weapons-manufacturing plant were established.

The truce talks, which began in July, 1951, and continued for two years, were finally concluded on July 27, 1953. Though a truce was concluded, the Communists have not given up their aggressive intentions. The Reds have launched a program to rebuild the units smashed during the intense fighting, and are receiving equipment from Russia and are busily occupied in increasing their armaments. To meet this menace, the ROK Army has been ceaselessly increasing its fighting ability, with wary eyes on the aggressive intentions and preparations of the enemy. The ROK Army, though comparatively young, is the greatest anti-Communist democratic force in the Far East, and is ready to discharge its responsibility to protect the peace.

The plan to withdraw United States troops from Korea was stated by President Eisenhower on December 27th, 1954. On March 14, 1954, the United States began to withdraw two divisions from Korea, despite strong protest from the Republic of Korea. But the gap opened by the withdrawal of actual military power from Korea was filled by the build-up of the ROK Army. On December 15, 1953, the First Army of the Republic of Korea (FROKA) was activated, and received operational and training control over its subordinate corps from the United States 10th Corps on March 15, 1954. On May 3rd the Joint Chiefs of Staff Conference was discontinued and a Joint Staff was established by Presidential Order 895. General Lee Hyung Keun was appointed Chairman of the Joint Staff, and Lieutenant General Kang Yung Hun, Director. Thus the chain of operational orders in the Armed Forces of the Republic of Korea was centralized.

In the meantime a series of military conferences among high-ranking officers and statesmen of the United States and the Republic of Korea were held: the United States-ROK Seoul Conference on March 30, 1954; FEAF Commander General Partridge's visit to Kyungmu-dae for the third Joint Chiefs of Staff Conference discussing build-up of the ROK Army on April 7th; the fourth Joint Chiefs of Staff Conference on April 26th, held just before General Van Fleet's arrival in Korea; the United States-ROK Military Conference attended by General Van Fleet on May 9th; the ROK Army Corps and Divisional Commanders Conference presided over by General Chung, Chief of Staff. All these conferences discussed the build-up of the ROK Army and defensive strategy in postwar Korea. In addition a special series of secret conferences between the United States, represented by Defense Secretary Charles Wilson, and a Military Mission headed by General James Van Fleet, and the ROK by National Defense Minister Admiral Sohn Won Il, General Chung, and other high-ranking military leaders were held till May 17th in Pusan.

On May 22, 1954, the ROK 6th Corps was activated, and with this corps the army had twenty active divisions. On May 26th the First AAA Battalion was activated. As a result of President Rhee's visit to the United States, and the United States-ROK Seoul Conference, the ROK Army organized ten reserve divisions in addition to its twenty active divisions. Plans to establish an arsenal for the army and a shipyard for the navy, as well as to reinforce the air force with jet planes and the navy with more vessels, were also stepped up. Moreover, dissolution of the Korea Youth Association and the organization of a militia by a presidential order dated September 16, 1953, as well as enlistment and special ten weeks' training for college students announced by the defense minister on June 11, 1954, and by a directive of the educational minister on June 28th, made possible military training for all people and the formation of a pool of officers necessitated by the organization of ten reserve divisions.

Establishment of a soldiers' college on January 26, 1954, under supervision of the Ministry of National Defense, for officers and men who discontinued their studies on joining the Armed Forces, greatly contributed to the advancement of the educational level and combat effectiveness of the ROK Army.

A Mutual Defense Treaty between the United States and the Republic of Korea was agreed upon by Secretary of State John Foster Dulles, who came to Korea on August 4th, a week after the conclusion of the Korean truce, and Foreign Affairs Minister Pyung Yung Tae, on August 8th, in Seoul. It became effective from January 17, 1954, when the American Congress and the National Assembly of Korea ratified the treaty. The treaty does not commit either country to go to war if the other is invaded, but seeks to provide for mutual assistance through constitutional procedures.

The Korean armistice agreement, which was finally signed after 24 months and 17 days of protracted wrangling, recommended the initiation of diplomatic talks for a peaceful solution of the Korean issue. Owing to obstructionist tactics by the Reds, however, the political conference failed to achieve results. Instead, the Geneva Conference took its place. At the Geneva Conference the Republic proposed an election for South and North Korea under supervision of the United Nations, but from the very beginning the Republic knew that it was impossible to bring about the unification of the South and the North through negotiations with the Communists, and had no choice but to wait for another chance to achieve unification.

General Chung Il Kwon, former Army Chief of Staff, chose the following major objectives for the ROK Army during the armistice: establishment of a logistical support system, including development and expansion of an arsenal; increased officer training; organization of additional reserve units; and the strengthening of mutual respect and good will between the people of South Korea and their army.

By the order of General Maxwell D. Taylor, then Commander of the Eighth United States Army, the United States 10th Corps was relieved of its operational and training control over FROKA, and FROKA received control of the 1st, 2nd, and 3rd Corps as independent tactical units on March 15, 1954. Earlier, on December 15, 1953, the First ROK Field Army was activated with a ceremony held on the parade ground of the United States 10th Corps, when Lieutenant General Bruce C. Clark, corps commander, presented the colors of the First Field Army to its commander, General Paik Sun Yup. In the next three months, First Field Army Headquarters, under its first Chief of Staff, Major General Kim Ung Su, received organizational instruction from the United States 10th Corps.

During the previous ten years, a division was the highest tactical unit of the ROK Army, and fought under the direction of United States corps in the early part of the Korean War. As the ROK Army increased the number of its commanders and combat-trained officers, and strengthened its fighting capacity, independent ROK Army corps were organized, but still under the control of the United States corps. Following the conclusion of the truce agreement in August, 1953, as a preparatory step to the transfer of operational and training control over the ROK corps, the United States 10th Corps was reorganized with the 1st, 2nd, and 3rd ROK corps and various divisions under its command for field training. When these corps, which were holding two-thirds of the front, became independent from its command, the United States 10th Corps Group reverted to its original status.

The highest combat unit of the ROK Army, the First ROK Army, will eventually relieve the United Eighth Army of its function. FROKA has now added the 5th Corps to its command, and in July moved its headquarters to Wonju.

In order to cope with an emergency, FROKA, which is established along more than two-thirds of the Korean front, holds full-scale maneuvers twice yearly. It is equipped with the most modern weapons, supplied by the United States Army, and is putting emphasis on the training of specialists, both officers and enlisted men. From January to August, 1955, the Commanders Orientation Course, in which General Park Chung Hee, Army Commander, himself enrolled; Field Ordnance Course, Engineer Course, Signal Course, Transportation Course, Field Medical Course, and many other technical programs, were established for the training of additional specialists for FROKA.

The Korean Army Training Command (KATC) was activated as the Korean Army Training Center on August 10, 1951, in Pusan, the country's logistical center, on the southern tip of the Korean Peninsula, while war was being waged close to the present cease-fire line. Since its activation as a training center, KATC has been making steady progress as the source of well-trained men for the army, and in 1954 it officially assumed all education and training facilities. KATC, which the ROK Army boasts is the biggest army training center in the Orient, is filled with soldiers gaining experience and hard training to swell the ranks of the ROK Army of more than half a million men.

On September 18, 1954, the activation ceremony of KATC was

held at Sangmudae, when President Rhee presented the colors of KATC to its first commander, Lieutenant General Yu Jae Hung. Upon the activation of the center, General Yu listed five objectives: combatlike training; emphasis on joint training; elevation of the educational level of personnel; standardization of principles; and accuracy of training administration. KATC has since achieved brilliant results in the training of tough, combat-ready soldiers.

In 1954 KATC took over three recruit training centers that were under the direct control of Army Headquarters, and fourteen service schools. As a source of manpower for the defense of the Republic of Korea, KATC has been named *Sangmudae,* "a place of military spirit." At the christening ceremony on January 6, 1952, President Rhee explained that *Sangmu* does not mean aggressive intention, but an appreciation of the necessity of military knowledge as a means of maintaining and securing peace and freedom for mankind.

As United Nations forces were gradually withdrawn from South Korea, the strengthening of the ROK Army became a necessity. On August 10, 1954, Lieutenant General Kang Num Bong, then 3rd Corps commander, was ordered to activate a second ROK Army, which would build up the Zone of the Interior. A committee for this purpose was organized, and when General Chung Il Kwon returned from the United States, the activation of SROKA was officially announced by General Order 8 of the Ministry of National Defense, on September 20, 1954.

The final decision as to what the mission and function of SROKA would be was reached by the Joint United States and ROK Military Committee meeting held on October 3, 1954. The activation ceremony, which was authorized by General Order 2715, Headquarters, the Republic of Korea Army, took place at Seoul Stadium on October 31, 1954, and was attended by President Rhee and other ROK and United States Government officials. Following its activation, SROKA began to perform its primary mission of logistical support for the ROK Army. SROKA also was charged with the responsibility of maintaining reserve forces for replacement of manpower, administrative support, and military assistance for the reconstruction of South Korea. With the activation of SROKA, the Korea Communication Zone was released from its function of logistical support for the ROK Army. Today SROKA has five military district commands, ten reserve divisions, security battalions, and many other technical units under its command. SROKA also is charged with the responsibility of mobilizing manpower by conducting the nationwide draft. When SROKA assumed all the AFAK functions, which had been operated by KCOMZ, on June 25, 1955, it initiated various Armed Forces Assistance activities, such as construction of schools, orphanages, churches, reconstruction of roads, and other technical assistance to rehabilitation.

IV

New Korea

♦ ♦ ♦ *"Newer is truer. Everything new is fine."*—PROVERB

MILITARY REVOLUTION[1]

As in most of the rest of Asia, power lies in the hands of the few who can apply force; that means the President, the army, or the national police. During former President Syngman Rhee's authoritarian government, the national police was a very powerful agency. Owing to the students' April Revolution against police brutality, and Prime Minister Chang's reduction of the police power under the "Second" Republic, after the downfall of Syngman Rhee, the Army of the Republic of Korea, being well trained, equipped, and assisted and advised by the United States, remains the only power group in South Korea.

The army coup in South Korea was motivated by dissatisfaction with the failure of John Chang's parliamentary government to root out corruption and intrigue among politicians. One charge against

115

him was that his government had not proceeded sternly enough in punishing the leaders of the Rhee regime. The coup was also directed against government plans to enact two security bills, ostensibly aimed at controlling unruly demonstrations and Communist activities, but opposed by Socialists and student groups as a threat to their newly won political freedom. In addition, the slogan "Give us jobs and bread!" was shouted repeatedly during the mass demonstrations, and pointed to the largest problem Chang inherited from Rhee: economic instability.

Since August 19, 1960, Chang had ruled over a deeply divided South Korean National Assembly, fighting a losing battle against new charges of corruption, of a weak policy toward the criminals of Rhee's regime, and of inability to solve the country's mounting unemployment problems. Although Chang government was the closest one to a democracy Koreans had known, he faced one political disaster after another. The Republic of Korea Army was angered by Chang's attempts to reduce its size; students were displeased by his soft attitude toward the members of Rhee's old government who were under arrest; and businessmen were angered by his attempts to close down the black market.

A Military Revolution Committee pledged continued tough anti-Communist policy and continued close cooperation with the United States. The ROK Army was one of the strongest anti-Communist forces in Asia, and its revolutionary leaders carried out the military coup efficiently and with practically no bloodshed. General James A. Van Fleet, former United Nations commander, who is called the father of the ROK Army, supported the army as being representative of the Korean people. Lieutenant General Song Yo Chan, former army Chief of Staff, also endorsed the coup, which was staged by his former subordinates, as necessary to save Korea from corruption and Communism.

The "democratic experiment" of the last year was thus brought to an end by discontent within the army, and General Park, with several other generals, engineered the coup. In April, 1960, the Army Chief of Staff, General "Tiger" Song Yo Chan, altered the balance of power within South Korea by tolerating student demonstrations. He also threw the army into a state of turmoil. Since his resignation a year earlier, there had been constant pressure from the poorly paid ROK

Army colonels for an all-around "purge" of generals to make room for ability and patronage at the top. In September sixteen colonels formally demanded the resignation of all eight generals, much to the dismay of the American UN commander, General Magruder, who made his opposition public. Under Rhee, some generals had organized army votes for the Liberal party and had had many opportunities for lining their pockets; but to oust them appeared to be a move that would weaken national security.[2]

The Democrats under Chang, in addition to a lack of leadership, were also vainly fighting corruption among the members of their own party, whose votes had been for sale during the Rhee period. In one sense the victory of democracy in Korea in April, 1960, was the signal for more people to share in the fruits of corruption. Another reason for failure was the Chang government's inability to allay apprehension in military circles in the face of growing public opinion for an economic and cultural *modus vivendi* with North Korea, an opinion that open discussion revealed as strong among South Korean intellectuals. Under Rhee's Korea, such suggestions would have been considered treasonous; under the present army regime it is undoubtedly considered a threat not only to the nation but also to the professional standing of the army.[3]

Although a revolution against a duly constituted government is not a venture to be undertaken lightly, the leaders of the ROK Army, with the highest ideals of patriotism, were forced to take this action in order to save the nation from complete disaster. The Korean people and their present military leaders are fully aware of the dangers inherent in military government. However, the ROK Armed Forces, hitherto aloof from politics, are the only remaining organizations that retain the people's respect; they alone are administratively capable of running the government; they are the only force strong enough to eliminate corrupt and self-serving interests; and they have no intention of abandoning the principles of real democracy. Rather, their determination is to convert these principles into actual practice.

The Military Government, strengthened by the resignation of General Chang Do Young, is now in general control throughout South Korea. The ROK Army coup leaders are able, dedicated men who want to remain on friendly terms with the United States, which should work with the new regime in every constructive way possible. Faced by multitudinous problems, the Military Government is determined to solve them, and has already achieved remarkable progress. Committees composed of civilians and of military officers are already studying the nature of the civilian government that will emerge after revolutionary tasks have been completed.

The new Korean Military Government has taken a number of long-needed steps: rice has been distributed to the poor; farm debts have been canceled; hoodlumism has been abolished; and full-time duty is being enforced among civil servants. There has been a stern crackdown on profiteering and corruption. There has also been an alarming abrogation of civil liberties; however, this phase may be only temporary, as the revolutionary government has now evidently begun to prepare for popular sanction for its rule in the form of a national referendum, the adoption of a new Constitution, and the announcement of new elections, to be held in 1963, for a civilian democratic government.

South Korea's deficit economy, its two million unemployed, and its shortage of resources are problems difficult for even the most capable rulers to solve. In the sphere of fundamental social and economic reforms, a comprehensive program has been planned with special attention to the depressed rural sector of the Korean economy. Poverty-stricken peasants have been given government subsidies to improve the productivity of their land, and more land has been put under cultivation. Marketing practices have been improved, and small industries have developed to an extent where they can absorb some of the unemployed in rural and city areas. The Military Government is planning to restore economic stability in South Korea, especially on some of the critical problems caused by the revolution.

General Park Chung Hee's statement that power will be returned to civilian hands when the Military Government's objectives have been realized is praiseworthy, and it is to be hoped that the junta will give way to civilian rule in 1963 through normal constitutional processes, as has been promised. This will minimize disruptions in the political, economic, and military fabric of South Korea. The firm determination of the present Military Government promises a Korea Tomorrow for the New Korea.

The following remarks on the necessity of the coup appeared in the *Korea Photonews,* issued by the Ministry of Public Information, in a Special May Edition, 1961:

. . . the recent military coup in Korea . . . was directed by the highest military officers in the nation. Dedicated (as they are) to the welfare of the country; inculcated (as they are) with the highest ideals of patriotism and discipline; the leaders of the revolution were forced—however reluctantly—to take this action in order to save the nation from complete disaster. The former government was incredibly corrupt; the executive branch so weak that all governmental processes were breaking down. The legislature was simply a congregation of small politicians too engrossed in petty quarrels for jobs to consider the welfare of the people. Business and industry stagnated; farmers were desperate; the vast number of unemployed steadily increased; hunger and starvation were abroad in the land. Beneath was the ominous undertone of Communism. Agents from Communist North Korea were actively spreading their false gospel; the utterly venal and completely irresponsible press poured fuel on the flames of unrest. It was—and is—the belief of the Armed Forces that if they had failed to act in this extreme national emergency, a different and irreversible revolution, probably Communist-directed, would have been inevitable. The military assumption of governing power is temporary. As soon as revolutionary tasks have been accomplished, it is the firm intention of the present regime to return power to a democratically elected, constitutional civilian government.[4]

Since the army coup, Korea has taken on a new look. In less than two weeks, the gangs of hoodlums that formerly infested all Korean cities were jailed and are waiting trial. Anarchic traffic conditions in Seoul and other cities have given way to the orderly, safe movement of vehicles and pedestrians. Work projects are under way; business and industrial firms are resuming operations; the "black market" and smuggling have been stopped. Householders, for the first time, no longer feel the need for barbed-wire barricades around their homes to exclude burglars. Rich criminals can no longer evade punishment for their crimes; neither can the poor. There is equal justice, under law, for rich and poor alike.

The period of national rehabilitation is beginning. Government offices are being reorganized on an efficient basis. Business and industry are being encouraged to expand their activities on a solid economic foundation in order to earn profits for themselves and to contribute to the welfare of the people. Every effort is being made to direct the country toward a self-supporting economy. Above all, it is the intent of the present government to strengthen the basic anti-Communist sentiment of the people, and to align this country even more strongly than in the past on the side of the United Nations and of the United States of America—the acknowledged leader of the free world against the aggressive forces of the international Communist conspiracy.

When the ROK Army generals overthrew a duly elected government in South Korea, the United States was taken aback. Army plans for a coup had actually begun in March, 1960, right after the rigged elections of the Rhee regime. However, the Students' Revolution forstalled the army plotters, and every Korean, including the ROK Army leaders, hoped that an era of honest and efficient government would follow.

When the coup leaders became convinced that the Chang government would not fulfill their hopes, the original group of nine leaders who had planned to overthrow Rhee's government met again to discuss and evaluate the situation. The ROK Army Revolution required only the courage of the few backed by the longing of the many. Later, the small group was enlarged to include about 250 officers of all ranks, and it was agreed to carry out a coup on April 19, 1961, the anniversary of the Students Revolution. Their expectation was that the students would again stage an "uprising" and that it would be necessary for the troops to restore order. The soldiers released from the United Nations Command would then take over the inefficient Chang government. However, the students remained quiet, and the coup was rescheduled for May 12th and finally postponed until May 16, 1961. General Park Chung Hee and General Chang Do Young, the Army Chief of Staff at that time, became involved later; General Park especially became a dynamic force in the uprising. The cost of the coup was 8,600,000 hwan, about $7,000, which was spent for travel and liaison purposes. The money came from an undisclosed businessman.

Because operations of the ROK Army were under the United Nations Command, headed by General Carter B. Magruder, the coup leaders, together with the ROK Army Chief of Staff, Lieutenant General Chang, had to use some 3,600 Korean troops in Seoul under the pretense of night maneuvers against student uprisings. Accordingly, the troops were released from the United Nations Command for the army's coup. According to a competent source, the plot, except for the date, was known to General Magruder, but the information was discounted, and countermeasures to protect the elected government were not employed. It was also reported that Lieutenant General Chang, Chief of Staff of the ROK Army, tricked General Magruder into ignoring the reports.

The Army junta's intelligence chief, Lieutenant Colonel Kim Chong Pil, one of the nine original planners of the coup, said that the coup succeeded because of inadequate or superficial American Army intelligence. Colonel Kim Chong Pil, who took paratroop training at Fort Benning, Georgia, in 1951, told newsmen that the Chang government would still be in power if the Americans had "dug a little deeper into the Korean situation: I feel that the U.S. Eighth Army's ignorance was due mainly to inadequate intelligence. They refused to believe that a strong organization with a united front could emerge from the Korean army."

The thirty-five-year-old colonel had some sound advice for the Americans. He told them to "develop a broader base of understanding with the Korean people. Their knowledge now is just superficial, based on limited information from a very few high-ranking persons." He cited as an example the fact that top United States Officers visiting Korea have contact with only a few higher officials; conversely, Korean officers sent to the States for training are only those "from the top who are corrupt."[5]

The ROK Army junta, violating the military understanding with the United Nations Command, moved troops secretly into Seoul with swift efficiency. At 3:00 A.M., on May 16, 1961, jeeps and trucks loaded with veterans began rolling into Seoul. Columns of paratroopers and marines raced practically unopposed to the center of the capital, surrounding government buildings, blocking intersections, and firing into the air to frighten the populace. The revolutionary army, comprising the 1st Marine Brigade, the Army Air-borne Unit, the 30th and 31st Reserve divisions, and the 6th Corps Artillery units, crossed the Han River and, although there was a negligible exchange of fire, seized the entire city.

By noon, citizens were going about their business as usual, and civil employees were reporting back to work. The radio broadcast that the ROK Army had assumed responsibility for the Republic of Korea was received quietly, but with satisfaction and hope by the majority of citizens, who were disgusted with the former Rhee and Chang governments. The nation reacted enthusiastically to the change of government. All branches of the military forces, including the cadets of the service academies, pledged their support. Veterans' organizations, students, teachers, business and civic groups voiced their approval.

Directly after the May 16th coup, the United States, in the person of Marshall Green, then chargé d'affaires and also minister in the American Embassy in Seoul, together with General Carter Magruder, then United Nations Commander, tried to save Chang's government, but their effort failed because the leaders of Chang's government bargained with the junta, and were determined to avoid bloodshed. After two days in hiding, Chang surrendered to the army.

The United States feared that its interests would suffer because Green and Magruder had backed the wrong horse. The consequence, however, was that the junta's admiration for America increased, and the bargaining position of the American Embassy and of the United Nations Command was improved, because of the acting American ambassador's respect for the constitutional government. It demonstrated that the United States Government had had no connection with the coup and that the United States Armed Forces in Korea were not involved in the country's internal political turmoil. To prevent civil strife and the dissolution of the South Korean army into warring factions, the United States decided to support the army and to assist it in establishing the reforms it had promised.

Upon seizing the legislative, administrative, and judicial machinery, the ROK Army junta issued its Revolutionary Pledges and won the full-fledged support of the entire nation. The six-point revolutionary program was as follows: anti-Communism would be continued as national policy; friendly ties with the United States and other free-world nations would be further strengthened; corruption would be wiped out; all-out efforts would be made for the reconstruction of a self-reliant national economy; unification of the divided land would be sought by all possible means; and eventually the army would turn over the reins of power to new and conscientious politicians, and return to their original duties.

Following is a partial paraphrase of the article "What Made the Revolution Succeed,"[6] by General Park Chung Hee, Chairman of the Supreme Council for National Reconstruction of the Republic of Korea:

The question "What has made the military revolution successful?" is likely to cause misunderstanding. The revolution has just started with the seizure of power by the military force; its full-scale development is now about to begin. The *coup d'état* has, of course, proved to be successful. The question of whether the military revolution will be successful or not, however, belongs to the future. In this sense it might be more appropriate to ask "Will the military revolution prove to be successful?" The success of the military revolution can be said to be a result of the failure of democracy in Korea. Therefore, the question "What has made the military revolution successful" really means "Why has democracy failed in the Republic of Korea?" Now let us review various aspects of Korean democracy in the past.

The history of Korean democracy was one of fifteen short years of successive failures. It was on August 15, 1945, that the Japanese imperialistic colonial rule over Korea was put to an end and democracy was "imported" to this country. Never before had the Korean people experienced Western democracy. Hence, Korea was a barren land for democracy. It was hardly possible that democracy transplanted here could reach fruition. In other words, Korea lacked the fundamental requirements for the sound growth of democracy. What are the fundamental requirements? We may look at them from four different angles: social and economic conditions, the national psychological attitude, the national moral conception, and finally, external tension.

For democracy to flourish, a nation should, first of all, maintain excellent social and economic conditions, and wipe out discontent among its people. In other words, democracy is bound to thrive where national life is stabilized and the educational standard is high. This is far from the case in Korea. Korea is a nation whose foundation has long been sustained by agriculture. What is the actual condition of the farming populace of this country?

According to the 1958 *Agricultural Year-Book,* published by the Agricultural Bank of Korea, the farming populace accounted for 62.8 per cent of the entire population of this country, totaling 21,909,-

742 persons. Those farming households who came under the category of from 0.245 acres up to less than 2.451 acres amounted to 1,610,-521, or 72.6 per cent of all farming households, totaling 2,010,900. The income of farmers constituted only 37 per cent of that of the entire Korean populace. This shows vividly what a miserable life the Korean farmers are leading. Such poverty exists not only in rural areas but also in urban areas. If one reads a UNESCO report that the annual per capita income of this country runs below $80 in American money, he cannot but deplore the fact that Koreans are among the poorest peoples in the world.

It is only too natural that democracy should fail to prosper in Korea, where the per capita income and the living standard of the people are so low. Korea has received enormous amounts of aid from the United States and other friendly nations of the free world. Thanks to this assistance the Korean people have barely avoided starving to death. Korea has received approximately $3 billion in aid from the United States. But what contribution has the aid money made toward the attainment of a self-sufficient economy in the country? The structural ratio of the nation's gross national product in 1953–1959 runs at 40.5 per cent in primary industry, 15.8 per cent in secondary industry, and 43.6 per cent in tertiary industry. This is a crippled structure. To think that tertiary industry should far outweigh primary industry in a nation that relies heavily on agriculture! Korea has neither adequate electricity nor ample water supplies. The man in the street satirizes this, saying, "The Korean reconstruction is a reconstruction of teashops, billiard halls, and bars."

Needless to say, reconstruction has been attained mainly with the aid from the United States. In other words, United States aid merely helped Korea to increase the tendency to consumption, rather than production, and fostered a consumption-first economy with an eye to attaining a demonstration effect. This ran diametrically counter to the direction the Korean economy should have taken for the attainment of self-sufficiency.

The nation's politicians gambled on this antinational course, and so did a good many businessmen, financiers, judicial officers, and government officials. Add to this, various types of corruption and irregularities in collusion with finance and politics. Judicial officers protected the "order" of corruption and irregularities with the process of law; educators advocated it among their students; and government officials bolstered it with their administrative privileges. In a nutshell, it was an order based on unsavory patronage and *sabasaba,* or disposition of matters by using underhanded means.

People called this "politics." All these things were done under the cloak of democracy. Such "politics," however, had nothing to do with the poverty-stricken multitudes of the nation. Neither did such "politics" have anything to do with democracy, even though it disguised itself under the cloak of democracy. Obviously, it was no more than an oligarchy bolstered by monetary influence.

From this stems the phenomenon of separation of the multitude from the ruling class, including politicians, who should have defended the people's rights. The discontent of the populace filled the nation. The statesmen were not aware of this. On the contrary, they were intoxicated with power, engulfed in self-complacency, and more engrossed in political swindling. The gap between the people and the statesmen grew wider and wider. Politics, when it loses the support of the people, is bound to fall back upon the terrorism of rifles and bayonets as a last resort. If things go on like this, signs appear signaling the downfall of the regime. A good example of this was the fourth-term and the fifth-term presidential and vice-presidential elections. The Liberal party, which desperately tried to maintain power by means of terrorism and blackmail, in the long run was expelled from power.

Then came into power the Democratic party, which played nothing more than the role of opposition group of the Liberal party. But though the Democratic party was an opponent of the Liberal party, it was in reality a collaborator with an oligarchy bolstered by monetary influence. No sooner had the Democratic party seized power than it showed the cloven hoof. Things had been better under the reign of the Liberal party than they were during the Democratic regime. The Liberal party could sustain itself in one way or another, thanks to a central figure, the bigoted old man Dr. Syngman Rhee, who was once looked up to by the Korean people as a great leader because of his career as an anti-Japanese fighter during Japanese rule. Unfortunately, there was no such leader as Dr. Rhee during the reign of the Democratic party.

The true nature of Democratic plutocracy appeared on the surface even more clearly in the early stage of its reign, and the people's hope became despair, which later developed into indifference. This indifference was vividly demonstrated in the elections for provincial councilors, including those of the City of Seoul, held less than four months after the government of John M. Chang was born; more than half the voters did not participate in the elections. This was a sort of silent resistance. The Chang regime's days were already numbered, and not only those of the Chang regime, but those of Korean democracy also.

The death sentence was declared from the Speaker's rostrum of the National Assembly Hall. The declaration was made, not by the House Speaker, but by a wounded April hero. In protest against the unfair ruling of the judicial authorities on the masterminds of the rigged mid-March presidential and vice-presidential elections in 1960, scores of wounded April heroes invaded the House of Representatives while it was in session, occupied the Speaker's rostrum, and declared the dissolution of the National Assembly.

It is said that in England even the queen cannot enter Parliament without permission. Yet in Korea, a riotous group swarmed into the Assembly Hall, sacred headquarters of the representatives of the will of the people, and occupied the Speaker's rostrum to declare the dissolution of the National Assembly! For this incident the Chang cabinet refused to shoulder responsibility. Such were the incapable and irresponsible politicians of this country in the past. It is not too much to say that with this incident the Second Republic, which was born of the April Revolution, was already doomed. Needless to say, amidst such social impoverishment, political irresponsibility, incapability, and corruption, the people could not display a high regard for individual responsibility in public life. In Korea, however, those who advocated individual rights and faithfully performed their duties and responsibilities were regarded as fools. But democracy can be achieved only when the entire nation is awakened to the fact that responsibilities always accompany rights.

What Koreans should bear in mind is the fact that their country is divided and constantly menaced by international Communism. No one knows when Korea might fall into a trap of direct or indirect aggression. At this very moment indirect Communist aggression is present in Korea, visibly or invisibly. In the past, the shortsighted politicians did nothing but strive to win political contests. They failed to strengthen the nation's anti-Communist front, and South Korea was forced into crisis. But South Koreans are not isolated in their fight against Communism. Friendly democratic nations are standing with them, and during the Korean War sixteen friendly nations heroically fought with them against the Communist agressors. In the event of choice between Democracy and Communism, there can be no room for Koreans to consider both North-South negotiations and neutralism.

The history of Korean democracy is, frankly, a history of failures. The success of the May 16th military revolution was the result of the failure of Korean democracy. But is the success of the military revolution intended to erase democracy for good in this part of the world? No. The revolution was designed only to revive democracy in this country. Is it not proper to say that when Communism has been expelled from Korean soil, corruption and irregularities and hunger have been wiped out, and the national morality has been awakened to the significance of freedom, responsibilities, and duty, democracy can revive in this country?

The revolution is designed to perform a full-dress operation for the revival of the freedom and rights of the state and the people at a time when the nation is confronted with destruction and the people's rights have been trampled down. The military revolution is not intended to strangle democracy in this country, but to suspend it temporarily; it is a remedial measure intended to restore democracy to its healthy function.

South Korea will have to undergo a series of drastic reforms of its economic structure in the endeavor to increase per capita income, invigorate the national life, and build up national education and culture. South Korea will have to do away with the easygoing consumption-first national philosophy, and make desperate efforts to lay a firm foundation for the attainment of a self-sufficient economy.

The sources of past social evils—corruption, irregularities, and injustices—should be rooted out, and a clean national morality encouraged. A free society, firmly founded on order, justice, and responsibility is the destination we are headed for.

South Korea must also bear in mind that their country is cut in half by the 38th parallel and that the northern half of the country is being illegally occupied by the tools of world Communism. South Koreans must ready themselves, physically and mentally, for the possibility of fighting, together with friendly democratic nations, to overcome the Communists. There lies ahead only one road that leads to victory over Communism. It is neither negotiation nor evasion. To win, South Korea must make its strength superior to that of Communism.

MILITARY GOVERNMENT[7]

As swiftly as the army junta swept out the Chang government, the Korean generals moved to tighten their control upon South Korea. President Yun Posun announced his resignation, but he was prevailed upon to remain in office, thus relieving the military regime from the necessity of obtaining diplomatic recognition. The continuance in office of President Yun Posun cleared the way for the military to work within a constitutional framework, and enabled the new cabinet to retain the good will of foreign countries as well as increase support at home.

The junta consisted of thirty-two generals and colonels, headed by the Chief of Staff, Lieutenant General Chang Do Young, thirty-eight, and General Park Chung Hee, chief of the junta. Announcing a new fifteen-man cabinet of members drawn from the ROK Army, Navy, Air Force, and Marines, General Chang became prime minister and defense minister as well. The military revolutionary administration formed a Supreme Council for National Reconstruction. An over-all government structure was outlined by the Council of State, the supreme organ under which the executive, judiciary, and Armed Forces were placed. The fledgling Reconstruction Government of South Korea suspended, "temporarily," the Korean Constitution, and in its place issued a Basic Law of National Reconstruction which, in the absence of a constitution, served as a basis of rule by decree. Its precise operational implication remained obscure, but it was generally understood that the maneuver was designed to remove any possible question of illegality of the *coup d'état* in terms of the national Constitution.

Following is a brief day-by-day summary of events in South Korea following the assumption of government by the ROK Army. After imposing martial law, the junta ordered, on May 17th, that the

National Assembly and all local councils be dissolved, and began arresting members of Chang's cabinet who went into hiding. President Yun Posun, apparently backing the junta, held a meeting with General Chang and appealed by radio to Prime Minister Chang to surrender. This was thought to indicate a possible mediation between the junta and the government of Chang. On May 17th the junta appointed a temporary cabinet of twenty-four officers, and took over complete control of the national police and Seoul police. An all-night curfew, news censorship, and control of rail and air transportation and of TV and radio stations were ordered. Schools were temporarily closed.

General Magruder and United States Chargé d'Affaires Marshall Green backed the Chang government and ordered ROK revolutionaries to return the government apparatus to John Chang, but Washington hesitated. Lieutenant General Lee Han Lim, Commander of the ROK First Army, heretofore neutral, joined the junta. General Magruder held back. Washington refused aid to Chang's government, awaiting developments, but promised to continue economic and military aid to South Korea.

North Korea increased its military personnel along the Demilitarized Zone, and the Soviet press assailed the United States as perpetrator of the revolt. The Japanese were dismayed, and feared that Korean-Japanese "normalization" would be set back. The Nationalist Chinese were jubilant, and the British looked for a more neutralist regime in South Korea.

Communist North Korea and Soviet Russia signed a mutual defense treaty in Moscow; next, North Korea signed a similar pact with Red China in Peiping. Kim Il Sung, the premier of the Democratic People's Republic of Korea, signed both ten-year treaties. Renewable every five years, the treaties stipulated that if either of the countries were "attacked and thus involved in war, the other contracting party would immediately render military and other assistance with all means at its disposal." A long-term loan to North Korea of an undisclosed amount was also hinted at by the Russian news agency Tass, which said the two countries had also agreed to consolidate economic and cultural relations. The presence of the top-ranking leader of North Korea in Moscow was considered a snub to Communist China, which was celebrating the fortieth anniversary of the Chinese Communist party in Peiping.

Russia and Red China had been separately attempting to attract

North Korea. In October, 1960, China loaned Korea $105 million as Khrushchev canceled his scheduled visit to North Korea. In November, 1960, Russia canceled a $190 million debt owed by Korea, and extended the repayment of another outstanding loan of $35 million. Recently, North Korea signed a treaty of friendship with Albania, one of the three Communist nations competing openly against Russian dominance, as a move to counter Western speculation about a Soviet-Chinese rift. Red China promised to raise its contribution to the North Korea economy to around $500 million as against $750 million from Soviet Russia. (See the North Korean treaties with the U.S.S.R. and with Red China in Appendix II, "Selected Documents on Korea.") South Korea considered its anti-Red posture well justified in view of the new pacts.

When the Korean Army junta secretly pulled more than 6,000 troops out of the United Nations Command in order to stage its coup in Seoul, General Magruder issued two peremptory orders to the junta: (1) Send back the 6,000 men withdrawn from the UN Command to stage the coup; and (2) Restore to their original commanders fifteen generals under arrest, or replace them with officers acceptable to General Magruder.

The UN Commander was annoyed by two aspects in the events: (1) the sacking of ROK generals whom General Magruder regarded as essential to his chain of command of ROK military units, and the appointment of men to the Supreme Council considered inconsonant with his needs, and (2) the potential weakening of U.S.-UN-ROK defense of South Korea by the withdrawal of key men from military positions to political positions in Seoul. The Park-Magruder agreement was intended to relieve this situation. After some disputes, General Magruder agreed to a new compromise under which the junta, on May 26th, retained control of 3,800 men, consisting of the 30th and 31st Reserve divisions, the 1st Air-borne Combat Team, and five MP teams. United States military supplies were being issued as heretofore to the ROK Army.

The junta generals established the thirty-two-man Supreme Council of Korea National Reconstruction, with General Park as vice chairman (later chairman), which replaced the National Assembly. On May 22nd all political parties, unions, and strikes were banned, and a seven-day work week was made mandatory. For the period of martial law, government offices were ordered to do away with all holidays in order to meet the revolutionary requirements. Government officials, aided by the enlightened leadership of the new cabinet members, were required to work full time to revitalize the life of the nation. Possession of American cigarettes and rice hoarding were banned. Arrests of those suspected of Communist leanings continued. Some of the 2,014 arrested to date were teachers and social workers.

To gain the United States' endorsement for the army coup, on May 23rd General Chang announced that he would go to Washington to explain the revolution to President John F. Kennedy in person, bypassing General Magruder and the American Embassy in Seoul. On May 24th the White House sent back word that President Kennedy was too busy preparing for his European trip to receive the visitor from South Korea, although it could fully understand Chang's wishes. The junta generals took the hint, began to relax censorship, released some arrested cabinet ministers, and toned down some of the harsher provisions of their martial law.

Nevertheless, the junta promised "swift and severe punishment" for corrupt government officials and businessmen, whose collusion had wrecked the nation's economy under previous civilian governments, the junta charged. At the same time, nine thousand government workers who had not served in the nation's Armed Forces were fired as draft dodgers. However, the junta ran into a snag in its new supreme law. The Constitution contains no provision for suspension, and General Chang Do Young, head of the junta, did not want to defy the Constitution.

On May 28th almost all small pamphleteering operations were banned, and more than a score of very prominent businessmen and top-ranking officials under the Rhee regime were jailed on charges of excessive profiteering. Other developments included an easing of curfew hours, lifting of oppressive news censorship, releasing of frozen administrative funds and the relaxation of the limit of withdrawals from banks. The people remained calm, almost apathetic, as their personal prospects of economic and social advancement remained uncertain. They were simply waiting it out. On May 30th the Council began appointing civilians to key economic and administrative posts, while maintaining military control by placing overseers from the army to watch the civilians. The Council of National

Reconstruction named civilians to head major government banks. This was designed to soften United States disappointment at complete military control of Korean affairs and also to provide trained personnel the military could not supply.

A special committee studying the cases of leading businessmen, former government officials and officers who had been arrested in the previous month on charges of allegedly amassing illegal profits, was told to decide upon the fines and punishments to be levied within a month instead of the original three-month period. The men awaiting trial were being held under a retroactive law passed by the John Chang regime that permitted punishment of officials or members of political parties who had made more than 50,000,000 hwan during the past eight-year period. Businessmen who made over $20,000 out of Korea in a like period could also be punished.

The government alleged that the arrested or wanted profiteers, numbering twenty-nine men, illegally made or misused some 129.6 billion hwan during the Rhee and John Chang regimes. The amount of 3,370,000,000 hwan was spent as political slush funds, and another 7,562,000,000 hwan were unreported in tax records. The seven-man special committee is headed by Major General Lee Joo Il, and has three university economics professors as advisers. The committee was divided into seven investigating teams, each being under the charge of a military officer but coordinated by a group of civilian prosecutors and accountants.

The junta backed up its promises to eliminate corruption with a new law imposing the death penalty for certain forms of illegal profiteering. "Illegal profiteers" were ordered to report their profits voluntarily to a special committee within ten days. Those who reported honestly would escape the death penalty but would face fines, back taxes, or confiscation of their profits.

The new law hit hardest at profiteers in the government by outlawing political kickbacks on bank loans and the secret movement of property out of South Korea. Persons who concealed property illegally acquired since the April Revolution, and who failed to report to the military government, could be executed, imprisoned for seven years, or have all their property confiscated under the new law. Twenty-six alleged profiteers have been arrested so far, and presumably will be the first to face trial under the decree. They include five generals and admirals, eleven businessmen, and ten former officials.

The junta arrested more than 3,500 political suspects, considered to be potential Communists or leftist hoodlums, and announced a new law, with a possible death penalty for Communist collaborators, as a warning to student groups who wanted a neutralized Korea. The military government arrested former Prime Minister Chang and his seven cabinet members, labeling them "pro-Communist plotters," and accusing Chang, a Catholic and anti-Communist, of assisting anti-state, pro-Communist activity by contributing the sum of $770 to a South Korean relief society, a pro-Communist organization.

The new government also brought charges against Chang and nineteen former officials for embezzlement of official funds and bribe taking. According to the Inspection Commission, Mr. Chang received a bribe of 3,000,000 hwan from the former president of the Seoul Electric Company last January. The commission also said that former Commerce and Industry Minister Chu Yo Han, former Finance Minister Kim Yung Sun, and former Communications Minister Han Tong Sook each accepted 2,000,000 hwan from the same source. The briber was identified as Yoo Tong Jin of the Seoul Electric Company. The commission also alleged that Mr. Yoo embezzled the bribe money from the funds of the Electric Fraternity, a trade organization of power companies, which spent over 100,000,000 hwan for political purposes.

The government spelled out charges of alleged corruption against members of the Chang regime and the Democratic party then in power in a booklet issued by the Information Office. Most of the men accused in the junta's report were in custody, including ousted Premier Chang. The booklet claimed that high officials in the Democratic party while in office took 4.5 billion hwan from businessmen for political use and that the officials illegally made or disbursed for personal gain over 6 billion hwan rightfully belonging to the national Treasury. High lights of the government accusations were as follows:

1. Election irregularities: Burned ballot boxes were found in districts in South Kyongsang Province during the July, 1960, elections.

2. Political funds: Over 2 billion hwan were secured from businessmen suspected of making illegal fortunes under Dr. Rhee; 117 million hwan thus collected were disbursed to local chapters, and each

party nominee was given a million hwan as a campaign fund. More than 4.5 billion hwan were obtained from various business sources for political use. Included among the contributors were: Textile Association, 2.5 billion; Petroleum Dealers Association, 130 million; insurance companies, 209 million; "illegal wealth hoarders," 545 million, including officers of Whasin Industry, Che Il Sugar, Tae Han Cement, Sam Ho Trading, and Tae Han Industry.

3. Loss to Treasury: Disbursed illegally (presumably for emoluments) were over 6 billion hwan, as follows: by the Education Ministry, 5 million; Transportation Ministry, 2 million; Foreign Ministry, 112 million; Health-Social Affairs Ministry, 6.6 million. Home Minister Shin Hyun Dong was accused of taking 24 million hwan from funds allocated for anti-Communist work.

4. Graft: Communication ministers Lee San Chul, Cho Han Bak, and Han Tong Sook received 1 to 2 million hwan monthly from the Korean Communications Association.

5. Favoritism: During nine months of the regime, 1,956 persons were put on government payrolls and 307 officials were promoted. Many pro-Communists and Communist agents were appointed to government jobs.

6. Exchange rate: The then-existing 650 to 1 hwan-dollar ratio was doubled in order to get $35 million in United States aid funds for Korea. This action was taken by Prime Minister John Chang and Finance Minister Kim Yung Sun without consulting the cabinet.

7. Abuse of power: Rights of office were abused in order to acquire government and private property. The Minister of Cabinet Administration "usurped" the government mimeograph office; the Minister of Agriculture and Forestry illegally occupied the home of the chief of the Farmland Reclamation Corporation.

8. The pro-Communist forces permitted 227 "seditious demonstrations" and 681 antigovernment assemblies, posted and distributed illegal bills and leaflets, and caused labor disputes in industry, disrupting national progress.

Former Premier Chang declared that he would willingly assume all blame for the failure of the Democratic party's administration, and would stay out of politics for the rest of his life. In return, he asked that talented men who were in disgrace for having associated with him be allowed to return to the service of their country. The deposed premier's remarks were recorded in a booklet, entitled "Speaking My Mind," which was widely circulated in South Korea. The small pamphlet was issued a few days after the new government released its charges of corruption and maladministration against Chang and members of his party. Mr. Chang's publication was quickly followed by a second government report listing additional irregularities of the former administration.

Chang confessed to the failure of his party to sweep out the tangled inheritance of the past, and its inability rapidly to reconstruct the nation. He said, however, that his party, from the beginning, was dedicated to the principles of respect for basic individual rights of all persons and of anti-Communism. He admitted that overstepping the bounds of freedom often led to license and subversion, sometimes permitting indirect Communist aggression and infiltration. Intemperate factional strife within the party prevented his properly controlling these and other irregularities, he said. Chang stated that he preferred peaceful measures rather than supraconstitutional acts to control irregularities. He said that it is contradictory to use dictatorial means to fight dictatorships, including the Communist type, and that he tried to preserve the principles of honoring basic human rights even when fighting Reds.

Chang appealed to the citizens to cooperate with the new government in its endeavor to accomplish political, economic, and social reforms and to reinstate democratic institutions within two years. He praised the new government's rapid strengthening of anti-Communist laws, merger of power companies, founding of a small-industry bank, and ban on smuggling. He also suggested that reconstruction be spread over a period of five to ten years.

With respect to the return of the government to civilians, Mr. Chang observed that the true way to cure Korea's past parliamentary ills was not to deny, but to improve its methods. He said utmost care should be exercised in renovating party organizations, changing National Assembly Laws, redrafting election laws, and reforming political activities. Mr. Chang declared that the most essential aspect of a successful parliamentary government is a reform in the minds of the politicians.

Rapid disposal of large numbers of criminal cases in Korea was anticipated as the government issued decrees setting up Revolutionary

Courts and Revolutionary Prosecution offices. A "Special Anti-violence Law" was issued that enabled the Revolutionary Prosecution to indict those charged with virtually all major crimes, including election rigging, abuse of official authority, "praising, encouraging, or otherwise abetting antistate organizations," as well as crimes of violence, smuggling, and embezzlement.

A time limit of five months was set for prosecution for trial by the Revolutionary Courts, and in the case of the profiteers, two months from the time of formal charge. Trials must be conducted within three months of formal prosecution. Other targets of the emergency measures were members of former President Rhee's party who were accused of election rigging, Communists, organizers of extortion syndicates, and hoodlums.

Hearings were continuing against sixty-seven men charged with election rigging and violence during the 1960 presidential election, publishing a pro-Communist newspaper, the *Minjok Ilbo,* bribe taking while in high office, and underground terrorism. Formal openings of the trials commenced in five separate courtrooms simultaneously in Seoul on July 29th. Handcuffed prisoners in white jackets and pantaloons faced panels of five judges of the Special Revolutionary Court attired in dark blue brimless caps and gowns with ROK medallions embroidered across the chest.

Among those on trial were ex-Home Minister Choi In Kyu, his Vice Minister Lee Sung Woo, National Police Director Lee Kang Hak, publisher of the defunct *Minjok Ilbo,* Cho Yong Soo, and Shin Do Hwan, who led a brigade of hoodlums to attack Seoul University students protesting the rigged elections. Among them, Choi and Cho had been condemned to the death sentence. All hearings were scheduled to be finished within a fortnight. Sentencing of the prisoners would follow shortly thereafter. Only those receiving death sentences were entitled to appeal their cases to a higher court under the Special Revolutionary law under which the trials were being held.

On August 27, 1961, South Korea's special Revolutionary Tribunal sentenced three former newspaper executives to death after convicting them of aiding Communist North Korea. The publisher, the editor, and an adviser of the defunct *Minjok* received the death penalty for urging student and reporter exchanges allegedly with the purpose of turning Korea into a Communist state. Two hoodlums were sentenced to death by the Revolutionary Court in two separate trials. Lee Jung Chai, famous underworld boss, was sentenced after twelve court sessions which found him guilty of organizing crime syndicates whose members committed acts of extortion and violence. Shin Chung Sik was found guilty of beating to death an eighteen-year-old student who demonstrated in the April Revolution.

At the same time, the prosecution asked the court for death penalties against two former First ROK Army colonels charged with trying to block the *coup d'état* that put the ruling military junta in power on May 16th. The two officers, Colonel Lee Kap Yung and Colonel Pak Sang Hoon, allegedly agreed to back the coup and then told the plan to their commanding officer, Brigadier General Lee Sang Koo. The prosecutor demanded a life sentence for General Lee's "counterrevolutionary activities." He was accused of taking information to Army Chief of Staff Lieutenant General Chang Do Young and sending soldiers to Seoul's City Hall Square in an effort to prevent the junta's coup. The junta also accused General Chang of seeking to use United States troops against Korean revolutionary forces. He was also charged with plotting, together with forty-four other officers, to kill Major General Park Chung Hee, the planner of the coup. Former head of the Korean Army coup, Lieutenant General Chang, who was later sentenced to life imprisonment, was replaced by General Park, Chang's former deputy and the real strong man behind the May army revolution.

General Park, a career army officer trained in Japanese military schools, was court-martialed for his association with Communists as a ROK Army officer in 1948, but escaped with his life to supply army intelligence with a list of Communist names and their activities in the ROK Army. He was a junior officer who was used to eliminate Communist elements from the ROK Army. Without the information supplied by General Park, the story of the Korean War might have been different, because a massive purge took place in the army just before its outbreak. After returning to uniform, he fought against the North Korean Communists, and was a front-line officer, a field staff officer and the First ROK Army's Chief of Staff.

General Park, master strategist of the coup, speaks English and has attended the advanced course of the United States Army Artillery School for the special training that has been the usual path to success for ROK Army officers. A man of few words, with an intense interest in national affairs, the forty-five-year-old officer was known as a man preoccupied with working his way up the military ladder, once he became Chief of Staff of the First Army. An indefatigable and a talented organizer, with a reputation for integrity, General Park is the kind of person that many ROK Army officers would like to pattern themselves after.

In order to reassure the United States, on July 4, 1961, General Park appointed an American favorite, retired Lieutenant General Song Yo Chan, forty-three, as the new prime minister. General Song had pressured President Rhee into resigning without a blood bath as army chief of staff in the Students' Uprising. Song was one of the first officers commissioned in the ROK Army, and rose to brigadier general in four years. As commander of the ROK Army Capital Division, he fought brilliantly for most of the Korean War, and earned from American General James Van Fleet the nickname of "Tiger." When he was chief of staff, he purged the army of 1,700 corrupt officers, including fifteen generals. He went to America to study politics and economics at George Washington University soon after his resignation in 1960, and was called back to Seoul by the junta to serve the new military government.

The new government formally dismissed seven diplomats, including Chang Lee Wook, Ambassador to the United States, and Dr. Channing Liem, United Nations observer, who were political appointees under the Chang government. Former ROK Army Chief of Staff, former Korean ambassador to France under Rhee and to Washington under Huh, General Chung Il Kown was appointed as the new Korean Ambassador to the United States. The retired general had been studying at Harvard University when the news reached him. Former ROK Army colonel and Deputy Minister of Foreign Affairs Lee Soo Young was appointed Ambassador to the United States.

Headed by General Park Chung Hee, chairman, the new cabinet comprises youthful and dynamic high-ranking military officers plus capable civilians. Departmental organization was left unchanged except for the Reconstruction Ministry, which has been retitled the Construction Ministry, and the Office of Public Information, which has been raised to the ministerial level. Such slight innovations apparently reflect the thinking that the corruption and inefficiency of past governments were due not so much to structure as to the men who ran it.

The United States has strongly urged General Park Chung Hee, Chairman of the Supreme Council of Korean National Reconstruction, toward liberalization of his tough military rule and the restoration of as many democratic institutions as practicable. On July 19th he asserted that the form of Korea's future civilian government and the restoration of political rights would be made public before August 15th, the anniversary of Korea's liberation from Japan in 1945 and also of Korean Independence. Furthermore, the ROK Military Government endeavored to set up a committee to determine the most effective use of American aid funds, and announced a five-year plan.[8]

Park released one-third of the 20,000 prisoners arrested in the early days of the military coup, including 2,560 of the 3,098 political prisoners. Major General Park was promoted to the rank of lieutenant general (later General), along with 55 other generals who were upgraded in the first large-scale military promotions since the retirement of 42 generals following the May junta. Among them, five of the new major generals and three of the new brigadiers are junta members. In addition, 3991 company and field grade officers were also promoted in the ROK Army, Air Force, Navy, and Marines.

At the request of the new United States Ambassador in Seoul, replacing former Ambassador Walter P. Conaughy, who became Assistant Secretary of State for Far Eastern Affairs, General Park released Lieutenant General Lee Han Lim, the ROK First Army commander who had refused to support the coup, former Premier Chang and 15,000 prisoners. General Park also agreed to cut his original plan for a military rule from five years to two years.

The Korean Military Government on August 12th declared that the country would be returned to complete civilian control after elections in May, 1963. The chairman warned that any political activities hindering the execution of reforms throughout 1962 would be "restricted as much as possible." All political parties were suspended, along with the legislature, in May, 1961. In the spring of 1963, political parties would be allowed to reactivate themselves for the general presidential election in May, 1963. In the meantime the present government will redraft the Constitution to make way for a single-house legislature, similar to the one Korea had during the Rhee regime.

Following is the complete text of the "Turnover of Government" statement of Lieutenant General Park Chung Hi, on August 12th in Seoul:

The Revolutionary Government, which has zealously studied when and how the government should be turned over to civilian control, achieving within the shortest possible date the revolutionary tasks of eliminating vice and establishing the foundation for new democratic institutions, as promised in Item VI of the Revolutionary Pledges, hereby announces to the people the final decision of the Supreme Council for National Reconstruction as follows:

1. Prior to the turnover of the government to civilian control, the Revolutionary Government will accomplish at least the following basic tasks in order to create true democratic political order and to prevent relapse into vice: First: It will eradicate all political and social corruption, enhance the new spirit, and establish the dignity of law. Second: It will reform and develop all institutions to the extent that they will be turned in the right direction. Third: It will rebuild the national economy, and positively carry out the first-year program of the Five-Year Economic Plan.

2. Turnover of the Government to civilian control is planned for the summer of 1963, for the following reasons: (*a*) 1962 will be a period of reforming all institutions and of enforcing the first-year program of the Five-Year Plan. During this period, political activities and popular movements that may weaken execution of revolutionary tasks will be restricted if necessary. (*b*) A new Constitution will be established and promulgated before March, 1963. (*c*) General elections will be held in May, 1963. After the election, the government will be completely turned over to civilian control in accordance with the provisions of the Constitution. (*d*) Political activities will be tolerated in early 1963.

3. The structure of the Government and National Assembly will be: (*a*) Form of Government: presidential system; (*b*) Form of National Assembly: unicameral system with 100 to 120 seats; (*c*) Election Management: public management by the government; (*d*) Former Politicians: A law will be enacted to prohibit corrupt and dishonest former politicians from returning to political office.

4. The duration of the Revolutionary Government as given above is believed to be the minimum length of time required for the fulfillment of the Revolutionary Pledges and the establishment of a firm foundation for

the democratic prosperity of the nation. As to the form of government and formation of the National Assembly, opinions of the people will be heard and will be reflected in the new Constitution to be established.

The following accomplishments of the Korea Military Revolution Government were described in the White Paper entitled "The Military Revolution in Korea," issued by the Ministry of Foreign Affairs on June 30, 1961.[9]

Public approval of the coup increased when the Military Government announced the six basic points of its policy. They were: (1) adamant anti-Communism; (2) belief in, and firm support for, the United Nations Charter; (3) indissoluble alliance with the United States of America as the leader of efforts to combat spreading Communist subversion and aggression; (4) eradication of corrupt elements in and out of government, enforcement of honesty and efficiency in the government, and the establishment of a self-supporting economy; (5) intensified efforts to unify the nation, in accordance with United Nations proposals, through peninsula-wide elections under UN supervision; (6) transfer of government power to a constitutional civilian government as soon as revolutionary tasks have been completed.

Since the coup, remarkable progress has been achieved. Corrupt elements within the government have been dismissed. Government offices have been reorganized on an efficient, businesslike basis. Thousands of redundant government employees who performed no useful duties, and who had secured their sinecures through nepotism, favoritism, or bribery, have been dismissed. Relief has been provided for the needy. The National Reconstruction Program is under way, and thousands of unemployed are now being paid living wages for useful work on projects of real and permanent value. Gangsters and hoodlums have been arrested, tried, and sentenced according to the severity of their offenses. Assistance has been given to farmers; arrangements have been made for the repayment of usurious loans at reasonable interest rates over a period of time; vitally needed fertilizer has been distributed promptly, at the established price, for the first time in the history of the Republic. The payment of the annual farm subsidies was announced on one day, and on the following day payments were made by county offices to farmers in full. In the past, such payments were delayed for six or more months—and in the end the farmers were lucky if they received half of the amount, the rest having disappeared by what might be called a process of osmosis into the pockets of officials all down the line.

Tax evaders have been located, and legal processes to enforce payment of delinquent and evaded taxes initiated. One group of thirteen businessmen alone publicly admitted evading the Hwan equivalent of more than $33,449,924 in income taxes, and voluntarily offered full restitution plus penalties. Law is being enforced. It is no longer possible to bribe police or prosecutors. Malefactors, rich or poor, receive the same treatment from the police and the courts. The Revolutionary Council recognizes that the principal problems to be solved are economic. They are also fully aware of the fact that military training and experience does not necessarily provide the best background for economic planning. Therefore, on June 22nd, the government relieved the military officers heading the Ministry of Finance and the Ministry of Economic Development. Mr. Kim Yu Taik, former governor of the Bank of Korea, was appointed Minister of Finance; Dr. Shin Tai Hwan, professor of economics at Seoul National University, was named Minister of Economic Development. Additionally, recognizing the need for expert advice in many specialized fields, the Supreme Council appointed an advisory council, initially composed of fifteen highly qualified civilian experts, to assist in drafting plans for immediate development in all areas of activity.

One action that has been widely misunderstood abroad was the cancellation of publication rights of a number of so-called newspapers. There are many well edited, responsible newspapers in South Korea. However, the principal, and in most instances only, business of some publications was blackmail. Their criminal activities were intolerable, and their publishing licenses were canceled. It should be noted, however, that not a single newspaper, periodical, or newsservice agency that existed before the April Revolution has been closed by the new government. Legitimate publications, without exception, heartily endorsed the government's action as necessary to restore journalistic ethics and prestige.

The new government in South Korea under General Park Chung Hee is showing signs of growing confidence that its administration would be a popular one, at least among those in the lower economic rungs, who comprise 95 per cent of South Korea's population. Signs of confidence were also evidenced in a popular survey taken by college students in Seoul. The answers were in favor of the new regime, and observers noted that the wide publicity given the project underscored the new government's confidence that the popular poll would be in its favor.

The government was also considering a nationwide refrendum on a revised "provisional Constitution." The vote will be taken on a new Constitution composed of two parts: a paragraph of the old Constitution that the junta thinks "survived" the coup, and the new Basic Law of National Reconstruction, which provided a legal basis for the junta's seizure of power and its subsequent actions.

The junta's Herculean efforts to clean up South Korea are in many ways admirable. The new government continued to push its plan of enforced austerity. It was determined to clean up Seoul; and some 8,000 families living in squatters' shacks moved to an emergency tent city outside Seoul. Two weeks of rations were allotted, but future rations must be worked for. High school students who live within two miles of school must walk. Boys must have their hair clipped short, and students are forbidden to frequent teahouses and pool halls.

The need for a long-range national rehabilitation plan was frankly admitted, and the junta began selecting a competent staff of leading university professors and professionals to set up three committees under the Supreme Council of National Reconstruction, fourteen subcommittees headed by core men from the council, and five subcommittees under the Planning Committee of the Council. More capable civilians must be chosen from the fields of political science, economy, culture, education, social welfare, public relations, rehabilitation and jurisprudence.[10]

Administration[11]

Stability following the Military Government's initial reforms has more than compensated for the minor inconvenience experienced by a few. The achievements of the first phase, a period of reform of the revolution follow:

A fund of some two billion hwan left over from the National Assembly budget was allocated for relief of destitute and disabled veterans; local council budgets provided for the welfare of each local populace. When the Supreme Council for National Reconstruction assumed the administration of the nation, fifteen political parties and 238 social organizations were dissolved by Decree Number 6. This was not a denial of the freedom of assembly, but a measure taken to stop their harmful activities. Nonpolitical organizations, except anti-state groups, are allowed to register, and freedom of activity is guaranteed. The establishment of a career service system prescribing, among other things, age limits and occupational specialties ensures the political neutrality of public officials, eliminates favoritism, and procures competent personnel. Corrupt and inefficient officials were replaced with conscientious and competent ones, and all officials were required to register their financial status. Some 6,700 officials who had not completed their terms of military service were dismissed. The Inspection Commission and the Board of Audit operated impartially, and the second supplementary budget allocated 12 billion hwan to carry out reasonable salary increases and a pension system for officials.

The Economic Planning Board was established with a vice premier as chairman, and the Office of National Construction was established under it. The Public Information Ministry was created to manage public-relations activities, and the Administration Management Bureau was established under the Ministry of Cabinet Administration to study and examine administrative affairs and personnel management. An Administration Management Committee was also established, under the same ministry, to promote efficiency and simplify administrative procedures and to retain officials.

The government plans to consolidate various administrative organizations at the county level. It will also establish model administration districts in every three counties, reform local tax administration, and expand welfare facilities. Heads of cities and lower administrative districts with a population of 150,000 or less will be named by provincial governors. Training programs for county chiefs and other officials has begun.

A nationwide manpower survey was to be conducted from August 17th to October 21st at eighty-nine Government offices and involving 28,000 officials. The minimum manpower required to carry out assigned workloads will be determined. A screening test for the employment of clerical officials was held on July 27th; 63,751 candidates applied. Training programs for section chiefs and higher offices were launched on July 10th. Emphasizing the revolutionary spirit, the programs were geared to train a total of 1,594 officials before August 18th.

There are 447 laws and ordinances, instituted before the establishment of the Korean Military Government, that are still in force. To recodify or discard these laws the Recodification Committee was established on July 18th under the prime minister. To reform traffic administration, traffic laws were revised. Operational permits for more than 500 vehicles were canceled. Suspension and cancellation of drivers' licenses numbered 200 by the end of July. Traffic accidents have decreased by 20 per cent since the revolution, and traffic regulations are being observed by pedestrians and drivers alike.

The police administration has been renovated, and arrests have been made in more than 3,200 instances of pro-Communist activities and spying, in 280 cases of major crimes, including murder and robbery; and 10,000 instances of violence. There have been over 270 prosecutions for operating unlicensed dancing halls, for 790 cases of building unauthorized houses, and for over 600 instances of smuggling, involving 1.3 billion hwan (about three times that reported the previous year).

Foreign Policy

The new government lost no time in carrying out reforms in the diplomatic field, and its initial efforts are now bearing fruit. Immediately after the May 16th revolution the government centered its efforts on: promotion of international understanding and strengthening of diplomatic ties with free nations; cooperation with international organizations; normalization of relations with Japan; promotion of economic relations with free nations; conclusion of a status of forces agreement with the United States; protection and guidance of Korean residents overseas; establishment of a career foreign service system.

Activities of the Korean mission overseas have been increased following the revolution, and the government has strengthened ties with foreign envoys stationed in Korea. The government has also extended invitations to the chief executives or foreign ministers of friendly nations to visit Korea. Good-will missions have been sent to all the continents of the world to enlist international understanding of and support for the Korean Revolution.

A three-member civic mission to the United States was highly successful in winning understanding of the revolutionary cause by the American Government and people. The mission was composed of the president of Ewha Women's University, Dr. Helen Kim; the publisher of the *Dong A Ilbo* daily, Too Sun Choi; and the Presbyterian minister Kyung Jik Han.

A good-will military and civic mission made a successful tour of the United States, Canada, Haiti, Brazil, Uruguay, and Argentina in July. Led by Major General Dong Ha Kim, the group is scheduled to extend its visit to Paraguay, Chile, Peru, Colombia, Panama, Costa Rica, Nicaragua, Honduras, Guatemala, and Ecuador. The mission will have visited a total of seventeen nations on the American continents.

A second mission, headed by Ambassador to London Yong Shik Kim, left on July 3rd for a good-will tour of seventeen European nations; Great Britain, France, Germany, Switzerland, Italy, Greece, Spain, Portugal, Belgium, Luxembourg, the Netherlands, Denmark, Norway, Sweden, Iceland, Ireland, and Israel.

A third team, sent to the African continent, began its tour of nineteen countries on July 5th, including Mauritania, Senegal, Sierra Leone, Liberia, the Ivory Coast, Nigeria, the Central African Republic, the Congo, South Africa, Ethiopia, and others. Headed by Ambassador Sun Yup Paik, the mission is striving for the promotion of friendly relations and exchange of diplomatic missions with young African nations.

Led by Ambassador Tchi Chang Yun in Ankara, a fourth mission is touring the Middle and Near East, Turkey, Iraq, Lebanon, Cyprus, Saudi Arabia, Jordan, the United Arab Republic, Libya, Morocco, Tunisia, and Iran.

Headed by Ambassador Duk Shin Choi, a fifth group is visiting Southeast Asian nations. By July 26th it had visited six nations: Japan, Free China, the Philippines, Australia, New Zealand, and Malaya. By August 23rd it was to have visited another eight countries—Vietnam, Thailand, Cambodia, Burma, Ceylon, Pakistan, India, and Nepal. Extension of the mission's tour to Laos is under consideration. Meanwhile, Bishop Ul Soo Yoon, of the Roman Catholic Church, paid a visit to the Vatican City on July 1st. These good-will missions have received more welcome and understanding than originally was expected.

Leader of the Army Coup, General Park Chung Hee. (*ROK, O.P.I.*)

A Korean mother is proud of her sons in the ROK army, navy, and air force.

The government also carried out a personnel reshuffle, weeding out corrupt or inefficient heads of diplomatic missions. The appointment of six ambassadors, including one to the London post, which had remained vacant for some time, and a minister to Japan, has reshaped Korea's diplomatic alignment overseas. Within the Foreign Ministry, some eighty officials were released either for failure to perform military service or for counterrevolutionary activity.

On July 7th the United States Department of State issued a statement confirming the bonds of friendship existing between the two countries and its determination to continue economic assistance to Korea. On July 27th Secretary of State Dean Rusk officially endorsed the Revolutionary Government, reconfirming closer cooperation between the two nations.

Following the revolution, prospects for improvement of relations between Korea and Japan became brighter; the new government was fully prepared to reopen the Korean-Japanese talks.

In order to promote economic relations with free nations, the government has taken the following measures: it became a member of the International Development Association to obtain development loans, on May 18th; it signed an agreement with the World Health Organization to receive technical assistance June 24th; and it has agreed with the Federal Republic of Germany on matters of principle for a treaty of friendship, commerce, and navigation. The two governments are now about to start discussing procedural matters for conclusion of the treaty. A working level conference was held in Bangkok for conclusion of a trade pact with Thailand on June 22nd. The agreement was to be formally signed in Seoul in the autumn. Negotiations are also under way with Italy for a trade agreement.

The government has made diplomatic approaches to India, to Arabic nations, and to other non-Communist neutral countries. Plans are being drawn now for exchange of diplomatic missions with Canada, Brazil, the United Arab Republic, Malaya, India, the Ivory Coast, and Iran.

To clarify the intentions and the effects of the May 16th revolution, the government has distributed overseas English, French, Japanese, and Spanish editions of *The Military Revolution in Korea* and *Korea Photonews*. Broadcasts, records, slides, and postcards are also used to inform friendly nations of the government's achievements.

National Defense

The government disbanded and reorganized part of the Defense Ministry for reasons of economy and efficiency. The Joint Chiefs of Staff was disbanded and a similar, yet smaller, staff was set up within the ministry. This alone saves 65 million hwan of defense outlay yearly, and eliminates 370 men. The National Defense Science Research Institute was dissolved, and its functions were assumed by the army and the office of Atomic Energy. Further study is now in progress for reorganization of other agencies under the Defense Ministry.

A Capital Defense Command was inaugurated on June 1st to strengthen Seoul. The government is pushing plans for modernizing combat forces with the latest arms and equipment. The military overseas broadcasting program, one hour daily, has been reshaped to convey the spirit of revolutionary reform and reconstruction.

The following measures have been taken, or are under study, for renovation of military service and personnel administration: A study is being made to reduce the army tour of duty from the present two years and nine months to two years, as stipulated by the Military Service Law. Reserve Officers Training Corps have been established at sixteen universities for volunteers from the junior class to maintain a necessary number of junior officers and other important staffs in reserve. The government has simplified procedures for military procurement. Under the new rules, the army supervises procurement programs for each branch of the service. The new system pares defense budgets, improvises the quality of goods, conserves labor forces, and developes domestic industries.

In order to promote veterans' welfare through simplified administration, a new office was set up under the direct control of the prime minister. The Office of Veterans Welfare Administration is solely responsible for welfare programs that formerly were administered separately by the ministries of National Defense, Health and Social Affairs, Communications, and the Military Welfare Association. New laws were enacted to give veterans priority in government employment and state-run enterprises, and to advance loans for resettlement.

Some 1,300 military vehicles leased or illegally released for civilian use were returned to the government after the revolution. The leases were responsible for illegal transactions in military-vehicle accessories on the open market. The government has also completed renovation of military-installation management. Private properties for military requisition will be purchased by the government in accordance with logistical needs.

The government established June 20th–29th as a grace period for military service draft dodgers to surrender. As a result, 494,982 persons surrendered during that period, and they will be given an opportunity to fulfill military-service obligations.

As a result of firm military discipline, accidents in the Armed Forces have drastically decreased, and the number of AWOL's has dropped noticeably. Other Armed Forces violations declined to one-half of the prerevolution level. The new government has made a saving of over 950 million hwan and 600,000 *suk** of rice, as a result of the new supply plan implemented in July, calling for partial use of barley in place of rice for Armed Forces personnel. Improved maintenance of military equipment has also contributed to reconstruction in flooded areas.

Legislative and Judicial Affairs

In accomplishing the revolution's first phase, the following achievements were made in legislative and judiciary fields: After the May 16th revolution, martial law was proclaimed throughout the Republic of Korea to secure public order. Public stability was established by banning assembly and reprisal. Airports and harbors were closed to prevent the influx of Communist agents and the flight overseas of capital and black-listed personnel. Faith with friendly nations was kept by protecting the life and property of foreigners in the Republic of Korea.

The fundamental principles of constitutional government were reaffirmed by respecting the independence of the judiciary and by ensuring just and impartial trials. This decree served to crush Communist activities, guaranteed security, and placed the nation on a firm anti-Communist basis. After the Military Revolutionary Committee was redesignated the Supreme Council for National Reconstruction on May 20, 1961, emergency martial law was replaced by security martial law.

* A *suk* = 2.5 bushels.

The SCNR enacted laws designed to achieve a social-welfare state, security of the people, and a higher living standard. New laws seek to provide a legal basis for the Revolutionary Government to reconstruct the Republic of Korea into a genuine democratic Republic, safeguards the nation against Communist aggression, and overcomes corruption, injustice, and poverty.

A special law covers virtually all major crimes, including election crimes, smuggling, abuse of official authority, organized violence, counterrevolutionary and antistate acts. It is designed to provide heavier penalties for specific crimes, notwithstanding provisions for punishment set forth in the Criminal Code, the Korean Constabulary Law, the Military Criminal Law, and other laws.

The Anti-Communist Law ensures national security and the people's freedom. Although hoodlums were used to perpetuate former regimes, the law now punishes terrorists. The Anti-Violence Law is designed to accord equal legal protection to everyone.

In addition to the aforementioned laws, eighteen decrees and four ordinances of the Military Revolutionary Committee, and fifteen decrees and forty-two ordinances of the Supreme Council for National Reconstruction were enacted and put into effect. Some sixty laws, including a law for disposition of usurious farm debts, were also implemented, covering politics, economics, society, and culture.

The Revolutionary Government also decided to enact laws for the reconstruction in the fields of politics, economy, society, and culture; for strengthening anti-Communist posture and counterintelligence activities; and for establishment of social order. About fifty laws are being drafted. They include a property-registration law for government officials, a law for appeal, and a law for disposition of charges filed by civilians. About four hundred old laws and decrees enacted under Japanese rule and the American Military Government were to be modified or replaced by new ones by January 20, 1962.

Laws such as the Court Organization Law, the Prosecutor's Office Organization Law, the Code of Criminal Procedures, and the Code of Civil Procedures—previously unrealistic and ineffective—have been amended and reorganized to accomplish fair and quick judicial administration. High standards have been enforced among judges, prosecutors, and officials of legal organizations, eliminating favoritism.

Efforts have been made to eliminate social vice. Proper guidance for juvenile delinquents and more effective administration of juvenile institutes has been implemented. Since May 16th, 3,550 actual and potential juvenile delinquents have been given corrective guidance. Among them 1,951 have been allowed to return home. Statistics show that 55 per cent of those rounded up were returned home, compared to 31 per cent before May 16th.

The Revolutionary Government also intends to establish occupational rehabilitation training in prisons. Recently a weaving shop was established as the first of such projects. Guidance for remolding character in terms of anti-Communism and patriotism is enforced at all institutes. A drive to eliminate illiteracy and improve moral and professional education to equip inmates with the necessary background for positive social roles is now in full swing. As of now, 63 of 619 juvenile prisoners have written their names off the illiteracy list. The principle of segregation according to crimes, terms, habitual criminals, and age will be strictly observed. At present jails are too crowded, and prisoners, regardless of their crimes, are lumped together, making proper corrective measures ineffective.

The Special Prosecutor's Office, created immediately after the April Revolution for prosecuting those involved in rigging the election and in possession of illicit fortunes, consisted of 30 prosecutors and 90 clerks. Simultaneously the Special Court was activated, with 120 employees, five trial panels and two sections. During four months the Court and Office investigated 818 cases, indicted 103, and completed 20 cases of those indicted. During the same period, the Prosecutor's Office spent 560 million hwan—76 per cent of the total amount allocated—and the Court over 400 million—82 per cent of its allocation.

The Revolutionary Court and the Revolutionary Prosecutor's Office were inaugurated on July 12th. The Court comprises 39 judges, or five primary panels and two panels of appeal, and the Office has 30 prosecutors. Indictments and trials must be conducted within a prescribed period. Presently the Office is investigating and preparing for trial 36 cases (involving 227 persons) indicted after the revolution and 76 cases (involving 193) carried over from the previous regime. The Revolutionary Court will independently try antistate, antinational, and counterrevolutionary activities, as well as 83 cases carried over from the previous Special Court.

Reform of Inspection Duties

The previous personnel of the Inspection Committee inaugurated on April 3, 1961, with 128 officials, completed only two cases despite spending 20 million hwan during one and a half months ending May 15th. As a result, after May 16th the committee sent teams to provinces three times to verify enforcement of government policies by local organizations and determine administrative irregularities and inefficiency. They recommended the roundup of hoodlums; the reappraisal of city planning, with compensation for those affected by the new plans; the regulation of the distribution of personnel in rural police stations; the establishment of an administrative telephone system; and improved rural conditions.

Recommendations were also made for a reappraisal of martial duties and the establishment of military discipline; the enhancement of anti-Communist ideologies for teachers on all levels; reorganization of middle, high, and college educational systems; increased allocation for school properties; and the protection of temples and other cultural properties.

The committee also suggested reorganization of the national development budget; improved factory facilities to secure supplies for the Armed Forces; training of agrarian leaders; promulgation of measures against forestry theft; timely release of farming loans; the merging of agricultural cooperatives and livestock owners' associations; and improving rice-liens programs.

Also recommended were: examination of the structure of fishery unions; granting of loans for the fishery industry; stepping up measures to attract tourists; reexamination of civil employees and of the civil employment program; implementation of resettlement measures for lepers; providing doctors for rural villages; and disposal of civic petitions and appeals. In mid-1961 civic petitions and appeals received by the Inspection Commission since the revolution totaled 1,188 cases. Of these, 915 cases have already been disposed of.

Since the revolution the Board of Audit has centered its examinations upon government offices or state-run enterprises that exercise considerable influence upon the nation's economy, including the Office of Supply, Office of Monopoly, Customs, Deahan Coal Company, Korea Tungsten Mining Company, Korea Power Company, the Bank of Korea and the Reconstruction Bank. The board has already dealt with 28 organizations and examined 3,151 cases involving 81.5 billion hwan. The new government ordered branch chiefs to process, not later than July 31, 1961, cases in arrears since the foundation of the board— a total of 7,967, involving 6,130 million hwan. Of these, 509 cases, involving 490 million hwan, have already been disposed of. The government plans to publicize audit results of investigations under way into various past governmental expenditures, including government contracts, disposal of major vested properties, and 6.3 billion hwan of past expenditures.

Public Affairs

Highway bridges and roads have been repaired and expanded, and flood damage rehabilitated under projects financed with 7.9 billion hwan. Projects completed as of June 30th account for more than 45 per cent of the total works planned, and mobilized 5,620,000 man-days in all.

To finance the program, the government earmarked 9.4 billion hwan. By the end of June, the projects were more than 50 per cent completed, with some 5,860,000 man-days mobilized. Projects undertaken included dredging, coastal dikes and levee construction, sluice installation, and flood-damage rehabilitation. Financed with 2.8 billion hwan, the program calls for repairing streets, water-supply and sewage systems; city zoning, constructing of tourist roads, and building a national park in Kyongju. By June 30th the projects were 38 per cent completed. Man-days totaled more than 2.2 million.

Financed with 3.3 billion hwan, new water-supply systems are being installed in 24 cities and existing systems are being repaired and enlarged in 29 cities, with 990,000 man-days already employed. Thus the NCS program is about 55 per cent underway. It has created employment opportunities for a total of 14 million persons. A five-year program calls for increasing the number of model villages from the present 380 in 20 counties to 620 in 60 counties. Sixty supervisors for model villages are being trained.

The government instituted the Economic Planning Board to bolster its economic policies and programs. The board is responsible for establishment and effective operation of over-all economic plans and programs. The creation of the board marks a turning point in the nation's endeavor for positive economic measures. With the inception of the board, economic activity and relief of unemployment are expected to become more active beginning in August.

A committee on disposal of illicit fortunes was set up and investigation teams were formed to complete investigation of illegal wealth within three months. Disposition of wealth illegally obtained under previous regimes is one of the most difficult of revolutionary tasks. As of July 20th illegally gained fortunes uncovered by investigation teams amounted to 72.6 billion hwan. The committee has released all businessmen held for investigation.

Facilities were added to waiting rooms at all railway stations; fans were installed and water-supply systems improved on passenger trains. Outdoor waiting rooms were built at the Seoul and Taejon stations. Efforts to eliminate burglary within railway station compounds and the theft of cargos were so satisfactory that compensations for lost cargo and baggage, which used to average well over 100 million hwan a month, were cut to zero in June.

The most noteworthy accomplishments in transportation are the opening of the Neungui rail line around Seoul and the beginning of construction on the Hwangji Line. Taxis in Seoul are operating on a two-shift system for the dual purpose of conserving gasoline and solving traffic congestion. Transfer of Kimpo International Airport control to the Korean Government will earn the government some 73 million hwan per year. Preparations are under way to reopen the Chosun Hotel as a tourist facility.

Regulations for telephone installation have been revised in order to ensure fairness and uproot the exercise of political influence. Airmail and parcel post exchanges are being expanded, and expansion of the international communications network has been completed.

Government policies on education and social affairs aim at building up sound foundations for a democratic welfare community in the shortest possible period. Four major policies aim at crushing indirect Communist aggression, remodeling the people's spirit, eliminating poverty, and reforming cultural movements. To realize these policies, conferences were held by representatives of educational administrators, teachers, students, and cultural and religious circles. Revision of the educational law and extraordinary measures on education are under study.

All forms of corruption and injustice have been weeded out among personnel, by prohibition of collection of PTA and other fees, by strict use of budgets, settlement of campus disputes, prohibition of political activity by students, teachers, and labor movements, and reshuffling of school principals responsible for overenrollment or illegal admission of students.

Over-all renovation of the educational system and administration is being contemplated, with advice from an advisory committee on educational policy reform. The semester system has been improved. In order to ensure the democratization and independence of education from politics, measures are being taken to consolidate city- and county-level educational commissions. Reform of the Education Ministry is also being contemplated, to improve efficiency of administration. Special seminars on anti-Communism will be included in university and college curricula. Lower-level schools will sponsor speeches on current affairs, and plans have been drafted to provide students with increased training in athletics and military skills.

Legal provisions to obtain funds for a five-year plan on completion of the second compulsory education program are under study. A total of 2,700 classrooms are under construction, at the cost of 4.4 billion hwan, and conversion of public buildings into school facilities will help solve the classroom shortage. Administrative action has been taken to close the gap in quality of students in primary schools and to perfect a school-zone system for all pupils above the sixth grade.

It has been decided to extend privileges to vocational-school graduates in examinations for college entrance. Vocational schools without adequate laboratory and on-the-job training facilities will be closed. In accordance with regulations governing university and college standards, twelve university presidents and college deans involved in financial mismanagement, politicking, and excessive enrollment of students have been dismissed. Merging of national and public universities and colleges and the readjustment of enrollment capacities will be effected. A law governing the management of private schools is under study to protect private educational institutes against exploitation.

Decisions have been made to pay a 4,000-hwan monthly allowance to all primary-school teachers and a special pregnancy allowance to woman teachers. Under the new system, members of war-bereaved families will benefit from loan scholarships totaling 45 million hwan, aside from government scholarships and loans. Children of war dead in primary school will receive free textbooks, and middle-high and college students will be exempt from admission charges and tuition fees, plus half of other school expenses. Better education of Korean residents in Japan is being sought by the dispatch of two educational supervisors and ten exemplary teachers. Some eighty students in Japan were also invited to visit their homeland. Necessary procedures have been completed to provide free education for more than a hundred students wounded during the April uprising.

On July 20th the government completed distribution of 2,600,000 copies of summer vacation books published in commemoration of the May Revolution. The summer books were provided at 40 hwan a copy. Meanwhile, the Munkyo Textbook Company was authorized as the sole publisher of elementary textbooks, thus avoiding confusion. Books for those engaged in farming and fishing, and for adult education will also be published.

The government seeks to establish a law designed to protect cultural objects, and also aims to reorganize the Daihan Athletic Association, reregister various cultural groups, purify religious organizations, dispose of unaccredited institutes, and provide for extension institutes. As part of the new plan, an art festival and an athletic meeting were staged to commemorate the May Revolution.

Efforts are being increased to obtain membership to the UNESCO "coupon" system, which will greatly facilitate academic research in the universities. Establishment of a library center for scientific books and association with the international copyright convention are also being sought.

Jointly, the Government, the military, and civilians are providing public summer preventive clinics. A total of 277 million hwan was expended for insecticides and for examination of water supply and wells. Twenty health centers were established in doctorless areas, with 347 accredited doctors participating. One thousand and ninety-six illegal medical practitioners and 1,420 illegal "pharmacists" were prosecuted. Sixty-eight water points have been installed throughout the country at a cost of 91,950,000 hwan. Limitations on drug sales were revised; and over 500 poppy fields were destroyed, and 13,000 boxes of narcotics.

One million destitute farmers were provided with 150,000 bushels of grain and placed on public-works projects. Six hundred and fifty vagrants were resettled in the Dai Kwan Ryung area, and 1,277 junk collectors were employed at a cost of 40 million hwan. Two thousand waifs were either sent to native homes or resettled. As emergency flood relief measures, 165 million hwan was appropriated for 57,089 flood victims. Eighty per cent of flood-damaged roads, bridges, and railroads were repaired as of July 31st. A loan of 2.5 billion hwan has been earmarked for rehabilitation of destroyed houses. The money will be repaid over a thirty-year period.

Special funds totaling 60 million hwan were provided for 400 disabled military and police veterans. Sixty disabled veterans were given medical care, technical education was given to 6448 men, and 121 artificial legs were made at a cost of 82 million hwan. Shortly before Memorial Day, an estimated 15.4 billion hwan was provided for annual subsidies for relatives of servicemen and police killed in line of duty.

Since the May Revolution, unemployed have been placed on national reconstruction projects at a daily rate of 463,618 men. An unemployment survey has registered 523,024. The survey provides data for placing unemployed. Relief, ICA, and government projects are now building 22,936 houses.

The National Reconstruction Movement was launched to carry through the government's revolutionary tasks. With headquarters in Seoul, the movement has consultative bodies throughout the country. The nationwide campaign aims at expelling Communist sympathizers, enforcing an austere life, increasing production and reconstruction, enhancing public morality, and advancing the people's physical strength. Based on a seven-point movement, 8,500 trained leaders were to lay the groundwork for rural and economic reconstruction before the end of the year. As part of the movement, nationwide fund-raising and relief projects are under way for recent flood victims.

A Ministry for Public Information was established by the government to provide impartial information promptly. The government lifted censorship of the press ten days after the May Revolution. The government also closed down 76 dailies, 305 news agencies, 453 weeklies, 240 monthlies, and 95 other news publications that did not have adequate facilities. Also, a supply-and-demand plan for newsprint was discussed between the Finance Ministry and Commerce Industry Ministry. Lowering of the tariff on import of newsprint and increased production of domestic newsprint was discussed.

To counter Communist propaganda and publicize the government's revolutionary tasks, broadcasting programs were reassessed and reorganized. A new program is a two-hour afternoon broadcast to the North Korea Communists. Nearing completion is a 500-kw. transmitter at Whasung County, Kyonggi-do. In addition, construction works are under way on a 50-kw. and two 10 kw. stations in Pusan, Suwon and Kwangju. Legal measures have been completed to expand amplifier relay networks for farm and fishing villages.

An opinion survey was conducted from June 1st to 3rd among 1,500 citizens of Seoul, so that the people's ideas would be reflected in the formation of new policies. The results of another survey, conducted from June 30th to July 12th, among radio listeners, were used in reformulating radio programs. The results of another opinion poll concerning government policies, collected from 3,000 persons throughout the nation between July 26th and August 2nd, are being assessed and analyzed.

On the anniversary of the outbreak of the Korean War, an entertainment troupe toured front-line areas for nine days, presenting eighteen performances for combat soldiers. Two mobile movie teams have entertained farmers and fishermen with films designed to promote understandings of the revolution.

Changes in the life of South Koreans created by the Korean Military Revolution were reported in the *Korean Republic* as follows:[6]

The Military Revolution has brought about an evolution that ordinarily would require a decade. The revolution put an end to centuries-old political corruption; but it was even more important in that it reformed the heart of the people. For example, an average office worker, before the revolution, woke up every morning about the time when he was supposed to report for work. No one would reproach him for tardiness, since tardiness was a common practice everywhere. After a breakfast that was far inferior to his social status, he dressed in a first-class suit that usually had cost him a month's salary. Then he would take a jitney, or even a taxi, to his office, since he shared the universal aversion to taking streetcars or buses.

During his office hours, he went a couple of times to a tearoom in the morning, since he did not have much to do, and, even if he had, he didn't care much about his work anyway. A few cups of coffee was a "must" during his work day, he believed, for social and physical reasons. He was, and is, a good smoker. Before, he was ashamed to buy Korean cigarettes. Though his monthly salary would buy him not more than ten cartons of American cigarettes, he felt he had to smoke them.

In the afternoon, he would leave the office for a couple of hours on private affairs. After office hours, he could expect someone or other to invite him to a bar or restaurant, where he could spend a whole month's pay in one evening. A taxi brought him home dead drunk almost every night. When he reflected on his way of living and the future of his family, he would shudder with horror. But in the next thought, he shrugged it away as unavoidable. "Everybody lives like this, and it's the only way I can live here in Korea," he would tell himself. May 16, 1961 was the date of his mental rebirth. In a few days he learned to live according to his means, but more decently and healthily than ever.

Now he wakes up when the air is fresh and cool. After sweeping his yard a little and eating a wholesome breakfast, he puts on simple but clean trousers and short-sleeved shirts. He is really glad he no longer has to wear necktie and heavy suit in this hot weather. Then he takes a bus or a streetcar, without being ashamed. Most decent people take them now. It is still agreeably cool when he reports to the office by 8:00 A.M. The day's work is done during the day—without delay. At noon, he eats from his lunchbox as the Revolution has taught him to do. He admits, without shame, that Korean cigarettes are as good as any foreign-made ones. He has also come to realize that coffee is not indispensable, as he once believed, in his vanity. He knows that in this way the nation is saving 6 billion hwan in foreign exchange for cigarettes and another 6 billion hwan for coffee annually. When the workday is over, and he boards the bus for home, he is really proud of doing his job, a feeling he had not known before.

Another example: A college girl has replaced her fancy parasol with a straw hat, her gaudy dresses with white cotton blouses with short sleeves, and black or blue skirt, and her high heels with sensible shoes. She has stopped going to tea rooms and dance halls. She is disgusted to recall that, shortly after May 16th, a few college girls were included among the twenty-two men and twenty-three women sentenced to prison terms for dancing at a secret hall one Saturday afternoon. She has renounced student demonstrations because she now realizes that a student's job is to study. She has even volunteered for a vacation program to help the rural populace with first aid, rice planting, building roads, and teaching the alphabet. She is now in the forefront of the national austerity drive.

A bus driver may witness the novel transition in his own way. In the old days his bus never left a stop until it was packed to the bursting point. Then it careened to the next stop. There was practically no time limit to the stop or to the capacity of the bus. Passengers were no more than two-legged cargoes, undeserving of service. The driver did no more than slip a few hundred hwan into a cop's pocket if he was picked up. Now he knows exactly what the regulations mean. His bus leaves as soon as passengers get off and get on. Not one passenger beyond capacity is allowed to board. His bus never squeezes past other vehicles on the busy streets. He says that the pedestrians, who used to dash across the streets regardless of traffic signs, now follow the go-stop signs meticulously, knowing that the signs are designed to protect their own safety. With the reckless drivers and jaywalkers gone, Seoul's title of "the worst traffic hell in the world" now belongs to the past.

Changes are evident in every other field. Some 880 refuse collectors in Soul organized into the Refuse Collectors Autonomy Association. These ragpickers were potential criminals, posing many social problems. They lived destitute, decadent lives, and the corrupt regimes of the past never succeeded in controlling them. Now these collectors work and live orderly lives in black fatigues and blue caps. Thousands of shacks illegally built in the Seoul area have been removed by the occupants spontaneously, clearing the way for new city construction. The old regimes repeatedly attempted to remove these obstacles for public works, but in vain.

Places of pleasure and resorts, such as tearooms, bars, cabarets, and pool halls, which, ironically, flourished in this impoverished nation, are almost deserted now. Smuggled foreign goods, mostly luxuries, are rapidly disappearing from show windows. Within a few months, no more of them will be seen. The day seems in the offing when chronic poverty will have disappeared, and the national economy will be securely established, as the revolutionary leaders have pledged.[12]

Economy[13]

In order to ensure free and honest business competition and encourage the creativeness of entrepreneurs, the basic task of the revolutionary economic reform policy has been to encourage special business privileges. As the revolutionary junta anticipated, social unrest, mass withdrawals of bank deposits, grain hoarding, and a rise in food and grain prices followed the coup. Measures curbing these trends were immediately put into force.

Immediately after the revolution, all bank deposits were frozen, a decree prohibiting a rise in food and grain prices was issued, and stringent controls against hoarding were enforced. Distribution of relief grain was stabilized, and grain prices were lowered. A social uneasiness gradually diminished, the government lifted the ban on bank withdrawals. Such emergency measures minimized economic confusion and paved the way for successful future revolutionary undertakings. The government's actions during the first forty days of the revolution demonstrated its desire to implement well-formed plans.

The new government's basic economic policy is that a free and competitive economy, participated in by free men, will surpass the forced economy of Communist countries. It seeks to prevent business monopolies detrimental to the public welfare, and endeavors to improve the economic conditions of rural and fishing communities.

In its budget reformulation for fiscal 1961, because of a drastic cut in various nonessentials large funds were made available for construction purposes. Most taxpayers had suffered from relatively high tax rates and tax-administration defects under previous regimes. As a result, tax evasion had become a common practice, hindering the development of honest business. The government indicted upper-bracket delinquent taxpayers in July.

In the past, taxpayers suffered from an arbitrary tax-assessment system. The system was abolished, and a policy whereby taxpayers filed tax returns voluntarily was adopted. The new method envisages streamlining tax administration, promoting business activities, and increasing income-tax revenue. The government intends to create a wholesome business atmosphere by implementing just and fair sharing of the tax burden, based on the principle of "taxation according to ability."

Control of luxury goods and implementation of an austere life had not been achieved under previous regimes. In order to encourage austerity, control the use of foreign luxuries, and stimulate savings, the government has banned the import of a number of foreign goods, causing greater consumption of domestic goods. Foreign cigarettes, which flooded Korea's markets since the Liberation of 1945, have finally disappeared from the domestic market. A saving of eight billion hwan is expected annually as a result of the ban, and a rise of three billion hwan in the sale of domestic cigarettes is forecast.

To ensure stability of the citizen's everyday life, the government effected stringent price controls immediately after the revolution. As the fear of rising prices diminished, the government lifted price controls on July 10th, with the exception of those on rice, barley, and coal briquets. Government-regulated public service rates, which play an important role in forming price levels of general goods, were lowered, and efforts are being made to curb upward trends in prices. For instance, bus fares, haircut charges, and the price of beverages have been lowered.

The government promulgated a law restricting the power of stockholders in banks and savings institutions, ending the abusive control by major stockholders. Interest rates on bank savings have been raised on an average of 50 per cent to attract additional deposits. Banking institutions have adopted various measures to improve management and reduce unnecessary manpower. As a result, the Bank of Korea alone is expected to save 600 million hwan in its expenditure account during the latter half of the year.

The ROK Government and USOM reached agreement on July 5th on the first phase of a five-year plan for development of hydroelectric facilities with a 580,000 kw. capacity. Construction of power plants at Samchok, Pusan, Yongwol, Chunchon, and on the Sumjin River is now in progress. Funds were secured in the second supplementary budget for the current fiscal year. Three substations were built in June at Susaik, Hannam-dong, and Suwon to eliminate power loss in the distribution system. Under the five-year plan for increase of coal production, the Daehan Coal Corporation recently set a record high production. Programs are being carried out to increase power output by 59,000 k.w. by January, 1962. Plans for transporting upward of five million tons of coal have been completed to meet the expected increased demands during the cold season.

A merger of three former power companies into the single management of the Korea Electric Company is expected to result in a reduction of operating costs of 4.5 million hwan. With reduced operating costs and increased efficiency, the new company is expected to net 15.9 billion hwan annually. With the depreciation cost estimated at 5.6 billion hwan, the company can reinvest 10 billion hwan for expansion and improvement of facilities.

With less manpower, government-operated enterprises are now operating at higher efficiency, and can save 3.6 billion hwan in wages and allowances alone as a result of reduction of personnel by 3,000. Construction of the Honam Fertilizer Plant has been resumed with an investment of 3.5 billion hwan by the Government.

In the field of agriculture, forestry, and fisheries, government policies are basically different from those in the past, and are bringing conspicuous results.

Shortly after the revolution, the government resolved to lift the burden of usurious debts from the shoulders of farmers and fishermen, and issued a decree concerning such debts ten days after the revolution, and implemented it on July 14th.

Government releases of farm loans were rapidly made available in large amounts. Funds released since the May 16th Revolution total 11.1 billion hwan, with an additional 12.1 billion hwan to be released by the end of this year. The government saw to it that the money reached the farmers' pockets and was utilized effectively. Such funds helped to ease the tight-money situation caused by high-interest private farm loans. With advance loans provided under the government rice-liens program, farm operation funds are expected further to improve the economy.

Efforts have also been made to ensure timely supply of fertilizer in adequate amounts. A major portion of fertilizer demand is met by government imports, and a system exchanging fertilizer for grain was instituted. Consequently, the government maintains a reserve of 3,650,000 bushels of grain. These measures contribute toward the timely and adequate distribution of fertilizer.

Government measures in this connection include: promulgation of a farm price maintenance law on June 27th; the purchase of summer grains to stabilize prices of summer yields; raising the purchase prices of export farm products, including peppermint, hemp, and silk cocoons; setting grain prices at prerevolutionary levels; releasing government reserve grain saved by military personnel; maintaining price stability through the release of five million bushels of rice under the liens program; and government purchases of grain crops to avoid a seasonal slump during the fall harvest. These measures aim at freeing farmers from heavy losses resulting from low farm prices. The government is well aware that an increase in farm incomes is a "must" for the development of the national economy.

An effort was also made to facilitate the sound development of farm cooperatives, which have been reorganized to include credit service, providing for the economic advancement of farmers. In revising the Farm Cooperative Law, the government provided legal measures to safeguard cooperatives from political interference.

Half of the four billion hwan earmarked for development of the livestock industry has been released and the other half was to be issued during the second half of 1961. The government banned imports of $3 million worth of molasses and ordered the raising of sweet potatoes to meet domestic needs. Similar measures will be taken where substitution is feasible.

Farmers with debts bearing over 20 per cent interest—normally loans to farmers bear from 35 to 65 per cent interest in money and crops, and sometimes go as high as 80 and even 100 per cent—are required to register with debt-assessment committees in their village. The committee checks the farmer's report against the claim of the creditor, who is also required to register the indebtedness due him.

The Bank of Agriculture of the Farm Cooperative asks the farmer to sign over his debt to the bank with an IOU that must be paid off in seven years and that bears 12 per cent interest. In turn, the bank will issue "farm bonds" to the creditors that also bear 12 per cent interest but may be cashed in three years. Bonds may thus ease the farmer's debt payment burden up to 150,000 hwan. Farmers who still are in need of money to tide them over until harvesttime—and most farmers are—may borrow up to 30,000 hwan per family from the Bank of Agriculture. The farmer must repay his loan when he has harvested his crop at the rate of a suk of rice, or 2.5 bushels, per each 3,000 hwans borrowed. The collection of grain will be used to stabilize prices when the rice supply dwindles in the market, usually every year before seeding time in the spring. The government expects to lend 11 billion hwan by the end of September.

The military government merged the Bank of Agriculture and the National Farm Cooperative Association into the Farm Cooperative. The Farm Cooperative will be a semigovernmental agency in which each farmer member may join with a one-vote privilege regardless of the amount of shares he may accumulate. Because shares in the cooperative cannot be put up for loans, loan sharks cannot accumulate them. The cooperative is also prohibited from engaging in political activities, and will serve as a bank for the farmer-member. It will also distribute and sell his crops, buy and process chemicals and tools for him, process other farm products for the market, provide him and his family with medical care, act as a collective bargaining agency on "economic or cultural matters," obtain technical experts, and set up reclamation and irrigation projects under government supervision. The Bank of Agriculture was established by the Chang government to provide low-interest loans to farmers. In fact, much of the current farm program was blueprinted before the military regime toppled the Chang regime. However, the coup is to be credited with the rapid implementation of projects which under past regimes in all likelihood would have languished in the idea stage.

The Korean farmer was and is the backbone of his country. He is also the miserable debt-ridden majority in his country. In South Korea 68 persons in every 100 workmen are farmers, and possibly 88 out of every 100 depend directly upon the farm for their very lives. Yet the Korean farmer produces only 38 hwan of every 100 hwan of goods and services produced in his country. He does own a third of all tillable land in South Korea.

Nearly half of all farmer-owned farms are only 1¼ acres in size. More than ¾ of all the farms are under 2½ acres. His tiny farm generally cannot support his family adequately; his family is always hungry; and his land is unfertile because of lack of fertilizers, poor irrigation, or too much undrained water. He has no modern tools, and he cannot afford better seeds or chemical fertilizers. He cannot pay his taxes, which run anywhere from 5 to 24 per cent of his total harvest, and he must borrow money to live while he hopes for a miraculous harvest next year. If sickness, drought, death, or a wedding occurs in his household, the farmer is nearly wiped out. There is nothing else he can do and nowhere else he can go. If the farmer cannot pay his debts or taxes, there isn't much the creditor or the government can do.

The government's speedy farm-relief programs are important steps, but they alone cannot cure the farmer's problems. When his land is paid off, his taxes are paid up, his debt payments stretched out, and his future loans bear smaller interest, he will have more cash and crops to live on. But the Korean farmer and his family will probably eat up the surplus. Other measures and additional means must be found to make the farmer save a portion of his harvest for future growth.

In the meantime, the long-range plan of the government for the

Korean farmer envisages a 30 per cent increase in farm production over the next five years. The Five-Year Economic Reconstruction Plan calls for only a moderate increase in rice production, but, wisely, will introduce diversification with barley, potatoes, and soybeans, and an immense increase in the raising of milch cows and goats, sheep and rabbits. Large irrigation plans are contemplated, along with land reclamation, and the introduction of government-subsidized fertilizers and seeds. The plan is nothing new. Like land-reform laws, rehabilitation schemes for farmers have been proposed anew almost every year since 1945. But there is encouragement in that the present regime may be able to put some of the plans into practice.

Of all the far-reaching reforms in fishery policies, the most important one is realignment and consolidation of numerous fishery organizations. Closely affiliated with past regimes, such organizations played a middleman's role, exploiting the already destitute fishermen by imposing excessive burdens on them.

An initial five billion hwan in emergency funds has been released to finance small and medium enterprises that had suffered from sparse capital. Another three billion hwan is slated for release by the end of September. On July 1st the government promulgated a law instituting a bank for small and medium industries. The new bank began operation on August 1, 1961. An industrial production registration system has been inaugurated to establish accurate production plans. At the same time, $800,000 in ICA funds, plus 25 million hwan, have been set aside for creation of an American-staffed advisory institute on improvement of business and industrial management.

Efforts are being exerted to reach a $340 million goal in exports by the end of 1966. Detailed procedures have been announced concerning issuance of permits for processes in the bonded area. Available export subsidy has been increased to five billion hwan. The postrevolutionary months have seen an increase in sales of domestic goods to the UN forces, as well as in general exports. The sale of eggs to the UN forces amounted to $200,000 by the end of June, and some 30,000 pigs were exported, earning $1.3 million.

At present, the people are intently watching the results of the revolution. They are especially concerned with disciplinary action against Communist sympathizers and counterrevolutionary elements, and those subject to disciplinary actions will soon face legal action. Economic reconstruction and the solution of unemployment, however, are the most crucial task of the government. Meanwhile, the public should reserve hasty criticism, and have confidence in their government.

Some irresponsible people recently spread rumors that the nation's industries had become bankrupt after the revolution. However, the following survey indicates the contrary. In private business, construction, barber- and beauty-shop closures were less than 1 per cent, while retail manufacturing, transportation, and printing businesses were at the low closure rate of 1.5 to 4.5 per cent. Though 70 to 89 per cent of cabarets and catering businesses closed, only 3.8 per cent of the nation's businesses have failed.

Government policy against tax arrears prompted the nation voluntarily to pay taxes, greatly helping to secure additional revenues. Luxuries were eliminated. The ban on foreign cigarettes resulted in a profit of two billion hwan for the Monopoly Office within two months. Employment rates in various fields, mainly National Reconstruction Projects, increased 5 per cent.

The present declining commodity prices and lowered government utility rates are evidence of the effectiveness of price controls. These are temporary causes of the current business recession. On the other hand, there are valid doubts, and measures to curb inflation as a result of releasing government funds are under study by the government.

Since the ROK Military Government, headed by a strong man, General Park Chung Hee, is aware that South Korea's economy is far from being well established, the junta is being forced to concentrate on some of the critical problems created by their own revolution. One was the heritage of all South Korean regimes—the intense and increasingly impatient demands of South Korea's people that the government in power do something about the country's economic illnesses, including unemployment, food shortages, and underproduction.

Highest on the list is the task of creating enough domestic confidence to inject life into a stagnant economy. The people with money must be persuaded that conditions are safe enough for them to invest it. Ever since the student-led revolution of April, 1960, people with money have been afraid to reveal their wealth by investing it, fearing that they would be arrested as profiteers. To restore economic confidence, the junta should announce that there will be no more arrests for past profiteering. It has unfrozen the bank deposits of more than a hundred wealthy men under investigation for profiteering, and has indicated that it would drop their cases.

Another major problem created by the revolution is the shortage of administrative talent. The experienced men of Chang's government are retired. Although army officers patrol the country, they have discovered that they badly need civilian help to run it. There are few indications yet of how successful the government has been in trying to restore economic stability at home. Meanwhile, the leaders of the coup are becoming concerned with their "image" abroad. They feel that it is a bad one, and complain of being "misunderstood," particularly in the United States. The junta members and the officers and civilians around them are concerned and annoyed that the rest of the world does not seem willing to accept their word that they are democrats at heart.

Since the devaluation of the hwan-to-dollar ratio under the John Chang administration, the national wholesale index went up 15 per cent between December, 1960, and March, 1961. During the same period, the cost of imported goods jumped nearly 40 per cent. Factors other than devaluation also contributed to the runaway inflation on the eve of the revolution. After the coup, the wholesale index spiral stopped, dipped a little, and is now slowly beginning to rise. Though the price of imported goods has slumped, harsh anti-import laws have put such merchandise under the counter. In addition, decrease in foreign export and a cutback in UN forces dollar spending since the beginning of this year curtailed supplies of foreign monies. Korea received $4 millions in January, only $2.6 million in March.

Against this background, the junta's arrest of businessmen who made large fortunes, the freezing of properties of some 450 wealthy families for tax indebtedness, the limiting of bank-account activities, the restrictions on usurious interest rates charged by moneylenders, and cutbacks in foreign trade all tend to inhibit the activities of some 85 per cent of the major industrial, commercial, and financial enterprises. The avowed 26 per cent reduction of civil servants, and the general unemployment resulting from decreasing business activity, have added to the psychological unrest of the general populace, already shaken by political uncertainties.

The Economic Planning Agency was set up by the government to plan and carry out strategic economic development projects in South Korea. The new agency ranks next to the Supreme Council of National Reconstruction and the office of prime minister in the government hierarchy. It took over the Economic Development Ministry and also absorbed the Bureau of Budget, Finances, and Statistics of the Home Affairs Ministry. The agency, directed by the former head of the Bank of Korea, Kim Yu Taik, is now operated by Prime Minister Song Yo Chan.

The Economic Planning Agency will blueprint a five-year development plan for South Korea calling for a 46.3 per cent increase in the gross national product by 1966. The vast economic resurgence program is scheduled to start next year. The government said that the project will create new jobs for 2,993,000 persons by the end of 1966. But it also forecast a population increase of 4,600,000 in the next five years, with 1,391,000 persons still out of work in 1966. At present it is estimated that 26.5 per cent of the work force, or 2,818,000 persons, are totally unemployed.

Aggressive population-control measures were promised that would attempt to reduce the current population growth rate of 2.88 per cent, but it added that the growth rate would still hover at 2.74 by 1966. The five-year plan hopes to change the capital investment pattern in Korea so that more funds would be directed to the development of new industries, such as coal, cement, steel, fertilizer, and oil refining. The report also envisaged a foreign investment capital requirement of $700 millions in the next five years to implement and sustain the plan. The government is hopeful of obtaining $423,800,000 from the United States, West Germany, and Italy. The five-year scheme also hopes to reduce the $261,900,000 balance-of-payments deficit to $186,800,000 by the end of the project.

The revolution has entered the second stage; it must exploit the lessons learned in the first stage to plan and prepare for the second. During the first two months of the reconstruction revolution, the fervor of the arbitrary clean-up campaigns that touched upon nearly every phase of the citizens' lives faded quickly. Two months later the man in the street was reacting coolly to the austerity credo. Everyone now stays home as much as he can. Shopkeepers have no business, and they can't get much merchandise. Bigger businessmen withdrew deposits to the tune of nearly 18 billion hwan.

The men in white shirts and dark suits playing at politics or business with American advisers and salesmen over Martinis at the Bando Hotel bar or in elegant *kisang** restaurants are gone. In their places are eager, harried young men in olive drab and shiny boots and sunglasses dashing about in dusty jeeps or working in their cramped offices till dawn. Government workers, from office boy to provincial chiefs, are scared of their jobs and of their bosses and of the investigators. Decisions are deferred, gathering dust, while the national economy stagnates. Even though all this is nothing new in Korea, the military revolutionists had hoped in vain that the reconstruction movement would fire the hearts of the people this time simply because the soldiers were sincerely devoted to making something of their country. But they are discovering that it takes planning, administrative talent, a viable and confident economy, and a cooperative citizenry to overhaul a sick country.

With such lessons learned, the second stage should gain greater popular support of the people, push economic rehabilitation as speedily as possible, and replace hastily picked military government agency heads with more experienced civilians. To secure greater popular confidence, investigators and police were told to be more civil and tolerant toward the citizenry. A thorough overhaul and consolidation of the mushrooming "investigating committees" was ordered, and the task was turned over to the Central Investigation Agency. The police were also cautioned to "learn to distinguish stones from gems."

To bolster the economy, the government should halt arrests for past profiteering; tax-evasion cases should be dropped and bank accounts released. Price controls should be withdrawn except on rice, barley, and coal briquettes. Liberal and low-interest loans for farmers and small businessmen should be provided by the government, and interest on savings accounts increased. Farm prices should be supported by the government for the first time in Korean history. Increased financial and technical aid should be sought by good-will missions touring the world. The government should maintain the present exchange rate and draw up laws aimed at attracting foreign

* *Kisang* are trained dancers and entertainers similar to the geisha of Japan.

capital. The need for increased austerity and savings to get the nation out of the near-permanent economic hole is required. Interest rates should be raised only on savings accounts. The spirit of free enterprise should be fostered, and businessmen should be encouraged by the removal of price and bank-deposit regulations.

A realistic recognition of a 10 per cent annual price increase is essential to any future planning. The inflationary spiral is almost inevitable, but the government should establish a price-stabilization fund to help control rising prices. The current stagnation of business and industry is principally due to a decline in purchasing power, lack of revolving capital, and an unrealistic taxation program. Lack of purchasing power left 18.8 per cent of all goods unsold during the first six months of this year, compared to 11.5 per cent last year. More than 65 per cent of iron, steel, textile and nonferrous metal stocks remain idle. Forty-four per cent of products sold in Korea were either on credit or consignment, resulting in an acute shortage of revolving capital. Further stimulation of business through better banking and commercial-note discounting systems is needed. A readjustment of present tax laws to encourage capital investment is necessary.

To secure more efficient administration, the coup should screen administrative heads, who are now all military men. Inexperienced soldier administrators should be replaced gradually by more capable civilian executives. The cabinet itself has six civilian members out of a total of fourteen.

United States Secretary of State Dean Rusk praised the new government in South Korea for the "vigorous and prompt steps taken in its efforts to root out corruption, to create a new atmosphere for national reconstruction and to provide a firmer economic base for democracy." He was encouraged by General Park Chung Hee's promise to make public by August 15th the form of Korea's future civilian government, which will be turned over to a democratic civilian government in 1963. He was also impressed with such prompt reforms as the unification of the power industry, the improvement of credit facilities for farmers and small businessmen, and adherence to international agreements.

Although there are still serious problems of inexperiences in the military administration, General Park's regime has shown commendable progress in clearing corruption, eliminating surplus officeholders, easing the farmer's lot, and promoting industry with a Five-Year Economic Plan. General Park has modified harsh repressive measures and has also shown every intention of permitting free and honest elections in 1963. However, he has important problems of maintaining unity among the ROK Army leaders, of preventing corruption in the new bureaucracy, and of dissatisfaction in some quarters with continued controls.

The South Korea Military Revolution is a "new" nationalism; in other words, it is an attempt to make 25 million South Korean people live a more righteous life. It would be dogmatic to call the ROK Army coup leaders reactionary because of their die-hard anti-Communist attitude, and they should not be accused of a lack of nationalism because they have done their best to get rid of unification movements operating under the guise of neutralism.

On September 12, 1961, President John F. Kennedy sent an invitation to Lieutenant General Park Chung Hee, Chairman of the Supreme Council for National Reconstruction of the Republic of Korea, head of the military group ruling South Korea, to visit Washington in mid-November, underscoring the President's decision to work closely with the ROK Military Government.[14]

As stated above, American support for the South Korea Military Government was the only way of preventing civil strife and dissolution of the ROK Army into warring factions. This support may well bear the fruition of his promise to restore democratic civilian government. General Park, of course, is expected to seek further American aid to ensure the success of democratic government, as well as help in bolstering the defense along the border with Communist North Korea. President Kennedy's invitation has added to General Park's prestige in Korea.

Diplomacy[15]

It is important that the Republic of Korea increase diplomatic, economic, and cultural relations with the free world. Her relations have been largely confined to the United States, the Philippines, Taiwan, and South Vietnam. South Korea also needs to make contact with the important neutralist states of Asia. It is imperative that relations be established with such major countries as India, Burma, and

Indonesia in Asia; with the newly emerging states of Africa; and with the long-established nations of Europe and Latin America. South Korea should push its campaign to establish a democratic nation concerned with and committed to the salvation of the Korean people, and to recast the image of New Korea abroad, broadening and strengthening international contacts.

The Military Government should be ready to undertake serious negotiations with Japan. A Korean-Japanese rapprochement would be of great advantage to both parties. The old pattern of superior-inferior relations cannot be allowed again, but Korea and Japan should be able to interact with mutual advantage politically, economically, and culturally. As in the dispute between Israel and the Arab countries, a vast amount of history and many complex problems affect relations between Korea and Japan. Korea and Japan have had the fundamental cultural differences. Korea, like most of Asia, has been influenced by the religions of Buddhism and Confucianism, which preach against bloodshed and advocate a meditative acceptance of worldly inconveniences while the mind and soul are purified by spiritual thinking. Japan has mainly followed the religion of Shinto, which teaches bushido and the code of the samurai, emphasizing patriotism and nationalism. (To die for Japan is to ensure eternal bliss to the believer.) Korean-Japanese discord has a long history of warfare, as in the dispute between Germany and France. Japan's forays against the Korean coast have been frequent for five hundred years.

While Western penetration brought both administrative turmoil and advantages to China, and tremendous industrial modernization to Japan, Korea withdrew into an isolationism so strict that the land became known as "The Hermit Kingdom," remaining aloof modernism until the Korean-American Treaty of 1882. On the grounds that Japan, by planting herself on the continent, could threaten the dangerously expanding power of imperial Russia, and that Korea had little of value for Western powers, the United States and Great Britain were content to leave Korea to Japanese exploitation when Japan challenged Russian power in the Russo-Japanese War of 1904–1905.

Japan prohibited Korean economical development, and the Second World War fanned Korean hatred of Japan, for the occupied country was squeezed mercilessly to help provide for the insatiable demands of the Japanese military forces. As soon as Japan was surrendered to the Allies, Korea expected as a matter of course that the United States military command in Japan would return gold, historical antiquities, and hundreds of ships that had been taken from Korea to Japan. Meanwhile, the Japanese were embittered against Korea by the forcible ejection from Korea, by American forces, of Japanese inhabitants, and by the turning over of their possessions, as "vested property," first to the United States Military Government and subsequently to the Republic of Korea Government.

The half-million Koreans resident in Japan, the bulk of whom had been taken there during the war as forced labor in factories, constituted another source of resentment. Since the Koreans were refused permission to take their possessions with them, and since land and employment in South Korea were inadequate to care for its burgeoning population and the inundation of four million refugees from the North, Koreans in Japan had little wish to return to their homeland. The Koreans who remained in Japan became "whipping boys" for a people much in need of reviving their self-esteem after their defeat, and the economic restrictions imposed upon them contributed to the infiltration of Communism amongst them. This "unassimilated minority" in Japan is one of several points of continual friction between the Koreans and Japanese.

Another cause of anti-Korean sentiment in Japan is the existence of a fisheries line that has been maintained midway between Korea and Japan since the end of 1945. General MacArthur originally established it as a means of keeping the Japanese closely within his jurisdiction, and to prevent their encroachment upon their resentful former colony, Korea. The line was reaffirmed by General Mark W. Clark during the Korean War, to reduce the danger of infiltration of South Korea by sea. And when the "Clark Line" was discontinued, following the signing of the armistice, ROK President Syngman Rhee reestablished it as a "peace line" to prevent Korean-Japanese imbroglios over fishing rights. Because the better fishing areas lie on the Korean side of the line, however, the Japanese are especially resentful, protesting the "illegality" of the "unilateral" proclamation of the "Rhee Line" by Korea. Korean coastal patrol craft have seized about a hundred Japanese fishing boats and several hundred Japanese fishermen on the Korean side of the line, some of whom are still serving prison sentences. Naturally, this makes difficult objective negotiations.

Still more difficult than the fisheries-line dispute, and far outweighing the heritage of ill-will from past history, is the question of claims and counterclaims between the two nations. The Republic of Korea has refused to specify its claims against Japan until Japan clears the way for negotiation by formally repudiating its 1905–1945 domination of Korea. But the government in Seoul has made clear that it expects a return of many priceless antiquities, of large quantities of gold, and of other properties taken from Korea during that generation-long period, especially in the months immediately preceding the surrender of Japan to the Allied Powers. Also involved are Bank of Chosun (Korea) funds that were held in Japan, of postal savings and insurance premiums paid by Koreans to Japanese companies, of back pay due Koreans who served in Japanese forced-labor battalions during the Second World War, and of embassy and other properties owned in Japan by the former Korean Kingdom.

Japan's claims against Korea were made explicit in an emotional outburst by Kubota, the Japanese delegation holding preliminary conversations with a Korean Mission in 1953, demanding the Japanese "rightfully" own fully 80 per cent of all the property and land in Korea. Therefore, it is impossible to enter formal discussions with Japan until after the complete renunciation of all such claims; otherwise they could be used as "bargaining points" to offset Korean claims upon Japan. And there, as of now, the matter rests.

In fact, Korean-Japanese difficulties are perhaps even more fundamental than these factors suggest. Essentially, what separates the two countries is not so much the hatreds of the past or the widely differing claims of the present, but fear of the future. Japan can scarcely have any real basis for fear of Korea, except that it may become strong enough to be an economic rival. Korea's fear of Japan is based on the rate of growth of the Japanese population of 90 million at an increase of over two million a year. Because Japanese people are simply too numerous to be able to live on their own islands, they must inevitably expand into Korea. Koreans are very much concerned, and also suspect Japan of planning an economic penetration of Korea as another means of reestablishing dominance.

The present Korean minority in Japan represents the residue of a much larger Korean community whose migration to Japan was the result of the Japanese expansionist policy in Asia from 1905 to 1945. As a means of making up the shortage of labor, Japan sought a supply of manpower in Korea after the Japanese annexation of Korea in 1910. Japan also drafted many young Koreans for forced labor when she was running her Greater Asia Co-Prosperity Sphere. This migration was set in motion by strong economic pressures exerted upon the agricultural population of Korea during the Japanese occupation. During the Second World War, the number of Koreans in Japan rose to approximately two million.

Following the surrender of Japan and the restoration of Korean independence after World War II, approximately 72 per cent of all Koreans in Japan went back to their own country. The division of their country and the outbreak of the Korean War made it impossible for the Koreans in Japan to be repatriated. In 1961 there were 611,000 Koreans in Japan, of whom 90 per cent were unemployed. Just as the Korean Peninsula is divided into North and South, so also are the Koreans in Japan divided into two groups: the Organization of Korean Residents in Japan (Mindan) and the Federation of all Koreans in Japan (Soren). Mindan, with about 150,000 members, support the Republic of Korea in the South, and Soren, with 200,000 supporters, North Korea. The remainder of 250,000 are neutral.

After the Pacific War, the Korean minority has been a constant irritant in Japan. Although greatly reduced in numbers, they have remained a highly vocal, emotional, and cohesive group. They have in no way identified themselves with the Japanese, and have considered Japanese law inapplicable to themselves. Factors such as these have deepened traditional feelings of hostility between Koreans and Japanese. The Koreans are accorded discriminatory treatment by the Japanese, and they harbor strong feelings of antagonism toward the latter. The Korean community has suffered the contempt of the Japanese people and has served as a scapegoat for popular dissatisfaction.

The Japanese, who have no love for Koreans, would like to send their Koreans back to overpopulated South Korea. The Koreans in South Korea, once oppressed by the Japanese, have no love for the Japanese, and the Republic of Korea Government insists that the Japanese Government must pay compensation for taking the Koreans for forced labor. On the contrary, manpower-hungry Communist North Korea wants to take in all the Koreans it can find in Japan.

The controversial program for repatriation to North Korea of Korean residents in Japan, which was due to expire on November 12th, was extended to October 27th, for another year. Red Cross representatives Masutaro Inoue and Busaburo Takagi of Japan and Kim Joo Yong of North Korea reached agreement on the details at the Japanese port of Niigata aboard the Soviet steamship *Tobolsk,* one of the two regular ferrying vessels used to transport the returnees. The agreement broke a long stalemate over the length of the extension. The Japanese side wanted only a six-month renewal, but the North Koreans insisted on a full year. From December 12, 1959, when the program began, through November 28, 1960, a total of 49,837 Koreans were repatriated at the rate of about 1,000 a week. The two Red Cross societies agreed on November 24th to step up the pace to 1,200 a week beginning March 1st.

The Communist-dominated Federation of Korean Residents in Japan stated that 60,000 Koreans in Japan were still eager to go to North Korea. ROK spokesmen contend that such Koreans are being duped into going to a virtual slave-labor camp in North Korea. There are about 630,000 Koreans now residing in Japan. The South Korean Government lodged a vigorous protest against the Japanese decision, and said that "if Japan should continue to push for Korean shipment to the North it is feared that it would constitute an obstacle in the way of friendly relationship between Korea and Japan."

Despite pressures from other countries to ease her demands, South Korea's new government intends to maintain previous Korean demands against Japan before she consents to a peace treaty. Korea's basic attitude on the issues of property claims against Japan and the Rhee Line, or "Peace Line," remains unchanged. Korea has demanded full payment from Japan for property and personal damage, confiscation, and services arising from the last world war and occupation before the war. In addition, the Koreans want valuable national relics taken from the peninsula by Japan returned to their native soil. They also demand full refund on postal savings and other bank accounts taken away from Korea at a discount during the war.

On the other hand, Japan has presented a bill to Korea for Japanese-owned land, factories, improvements, and properties the former Japanese owners were forced to abandon when they left Korea after the war. Korea's claims against Japan are about five and one half times Japanese claims against Korea. Japan has offered to pay cash for the services of Korean laborers conscripted during the war, and monies due on Japanese bonds and securities, but wishes to settle all other claims with nonrepayable economic and technical-aid funds and services.

Koreans claim that reparations disguised as grant-type aids is an absurd way of paying off outstanding obligations. Koreans maintain that repayment of occupation and war damages is one thing and economic and technical assistance another, and that Japan intends to kill two birds with one stone by paying off her indebtedness to Korea while declaring to the world that she is helping Korea.

Attempts to renew talks between Korea and Japan again got off to a bad start. The Japanese representative of the Foreign Ministry, Yujiro Izeki, asked Korea to permit Japan to open an observation mission in Seoul because Korea has one in Tokyo. Japan says that she lacks firsthand information about Korea, especially since a new government has taken over. The Korean minister to Japan, Lee Dong Hwan, replied that ROK has always insisted that a Japanese mission can be received in Korea only after normalization talks have ended. Both sides stalked away mad, and it may be some time before both nations decide to resume overtures.

But there are bigger factors that must also be taken into consideration. A free Korea and Japan must live together in peace if there is to be peace in Asia. They can be mutually helpful, if there is enough understanding and good will on both sides. The Japanese do not like to see their privileges curtailed by what they regard as pure Korean chauvinism, and the Koreans do not propose to be a dumping ground for cheap Japanese manufacture detrimental to the development of their own industry. There are half a dozen other sharp issues to be solved before Korea and Japan can become good neighbors. Although the Republic of Korea protested against the Japanese repatriation of Korean residents to North Korea, Japan carried out her plan, without the consent of the free Republic.

The Japanese government should protect Korean refugees, furnish them with employment, and guarantee their livelihood; Korean students in Japan should be given educational aid. While immediate steps should be taken to eliminate the discriminatory practices of the Japanese, on the other hand, Koreans should not expect to continue a dual nationality status in Japan.

An Army paratrooper hangs a sign designating the Headquarters of the Supreme Council for National Reconstruction on the wall of the National Assembly Building. (*ROK Photonews, May, 1961*)

Commemoration for Liberation, proclaiming the unification of North and South Korea. (*ROK, O.P.I.*)

The repatriation problem ought to be left alone until a better climate of agreement can be created. While efforts should be directed toward promoting the largest possible degree of moderation and patience on the part of both Korea and Japan, in the meantime the United States might propose some compromise solutions for current Korean-Japanese differences—solutions that would involve some commitments as well.

American Aid[16]

Honor and compassion commit the United States to Korean rehabilitation. Many Americans feel a strong bond of friendship with the Korean people, are anxious to bind up the wounds of a stanch ally, and want to help them achieve a more tolerable material condition. The United States has a direct interest in the strength and internal stability of the Republic of Korea. A young nation of 22 million people of proved courage and military talent, a rich heritage, energetic, and with a significant and potentially substantial productive capacity, its mineral resources are strategically important to the West. In addition, the integrity of South Korea's stand against the Communists has become known throughout the world. The greatest service the United States has rendered to South Korea is not merely financial; it appears in the commendable training, physical, moral, and technical, that America had bestowed on the ROK Armed Forces.

The Republic of Korea could not survive without continued support from the United States, which has given more than $3 billion worth of economic aid to the country since the Second World War. This aid, in effect, has seen Korea through occupation since World War II, independence, the crises of civil war, famine, and rehabilitation.

There are several principles upon which the United States conducts mutual security assistance programs throughout the world—ideas that had their origin long before the cold war. American foreign policy is rooted in the belief that peace must be maintained through a strong free-world defense against aggression. Global defenses of the free world have required the United States to assume many responsibilities in many places, responsibilities that are shared with allies all along the frontier facing the iron curtain, from Norway to Korea. To meet the Communist threat, the United States keeps sizable forces of its own troops far from home. In addition, it helps allied countries to meet the burdensome costs of maintaining effective fighting forces of their own. This is the kind of cooperation—a co-ordinated defense effort—upon which the security of the free world depends today.

But this is not enough. The Communist threat also takes the form of subversion and economic sabotage of independent countries. For this, another kind of defense is needed: economic development. The hope for free society in the future—for the happiness and life fulfill-ment every man seeks—cannot be realized without material advance-ment, without the security that comes from economic well-being, without the banishment of hunger, without the establishment of opportunity for all. The free world must achieve these goals if it is to remain free. In this struggle for freedom, the United States has still another mutual security program: economic and technical assistance.

In Korea, the invasion of the Communists from the North in June, 1950, was followed by a tide of destruction that wrought havoc for millions of people throughout the country. The ebb and flow of war traversed some areas as many as four times. Damage was so extensive that in the twelve years that have since elapsed, assistance required by the Republic of Korea from nations of the free world has totaled sev-eral billions of dollars. And many of these nations had sent their sons to fight and sometimes to die for Korea's independence.

Agriculture is the most important sector of the South Korean economy, and over two-thirds of the total labor force is dependent upon it for a livelihood. Smaller segments of the population are en-gaged in mining, industry, commerce, fishing, transportation, and government and professional services. The importance of Korea's economic sectors may be measured roughly on the basis of the esti-mated gross national product as a percentage of the total. On this basis, agriculture and forestry would account for 47.1 per cent; fish-eries, about 3.7 per cent; mining, 1.3 per cent; manufacturing, approximately 10.6 per cent; construction, close to 2.2 per cent; wholesale and retail trades, approximately 7.8 per cent; public utilities and transportation, 2.5 per cent; services (foreign trade and finance), 14 per cent; government, 9.2 per cent; other services account for the remainder. In South Korea's efforts to overcome the obstacles to reconstruction and self-support, it has received a large amount of foreign aid since the end of World War II, the greater amount having been provided by the United States Government directly or through the United Nations.

Coordinating the monumental effort of administering United States aid to Korea has been the responsibility of the United Nations Command Economic Coordinator for Korea since August 7, 1953. At that time a presidential directive established the Office of the Economic Coordinator for Korea (OEC). On July 1, 1959, the name was changed to the United States Operations Mission to Korea (USOM/K). While an artificial barrier to national unity has been created by the North Korean Communists—with the direct support of the Soviet Union and the Communist Chinese regime—independence, successfully repulsed aggression, freedom from starvation and epidemic disease, and economic growth are the Republic of Korea's achievements today.

Now Korea's economic progress, while steadily improving the standard of living, should be measured against three basic problems: division of the country, with the bulk of power and industrial facilities located in North Korea and agriculture situated in South Korea, devastation caused by the 1950–1953 Korean conflict, and the sharp population increase caused by an influx of about four million refugees from the North. These problems have created a most difficult economic situation. The goal of the American aid program should be to enable Korea to become self-supporting. This should be a long-range program, the success of which depends on increased exports, industrial production, power, management, and capital resources. United States assistance to Korea should seek to help raise living standards, to expand capital investment in projects contributing directly to agricultural and industrial productivity, and to enable the Korean Government to maintain its Armed Forces. It consists mainly of Resources Development, which makes direct material contributions to industries; and Technical Assistance, which provides specialists to train Koreans in latest techniques. The American people are assisting the people of South Korea to build a young nation that is strong and secure.

The source and the value of this economic aid furnished by the United Nations are known to and well appreciated by the people of the Republic of Korea and their government—from the farmer, who has direct knowledge that his fields were irrigated through a United

Nations project; or the purchaser of cement who identifies the name stamped on the container with a new United-Nations-constructed plant; to the country's economists and planners who calculate the product and requirements of the economy. The United Nations economic aid that was provided to the Republic of Korea through UNKRA, supported by the contributions of thirty-four member and five nonmember states, represented a bold new action to bring assistance of a new dimension to a nation that found itself in economic ruins as the result of aggression.

The last stage of the planned program carried out by UNKRA in the furtherance of that aim is almost concluded, and the agency's accomplishments and success are even now largely a matter of history. This fact, however, does not diminish its value; the United Nations can derive full satisfaction from knowing that what was accomplished has played a positive and active part in the task of restoration and rehabilitation. United Nations economic assistance not only has made, but is continuing to make today, an important and most beneficial contribution to the Republic of Korea and its people. The approaching closure of UNKRA does not end that contribution, for through the completed UNKRA projects, and the large residual fund UNKRA leaves for the government of the Republic of Korea for use on still more projects, it will continue steadily into the future, providing further help in the efforts of this young nation to build a viable and stable economy.

The United States aid operates both project assistance and nonproject assistance. Each covers the whole range of Korean economic development. Under project assistance, specific enterprises are programed, with the aid mission providing needed imported materials, equipment, and technical advice. Korean entrepreneurs ultimately pay all costs in Korean hwan, including the equivalent value of dollar expenditures. These hwan payments are deposited with the ROK Government in a counterpart fund which the United States and Korean Government officials jointly administer to finance local costs of further economic development. The salables program supplies a wide range of machinery, equipment, petroleum, fertilizer, and raw materials from abroad. These were sold for hwan to Korean enterprises, extending from large manufacturers to farmers, and the amount of hwan received also is put in the counterpart fund for further local-currency financing of economic development. Through this program, which totaled $185 million in one year, the United States aid has reached into many major industrial and agricultural activities in South Korea.

In the eight years that have passed since the Korean armistice agreement was signed, those facilities within the Republic of Korea damaged by the war have been almost entirely reconstructed, and the greatly improved state of the economy has now enabled the authorities concerned to give more thought to long-term economic development. In the period under review, a joint United States–Republic of Korea Economic Development Council was established to study problems associated with such development. A major economic problem confronting the Republic of Korea is the balance-of-payments deficit, amounting to some $300 million annually, which must be reduced if the country is eventually to support itself at current living standards.

As the Republic is predominantly an agricultural country, there are some prospects of exporting agricultural commodities, such as grains, fruits, nuts, and livestock, particularly cattle and pigs. For example, there is an exportable surplus of rice that is capable of expansion, but at present prices rice intended for export would have to be subsidized. Moreover, it would not be easy to find large markets for Korean rice, for not only is there increasing competition among grain-exporting countries, but also good harvests in Korea quite often coincide with good harvests elsewhere. A further difficulty is that, as more than 65 per cent of the increasing population live on the existing farm lands where the average family farm is less than two acres, salable surpluses are becoming harder to produce. It would be possible to increase the area under cultivation significantly only by using more of the hill lands in the river valleys and of the lower slopes of mountains, but such a program would require substantial capital investment. As for the possibility of large-scale livestock breeding, it is thought that the hilly country may be unsuitable for this purpose without considerable expenditure on soil preparation, but that some future increase in the number of cattle is possible within the present domestic pattern of agriculture.

The fisheries of the Republic of Korea are also a possible source of increased earnings of foreign exchange, but before substantial exports of fish are possible it will be necessary to exploit nearby deep waters to a greater extent than at present. Further repair and modernization of ships are necessary; fishermen have to be trained in their use; new methods have to be introduced and sufficient processing and refrigeration plants installed—although progress has been made in these fields. Here again, capital formation is difficult, for the fishermen themselves cannot provide the necessary funds to make the fishing industry a major source of foreign currency; some fisheries loan funds are, however, at present avaliable.

Before the prospects of industrial development can be fully known, surveys yet to be completed must determine whether iron and coal are present in sufficient quantities to support the development of heavy industry. The possibility that they will prove insufficient is one that should be faced. Surveys are also being made to discover or estimate the extent of deposits of exportable minerals. The formation of sufficient capital is of primary importance in all efforts toward economic development. Some of the substantial and increasing private capital in the Republic is now being invested in productive enterprises, although short-term commodity and financial transactions, unproductive in themselves, are generally more profitable. An increasing number of people now have incomes that allow some component for savings. It is necessary to maintain their confidence in the economy and to instill the concept of investment into the public mind.

Another difficulty is the shortage of technicians despite considerable promotion of technical training in the Republic and overseas by the government, often in cooperation with the various exchange programs. One major problem in the way of meeting the growing need is, however, the dearth of Korean-language books on technical subjects, which imposes on trainees the additional burden of studying in a foreign language. One of the potentially valuable resources of Korea is its large labor force; it may eventually prove possible to use this as skilled or semiskilled labor in the manufacture of goods for export.

The period 1953–1957 was characterized by efforts for reconstruction directed both toward regaining the 1949 level of production and income and the solution of problems inherited from the Korean conflict, such as the influx of refugees from the North and the severe inflation that ensued. These immediate aims had to be accomplished before primary attention could be given to the long-term planning necessary to develop the economic resources of the country. While it is difficult to differentiate clearly one stage of economic life from another, it may be said that by 1958 the reconstruction phase had largely been fulfilled and that the present phase is one of development and growth with an intervening period of adjustment.

Reconstruction must draw attention to the economic importance of the question of unification, particularly in relation to the problems involved in drawing up comprehensive long-term plans for economic development. Further, in present circumstances the continuance of foreign aid either from individual countries or from international agencies is necessary for the maintenance of economic stability in the Republic.

In assessing the financial condition of Korea, two favorable facts stand out. First, the nation as a whole has considerable natural resources adequate to provide a high standard of living for the whole population. Even South Korea, considered alone, normally has exportable surpluses of rice, fish, and other products. Second, the Korean people are eager to deal with their problems.

The unfavorable elements are more transitory, but are sharper in their immediate effects. First, the economy of the country has suffered drastically from the separation into two zones, cutting off the industrial North from the agricultural South, and from the handicap of twelve years of inefficient government rule. Second, South Korea alone among the "friendly" nations of the world was excluded from such hugely beneficial international programs as Lend-Lease, the United Nations Relief and Rehabilitation Administration, and the World Bank. Third, American aid should not be mostly in the form of food and other consumption goods, rather than basic supplies needed to rehabilitate the country's economy. And fourth, South Korea has had to exist in an interim condition without a good government to establish the long-range policies and to take the measures essential in any nation for the development of trade and industry.

Remedies for inflation must necessarily be drastic and painful. The basic goal is greatly increased production, both for home consumption and for export. To achieve this, every encouragement will have to be given to stimulate industrialization, since some 80 per cent of all corporate wealth in Korea is in expropriated Japanese properties, held in trust for the new government. Or increased production might occur through encouraging foreign investments and leaving industry

relatively free from heavy taxation and from labor restriction while
it is getting started. Currency and price controls will doubtless be continued. Additional aid is being extended by the United States as part
of its program of supporting democratic bulwarks against the further
spread of Communism. In any event, it is axiomatic that the difficult
situation into which the Korean economy has deteriorated cannot
easily be redeemed.

The Conlon Report of the United States Senate made the following suggestion to tighten the efficiency of the South Korea Aid Program:

A strong case can be made for the thesis that these funds have not
been used as efficiently as they should have been, that American interests
and objectives in connection with their use have not been sufficiently
defined and defended, and that our generally weak position has created
serious problems. The charge is common that American aid has created
too many Korean millionaires and sustained too many corrupt practices.
There is some validity in this criticism. Basically, we have had a weak
policy toward Korea in terms of stipulations, controls, and supervision.
We have usually invoked the time-honored maxim "non-interference in
the internal affairs of another state," despite the fact that massive aid
obviously is interference and our responsibility for overall trends in Korea
—and its ultimate defense—cannot be avoided. Clearly this is a complex
and difficult matter, and one not confined to Korea by any means. It is
one of the truly urgent problems in connection with economic aid to
late-developing societies. In Korea, the difficulties were doubtless compounded by the rivalries and divisions of authority that have prevailed
among our separate diplomatic, economic aid, and military missions;
recent administrative changes may bring some alleviation. But the
broader elements of the problem will remain, and need to be faced
squarely. These issues must not be used as the basis for underestimating
economic assistance as a major weapon in the worldwide struggle against
totalitarianism. But our techniques of aid, and our responsibilities in
connection with aid, need to be basically reassessed.

In Korea the American aid program should be reexamined with
respect to the following questions: 1. What form of aid is most conducive
to stimulating indigenous energies and capital formation? 2. To what
extent should assistance be geared to long-range plans and what should
be the American responsibility for checking the validity and progress
of such plans? 3. What is the proper balance between military and
economic aid, in terms of the security and welfare of Korea?[17]

United States aid to South Korea required further over-all planning for new projects to be justified on basis of need and resources. The history of American aid has been considerably criticized by both Koreans and Americans. The most frequent criticism was that a large part of the funds was siphoned off by corrupt Rhee and Chang government officials and that contracts were awarded to former President Rhee's favorites, who speculated with the funds. Both Rhee and Chang governments were to blame for corruption, but America shares the responsibility for the inadequate planning and insufficient supervision. The United States Aid program toward South Korea was discussed in the *New York Times:*

The time has come for taking a more disciplined approach to Korean aid, and the following changes are to be made: New projects must be justified on the basis of a surveyed accounting of the need and resources of the South Korean economy and the ability of local finance and management to keep them going once they are built. Economists of both countries agree that the time is long overdue for over-all national planning instead of project-by-project planning. No more money will be put into industrial expansion until the present industrial program, which is most often described here as "faltering," is going at full capacity. At the moment, ten plants built by United States funds are idle and about twenty more are running below capacity.

There is to be a tougher approach to both American and Korean contractors who fail to meet estimates of cost and speed. One fertilizer plant, the largest single industrial project in the country, cost about $36,000,000 instead of the original estimate of $16,000,000. Moreover, it was finished about a year behind schedule, according to information here. The United States' aid staff, totaling about 500 employees, is to be pruned. This year and next about 100 jobs will be eliminated, some because their mission will have been accomplished and some because officials are no longer convinced they were ever needed. There is to be tighter scrutiny of already approved projects. So far the United States has canceled $80,000,000 worth of plant building projects, largely because it believed the Koreans who were to have run them did not have the managerial talents nor the bank accounts to keep them going.

Programs that interest Americans more than Koreans are to be reexamined. Some Americans are beginning to think there are too many projects that were started simply because they fitted in with an American vision of society rather than Korean needs or interests. Among those mentioned is a teachers' training school that in one year turned out 200 graduates but was able to find teaching jobs for only five. There is to be emphasis on the theory that an aid program cannot be divorced from specific sociological and psychological patterns of a country and its traditions. At the moment, there are only two persons on the United States' operation mission staff qualified as psychologists or sociologists. Detailed studies are said to be lacking on one of the most important day-to-day problems facing Americans here—the roots, traditions and practice of corruption in Government and business.[18]

Korea has been regarded as responding to treatment rather than as on the road to recovery, although the economic situation gives evidence of vitality and the substantial success of United States economic aid is apparent on every hand. The international balance of trade of Korea is more unfavorable than that of any other country in the world, and it continues to be necessary for the United States to augment the revenue of the Korean Government to the extent of some 30 per cent of the annual Korean budget. In Korea, where many industries are government-owned and where many others are financed almost entirely by government loans, the normal profit-and-loss incentives and penalties cannot be accepted as adequate controls of management, and the elaborate and time-consuming machinery of bureaucratic review has to be relied on. If it is possible for the United States, with the cooperation of the Korean Government, to redirect its policies and procedures so that the prudence and self-interest of the entrepreneur can replace the alertness and skill of the government official in policing the economic aid program, the United States may reasonably expect better results.

Economic aid to Korea should be related to a number of specific objectives. About 50 per cent of it has produced local currency which has been used to underwrite part of the budget of the Korean Government. About 35 per cent of the Korean budget is spent on the Korean Armed Forces. Unless the United States is willing to see expenditures of the Korean Government for its military forces reduced, economic assistance to underwrite the Korean budget presumably should be maintained at a level sufficient to produce the necessary hwan. The balance of payments to Korea is more unbalanced than that of any other country in the world. The United States has to underwrite the deficit if the Korean economy is to operate; otherwise imports of fuel, raw materials, and foodstuffs would stop.

Aggressive West German businessmen are making deep inroads in American sales to South Korea. The pain is doubly acute because all purchases are made with American aid funds. While Korean Government procurement of German goods has risen 1,000 per cent, government purchases from America have fallen 20 per cent. Korea's procurements, with United States funds, from West Germany amounted to $700,000 in 1958 and $7,800,000 in 1959; procurements from America totaled $25,000,000 in 1958 and $21,000,000 in 1959, according to the *New York Times*. The reason is simple: German businessmen are more aggressive. There are thirty German businessmen in Seoul, and the corps is growing by leaps and bounds. German equipment is good and prices are competitive, below American quotations.

The American policy in Korea should be not only to provide sufficient economic assistance so that Korea can maintain a military force, together with a small United States force, adequate to defend the armistice line, but also to push the development of the Korean economy so that Korea may become increasingly able to support itself. Korea can never maintain a decent standard of living for its people if it isolates itself from the world and lives off its limited natural resources. The future welfare of Korea depends on the country's making a place for itself in the world in which the abilities and energies of its people can be utilized in agriculture, industry, and commerce. An economic failure in South Korea could be extremely costly to the United States and to the rest of non-Communist Asia.

V

Conclusion

DEMOCRACY[1]

Korea can lay just claim to being the most devastated country of modern times. The Korean War ruined rice paddies, gutted factories, and charred villages. Out of a prewar population of 30,000,000 about 3,000,000 became refugees and 100,000 children were left orphans. Furthermore, the Korean people have been brutally torn by civil strife, political unrest, and public disorder. A decade of frustration exploded into anger and bloodshed in South Korea. The new nation is so steeped in poverty that any change would seem an improvement. Finally, a Students' Revolution brought about the downfall of Rhee's regime, and a courageous Military Revolution brought the downfall of Chang's regime. Seldom in the history of a nation does so much happen in so few years.

The kaleidoscopic changes that have taken place in Korea involve complex economic, social, and political forces that are difficult to

190

identify. Korea has not escaped the relentless pressures that have been breaking the bonds of custom, manners, and tradition. Swept along by the tide and unfamiliar crosscurrents, the Korean people are being drawn into the vortex of violent changes that seem to characterize our time. They look, not back at leaders who have lost their equilibrium, but toward new personalities who may be able to guide them into calmer waters.

Korea's area is vast even in the context of today's rapidly shrinking globe, and important despite the trend toward automation, atomic energy, and space exploration. It is the people who make Korea a compelling factor in world affairs. They inherited wisdom without wealth, acquired political freedom without economic independence, and assumed responsibilities in international affairs beyond their visible capacities for fulfillment. The Korean people are just beginning their struggle to solve their problems.

In spite of their unfortunate past and their present uncertainty, the Korean people are determined to turn evil into good by their incessant and unfailing efforts to build a new, democratic society. They hope to transform their war-torn, battered, and disorganized country into a self-sustaining nation. They also hope to exercise their individual wills in politics.

The basic democratic definition, government by the full and free consent of the governed, has rarely been challenged in Korea. The test of a new young Korea must be how well that ideal is kept alive. It is therefore hoped that military rule in South Korea will be implemented so as to counter the threat of enemy subversion without hindering development of democratic institutions and processes in a free Korea. The people have sacrificed much for the cause of a free, democratic, and unified Korea, and Korea should be a symbol of real democracy in Asia.

Democracy is revered in South Korea as the best and only form of government that will alike guarantee the rights of citizens and provide an efficient government reflecting the will of the people. Democracy, as "government of the people, by the people, for the people," is obviously not the easiest way to run a country like South Korea. But it is the only way for men who want to be free. The history of the United States showed that an enlightened democracy can survive all difficulties, including revolts and civil wars. However, this does demand a great sense of responsibility on the part of both the governors and the governed, of the majority party as well as the minority party, and a willingness to settle differences by compromise even in countries where compromise is regarded as a derogation of principles. For only thus can the body politic arrive at decisions acceptable to the majority without crushing the rights of the minority.

America's progress has been sufficient to justify her in offering sympathetic aid and advice to younger nations. These can learn from America's experience. This is especially true of South Korea, sponsored, aided, and defended by America. But there is no reason for America to expect new states to function with a perfection that would have to jump centuries of education, experience, and experimentation. Korea does not have as many trained administrators, technicians, and skilled workers as the Army Military Government will need to develop South Korea's resources, both social and economic. Unfortunately, real democracy has not existed in South Korea, even after liberation from the Japanese autocratic government.

The temporary suspension of democratic government in the Republic of Korea need not and should not imply the permanent destruction of democratic principles. Both the present ROK Army leaders of the Military Government and the peoples in South Korea, as well as the United States, are determined to set up a constitutional civilian government within two years. The Supreme Council of Korea National Reconstruction should establish a committee composed of civilian and military officers to study the nature of the civilian government that will emerge in 1963 when military revolutionary tasks will be completed. This is a most difficult task, which must take into consideration innumerable tangible and intangible factors. The present South Korea Government might well study the West German Constitution, which meets the danger of a multiparty system by providing that Parliament can overthrow a chancellor or premier only by electing his successor in advance. This provision has not only assured West Germany of a stable government but has also set it on a course toward a virtual two-party system that promises stability.[2]

The revolutionary slogan "Crush Indirect Aggression" can be interpreted as a crusade for social justice and welfare through bolstering inner vitality. Elimination of subversive elements and other cankers of the body politic is certainly the most effective way to counter Communism, thereby cementing the democratic foundation of this country. However, General Park, Chairman of the Military Government in South Korea, made startling charges of pro-Communist activities against former Prime Minister Chang and many of his cabinet members.

General Park and his zealous young leaders have undertaken formidable tasks in tackling the problems of social and economic reform in South Korea while simultaneously resisting pressure from the North. In the circumstances, the use of strong methods is inevitable, but those being employed by the new junta sound excessive. South Koreans revolted against President Syngman Rhee because his regime, among other deficiencies, was too oppressive. The junta at Seoul, however, must guard stringently against overdoing its purge campaign. A regime imposed by force can easily forfeit popular support by harsh and arbitrary actions. The South can win in competition with the North only by making itself "superior in every way." The South will not be superior unless the new military rulers respect basic freedoms, permit the expression of political views, and commit themselves more definitely than they have thus far done to the eventual return of constitutional, democratic government.

Though the new government must expose and eradicate intrigues undermining South Korea's stand against Communism, it risks the danger of destroying itself if it falls prey to a Korean form of McCarthyism, and if it uses the blanket of "anti-Communism" to stifle opposition. If the Military Government in South Korea does not act with regard for popular rights and for democracy, the people of the South will find little to choose between two repressive systems and little reason to give the new government their loyalty. The Korean students who hopefully ran Syngman Rhee's seemingly indestructible administration out of power in April of 1960 may see their revolution produce, in General Park's regime, something suspiciously like an absolute military dictatorship.

RECONSTRUCTION[3]

Economic stability is a prerequisite for a true democracy. Poverty-stricken, hungry, and insecure people cannot be expected to exhibit a healthy concern over national and political affairs. This is especially true of a young, undeveloped, and divided nation like South Korea. South Korea economic problems are no simple ones; many of the difficulties faced by the Republic are similar to those encountered by other underdeveloped countries, but the major difference is that, despite enormous amounts of foreign aid, the situation continues year after year to be grave. Complete breakdowns of ordinary business transactions have not been uncommon. American economic aid is being gradually terminated, and the ROK Government is dismayed at the prospect. Military aid in the amount of $200 million per annum is granted separately.

American military aid corrupted Korea almost as much as it helped that country, according to United States Senator J. W. Fulbright. It is undeniable that the management of United States aid was not perfect under the corrupt former regimes. But, comparatively speaking, South Korea has wisely used such aid for anti-Communist defense. The Korean Armed Forces have received fine training and excellent combat experience, and, along with the United States Armed Forces, they are one of the strongest anti-Communist forces in the world. It is hoped that now they can guide their country toward economic rehabilitation. The new government is cooperating with the United States Aid Mission to clean up the Mutual Aid program in Korea. Both Koreans and Americans know that American dollars were diverted from Korean farmers to make political capital out of local irrigation projects or to put into the pockets of politicians some of the money intended to promote industrialization.

The situation in North Korea was reported in *Time* in November, 1960, as follows:

In the seven years since the fighting stopped, North Korea has become something of a showcase with plenty of window dressing for Communism in Asia. Pyongyang (population 800,000) has a Stalin Allee just like East Berlin's, a vast opera house and a vaster sports stadium. Forests of swinging cranes constantly add to the number of workers' apartment houses. The national emblem is a flying horse that decorates everything from matchboxes to tractors: the horse is supposed to be charging toward socialism at 300 miles a day. Premier Kim Il Sung's proclaimed ambition is to "reach and pass Japan's per capita production in ten years."

The drawbacks to life in this dynamic workers' paradise are many.

The apartment houses exist amid shacks, slums and vacant lots that still make up most of the city and never appear in the propaganda. Gaunt and suspiciousy prisonlike on the outside, the barracks-like apartment blocks have mess halls and community toilets but neither heat nor running water in the apartments themselves. But by rigid regimentation and the help of technicians from Eastern Europe, Communist North Korea has made impressive economic progress of a sort. Ninety-five percent of the peasants are herded into Soviet-style communes. Factory workers toil 12 to 14 hours a day for wages that average $21 a month in plants that often operate round the clock.

With the usual dazzle of unconfirmable statistics, the North Koreans proudly contrast their achievements with South Korea. The North has less than half the South's population, but the Communists fell heir to 70% of undivided Korea's heavy industry, 90% of the electric power, 70% of the coal. Much of this capacity was destroyed during the Korean war, but the Reds say that by 1956 it was already back to prewar levels, and that since then output has doubled and even trebled. They claim that last year the North produced ten times as much steel as South Korea, five times more cement, just as much grain. Unfortunately, South Korea, badly led in the last days of Syngman Rhee and hardly led at all now, is suffering from economic confusion. It has received $2.5 billion in American aid and is urgently asking for more, yet has announced a further devaluation of its debased currency. Many of its United States-built factories are not working. There are more than 1,500,000 unemployed—an eighth of the labor force. The temper of the North is ruthless purpose; the mood of the South lacks decisiveness and even direction.[4]

The urgency is generated by impressive evidence that the North Korean dictatorship is forcing North Koreans into stepped-up industrial progress. Those who cite the Republic of Korea for democratic leadership in a new resurgence of a reunited Korea do it a disservice if they fail to attempt an appraisal of progress in the hostile camp north of the border.

South Korea's military leaders should move fast to deal democratically with South Korea's poverty, unemployment, inflation, overpopulation, and underdevelopment. The pitfalls before them, of course, are enormous. Maintaining unity within their own ranks will be a problem; military officers often make poor civil administrators; there will be the danger of army morale and discipline suffering from the involvement of its leaders in government affairs; government power and access to government funds will offer temptations that some army men will find it hard to resist; and South Korea's deficit economy, its 2,000,000 unemployed, and shortage of resources are stubborn realities hard for even the most capable rulers to solve.

The new Military Government must show great ability in the sphere of fundamental social and economic reforms. It is not enough to cancel farm debts and take other one-shot actions of this nature. A comprehensive program with special attention to the depressed rural sector of the South Korean economy is vital. South Korea's poverty-stricken farmers must be permanently protected from usury and other forms of exploitation. They must be given the means to improve land productivity, and more lands must be put into cultivation. Marketing practices must be improved and small industries developed to employ the jobless in rural areas and correct the drift toward the cities.

To prevent economic disaster, the following steps are urgently needed: (1) expansion of public-works projects to reduce unemployment; (2) payment of adequate wages to public servants to eliminate corruption; (3) control of commodity prices to the level of the wage scale, and vigorous prosecution of black-market activities to curb the ever spiraling inflation; (4) operation by the government of enterprises that stopped production, and freezing of their assests and credits until proper investigation is completed; (5) resetting of the hwan-dollar exchange rate on a realistic basis to check illegal dealings. Halfhearted measures will only bring a graver crisis. Poverty and discontent breed Communism.

Improved transportation should be a major goal, with emphasis on maintaining the Korean national railroad at a level of operational capability and efficiency necessary to support economic development and defense forces. The maintenance of track structure, harbor rehabilitation, modernization of aeronautical meteorological networks and airports are necessities. Telephone and telegraph service should be increased to meet growing industrial demands for improved and efficient communications. Power plants and dams should be constructed to cope with the shortage of electric power in South Korea. Primary industry should be developed to use a maximum of local raw materials and to minimize imports of finished materials, and still be diversified enough to meet essential consumption and alleviate national unemployment.

Mining production and export of minerals should be increased; mills should be built to permit extraction of copper and other base metals now lost in small workings for gold, copper, lead, zinc, and tungsten. The stress of modernizing and expanding all phases of farm life is necessary, and technicians should be chosen to serve as the nucleus of a future soil- and water-conservation technical staff. In livestock production and care, breed improvement, better feeds and nutrition, livestock product marketing, and animal disease control should be stressed.

The war-damaged waterworks systems and uncompleted sanitary facilities should be rehabilitated, and highway, bridges, and drainage systems in urban and interurban areas should be constructed as soon as practicable. Owing largely to war damage and heavy population increase because of the influx or refugees, South Korea has a critical housing shortage of some million units. The major obstacles in overcoming the deficiency are the shortage of basic building materials and of credit capital for housing construction, as well as the lack of a well-organized Korean home-building industry. An expanded credit system, tax reforms, a rigorous campaign against corruption, waste, and inefficiency are all necessary. A program for the utilization of manpower also is necessary to help solve the problem of unemployment and underdevelopment.

Fishing waters adjacent to Korea are reportedly among the best in the world. A path for migratory fish is provided by the Straits of Japan, and the shallow waters of the Yellow Sea are excellent for net fishing. Fisheries rank second to agriculture in supplying food for the population and fish provide a substantial proportion of the animal protein in the Korean diet. In the past, fish and seaweeds, including laver, have been a fairly important source of foreign exchange. Furthermore, the industry has been the principal means of livelihood for a sizable segment of the population. In pre–World War II years Korea ranked sixth among the principal fishing nations of the world, and produced substantial quantities of fish for export. Some reductions have occurred in the catch in recent years partly because the fishing fleet has been confined to inshore areas owing to the shortage of seaworthy boats. War damage to fishing facilities has been estimated at $6.7 million. A measure to rehabilitate and expand Korea's fishing industry provided vessels, equipment, and supplies to the fishing industry.

Sizable deficits have occurred in South Korea's balance of trade for several years as a result of the domestic shortage of natural resources and increasing economic and other requirements. The United States, Japan, and Hong Kong are South Korea's leading suppliers as well as its principal customers. These three countries were the recipients of practically all of South Korea's exports, and provided the greater proportion of its imports, the United States supplying about one-third of Korea's imports by value, including aid goods.

No investments of foreign private capital in South Korea in the past decade have been reported. Local private investment was made chiefly with funds borrowed from the Reconstruction Bank and the commercial banks. Such loans more than doubled in 1955, with manufacturing accounting for a substantial portion of the total. Yet very little has been accomplished regarding the encouragement of direct private capital investment in industry out of profits and savings, and the attraction of foreign private capital. Among the factors that tend to discourage United States private capital investment are the political uncertainties and the uncertainties stemming from the absence of a Korean foreign investment law and a treaty of friendship, commerce, and navigation with the United States. Economic and financial factors discouraging foreign investment include the limited local market for many commodities owing to the low per capita income, limited natural resources, and inflationary forces.

In support of the reconstruction effort, there must be a heavy emphasis on the more practical and technical brands of knowledge. The bulk of Western technical aid should be delivered in Korea. A much-needed area for improvement is that of administration and management. In the case of study abroad, efforts should be made to curb the traditional anti-Japanese prejudice. Because of cheaper transportation costs to, and living costs in, Japan, plus the slighter language barrier, study there can be made available to many more Korean students than could be sent to America or Europe.

Foreign aid remains essential for the Korean economy because it renders possible a continued economic growth and at the same time helps maintain an adequate standard of living. A large proportion of foreign aid is still contributed in the form of consumer goods. This makes possible the diversion of domestic resources from consumption to investment. Without underestimating its importance, however, it should be noted that foreign aid is a temporary expedient. Its effective use depends in a large measure on internal economic stability, on the determined efforts of the Korean people, and on the channeling into productive investment of the largest possible proportion of domestic resources. No effort must be spared to push Korean economic development at an accelerated pace. Americans found that technical knowledge and assistance can serve a major purpose when shared with their Korean counterparts. Other foreign countries can also render aid. Korea has barely begun to explore the possibilities of support from other nations, such as Japan and West Germany.

Whatever its resources, a nation needs to administer them effectively if it is going to realize its full economic potential. Its predominant values, its politics, and its producing, marketing, and governing organizations all must be conducive to development—or at least cannot be positively obstructionist. In these respects, the current Korean picture is not reassuring. The present institutional pattern is a curious amalgam of the very old and indigenous, particularly in the family-dominated rural communities; an overlay of Japanese organizational forms is found in the larger industrial and financial enterprises, government ministries, the police, and the rest of the bureaucratic hierarchy; a further overlay of American political forms stems from the United States interwar occupation, a United States-modeled military, and expediencies born of crisis. In many ways, so far as its modern sovereign government is concerned, the South Korean nation has had to run before it could learn to crawl. Social and value patterns were dislocated by the war, and the weakening of the family as the basic social unit was greatly accelerated. The spell of the new nationalism was intensified. Contact with American GIs and with a new phalanx of Western civilians vastly speeded up the "Westernization" of material wants, extending this phenomenon even into the countryside, far beyond the sophisticated fringes of the population, until the Sears, Roebuck catalogue became, almost literally, the most popular book in South Korea. And wartime inflation reduced the economy's production and marketing system to a crazy quilt of distortions, patchwork controls, and special arrangements. As a result, current

South Korean institutions seem to reveal only disarray and inefficiency. Despite its reforms, the government is arbitrary, and power, to an exceptional degree, is concentrated in the hands of General Park. Minute decisions and lowly appointments require his approval. Most of the ministerial and subministerial officers of the government, and many of the army's generals, are personal creatures of the chairman, with little or no independent political stature. Although there is some criticism of the present regime, Park's patriarchal appeal is greater, and his junta discipline more effective, in the politically more subservient rural areas, where there is no coherent or cohesive opposition. No one but the government really has a workable program. And all available instruments, including the army, the national police, a censored and subservient press, and students, veterans, and other groups are used to perpetuate the situation.[5]

While affording some localized and temporary relief from inflation, barter contrivances have compounded the inflexibilities and dislocations in the economy. By narrowing the scope of the free market, they have accentuated the intensity of inflationary pressures on the goods and services that remain in it. Worst of all, like other wartime expediencies, they have routed more and more of the earning and trading in the economy into undercover channels, out of sight or reach of the taxgatherer. Such is the present institutional panorama. Its implications for the indigenous Korean side of the rehabilitation endeavor are too plain to require extended comment at this point. The situation gravely compromises the South Korean Military government's ability to support further economic expansion with anti-inflationary policies. It clutters up enterprise with a snarled web of controls, distorts incentives, and mocks efforts to plan a closely calculated use of resources. However generously endowed it may be, no South Korean rehabilitation effort can succeed without extensive internal reform and moral stamina.

The inaction of South Korea's government has already caused an economic setback and a rise in commodity prices, and has thus brought more suffering to the already hard-pressed people. The tide of events has been running out, and time has not been our friend. Things will get worse before they get better, and South Korea should prepare itself now for the worst.

The Korean people, and particularly the youth, cannot avoid

some responsibility in the national reconstruction. They too must show a dynamism, capacity, and devotion for reform. The idea that vocational work or labor is degrading must be eliminated. The will to work is as important as the right to work. Korea cannot be built by scholars and government officials alone, any more than it can be protected by military men alone. The modernization of Korea will also require dynamic engineers, business administrators, technicians, and skilled workers. If the tasks and missions are to be accomplished successfully, they will require hard work, even sacrifice. But sacrifice can only be honestly demanded if it is practiced by those who preach it. Sacrifice in South Korea must begin at the top, practiced by government officials and business leaders. A new moral stamina is needed, a new sense of obligation to one's people—not just to one's self and family. And those who fail to meet the standards of this new stamina should be exposed promptly.

Before the ROK Army coup, black-market activities, beggary, or theft were the only expedients for some. Homeless, unemployed refugees, without money and removed from their friends, have created a specially heavy problem. Bribery has proved as expeditious in some instances under later government as it was necessary under the Japanese, Rhee, and Chang rules. Terrorism has seemed to some the only available substitute for the lawful self-determination that, as a people, they have been denied. Consumer goods have all but disappeared from the markets; factories have fallen into disrepair; food production has been inadequate; housing and clothing have been far below minimum needs; and inflation has mounted to dangerous levels. Accompanying the political and economic disruption has been an inevitable weakening of the moral climate. A people without direction of their own affairs, and without a chance to feed and clothe their families by honest endeavor, has become understandably tolerant of questionable means.

Such problems as these are dangerous infections which the new Korean government will have to deal. It is readily apparent that the long-delayed independence of Korea is arriving at last, but under circumstances of stress. The opportunity exists for the creation of a healthful and vigorous state, but the handicaps are severe and the external pressures will be strong. Both the people and their leaders

are faced by a challenge that many more experienced nations might
be unable to meet.

How to organize the energies of the people and resources of the
country to meet the challenge of independence is the first problem to
be solved. The Russians have introduced one method with the
Communist regime they have established in North Korea. The Americans have suggested another with their program of teaching the ways
of Western democracy. In both zones there has been a tendency to
accept the methods and ideologies of the occupation armies, with
the significant reservation that as soon as the local populations are
free to do so they mean to solve their own problems in their own way.

The Korean political pattern is not that of the old monarchy, for
that is completely gone; it is not the Japanese governmental system,
for that was bitterly hated, and almost no Koreans had a large enough
part in it to be able to continue it. Nor is the Korean way allied either
to Communism or to the present Western-style democracy. The
Korean political traditions are almost as remote from present American
political organization on the one hand as they are from Karl Marx
on the other. Sheer totalitarian power has been able to impose one
alien pattern in the North, and real democracy tries to take root in
the South. But the masses of the people were affected very little by
either in their ways of living and thinking before the Military
Revolution. Very little has changed in contemporary Korea since a
young, fiery, American-educated Korean, Tachi Ho Yun, expressed
in his unpublished diary the following bitter and candid observations
on his times of the end of the nineteenth century:

> Rotten, rotten, all of rulers are rotten. The people are in so miserable
> a condition of poverty and of slavery that they are willing to serve any
> master, be he Russian or Japanese or Hottentot, who would give them
> security of life and property. Poor King! He is surrounded by hundreds
> of people who are hurrying him and his country to ruin. Yet what can
> be done with a gentleman for whom experience has no lessons; patriotism,
> no meaning; and honesty, no attraction? Everybody in the Palace crowd
> seems to feel that this is his last chance (amen!) for devilment. From the
> Minister of Household down, all the hangers-on reflect on their dirty faces
> the greed, treachery and meanness with which their hearts are possessed.
> Only one thing hopeful in this hopeless country is the growing activity of
> young men as shown in societies and in schemes for newspapers.

The only hope for Korean reformation is another cleaning out like that of 1894, manning the government with the youths now in Japan. Every old official in the government is either a fool or a rascal or both. Korea is the land where children have no toys; women, no flowers; men, no independence. Long centuries of dependence on China has made Koreans think and feel that Korea can never be anything but a dependency on some great power. A Korean takes to national vassalage as naturally as a duck takes to water. As I have no influence in the government no influence worshipers come to see me. But lots of poor relatives come and ask for some money. A young man named Hong shows a deal of attention to me, calling me his elder brother on the ground that he is related to me through my great-grandmother from whom [he] is removed only some 20 degrees.

The Queen had a house bought in Shanghai prepared as a place of refuge. Could anything more unkingly or unqueenly be imagined! Instead of trying to establish their throne in the love of their people they spend ill-gotten riches in preparing refuges in which they hope to find safety from dangers all of their own making. What a pity that so clever a woman as the Queen should have been so blinded by selfishness! The most deep-seated and at the same time the most widespread evil in Korea is lying. The King may issue the most solemn edicts in favor of good government, etc. Not a fool in Korea would believe a word of it. I would not risk five cents on the promises of one or all of the ten Ministers of State. A thorough cleaning out of the whole misgovernment by putting into power honest men of real stamp will save this country for that day. Korea would go better if everybody worked more and talked less—politics. The people are now squeezed by governors, magistrates, royal inspectors, departmental inspectors, police and soldiers. The stories of wrongs which we can't but hear every day make us shudder.[6]

The law governing the National Movement for Reconstruction in South Korea stipulates in Article 2 that "the people's movement for national reconstruction under this law means a pan-national movement designed to let the entire people of this country cultivate a new morale, adhere to a new life system, and cement the concept of anti-Communism in line with following principles: (1) any pro-Communist and neutralistic thought will be denounced; (2) austerity will be encouraged; (3) the spirit of diligence will be inspired; (4) the aspiration for production and construction will be promoted; (5) the national morality will be enhanced; (6) the physical standard of the people will be improved." The National Movement for Reconstruction is a pan-national drive designed to help the Korean people qualify themselves as citizens of a democratic nation in the shortest possible span of time.

Today security and social justice are the first priorities for the Korean people, and one of the problems is going to be that of striking a compromise between justice and freedom. There has to be a compromise between these two desiderata, because each is inimical to the other, yet mankind cannot live without enjoying a balance of both. The continuing emergency in South Korea is a challenge to the effciency of a democractically administered society as contrasted with the regimented society of North Korea. South Koreans must retain internal liberty while developing the order and unified endeavor necessary to outstrip material success achieved wherever totalitarianism has sacrificed freedom for strength. The Student Revolution of April, 1961, and the ROK Army coup of May, 1961 gave important impetus to the New Korea, but the difficult task of national reconstruction remains. In order to strengthen South Korea, her people must combine efficiency with morality. What tomorrow may bring for a permanent solution of the Korean problem lies within the will of the Korean people themselves.

UNIFICATION[7]

Korea remains divided. The United Nations has kept a commission in Korea working toward unification of the country, but it has made little headway owing to the difficulties of direct agreement with the Soviet Union. Korea will remain under occupation for an indefinite period unless a radical change takes place in the policies of Washington or Moscow. Divided Korea remains a symbol of a divided world.

The armistice signed on July 27, 1953, included the provision that each side would cease bringing in military personnel except for replacement and rotation and that there would be no reinforcement of military equipment, such as weapons and enlarged or new airfields, on either side of the demarcation line. But the North Korean and Chinese Communists engaged in a steady build-up of additional weapons, light and heavy, and greatly expanded their military establishments and airfields in North Korea, thereby violating the terms of the armistice. On the other hand, the United Nations Command scrupulously honored the armistice terms by keeping its personnel well within the prescribed limits and by reporting to the commission all replacements of men and equipment. In order to restore their relative balance of military strength that the armistice was intended to preserve, however, the United Nations command modernized its forces in South Korea in 1957.

On the Communist side, the Chinese Red "volunteers" are supposed to have been withdrawn completely. But they are understood to have introduced artillery of "atomic capability." The United Nations has brought in rockets, guided missiles, and atomic cannon to maintain the balance of power. Both sides have imported weapons of mass destruction in violation of the armistice, and most of the more than three hundred meetings of the joint armistice commission and its secretariat have been devoted to an exchange of charges and counter-charges over violation of the terms of the armistice agreement.

The internal struggle between North and South Korea originated in the great powers' interest in strategic Korea. Soviet advocacy of Korean independence from Japan influenced Communism in Korea after the Bolshevik Revolution. The Soviet Union gave organizational and financial assistance to leftist Korean nationalists living in Asiatic Russia and Korea, and many Communist leaders in North Korea were Russian-oriented Koreans educated in the Soviet Union. Industrial North Korea's economy has been stimulated by Soviet aid and trade, and Korean Communists inclining toward Peiping rather than Moscow have been purged. The present Communist ruler in North Korea is typical of the close relationship between the Soviets and the Korean leftists.

Russia made a separate treaty with Korea immediately after Korea was opened to the Western world in 1882 by the United States, and Russian influence in Korea was not displaced until 1905, when Imperial Japan took control of Korea following the Russo-Japanese War. Troops of the Soviet Union entered Korea as far as the 38th parallel as soon as the Japanese surrendered in 1945, and set up the Communist system in North Korea. Owing to United States determination to fight against the North Korean invasion in 1950, South Korea was not influenced by the Soviet system.

At the time of the South Korean Military Revolution in May,

1961, the North Korean Communist Government was caught off guard by the sudden power change in South Korea. They at first applauded, believing that the military revolution was a national uprising against America, but finally adopted the line that General Park Chung Hee is an American puppet. Soviet Russia countered with a new ten-year mutual defense pact with Communist North Korea, and shortly afterward Red China followed suit. In the South, after establishing an anti-Communist government, the ROK Army controlled Communist subversion and neutralistic movements, arresting two thousand persons charged with activities ranging from spying to fellow traveling. Internal strife among Koreans for unity between North Korea and South Korea has never ended.

The time has come for Koreans to settle their national problem. They must now try to iron out the difficulties confronting them. There is no third party strong enough to break the deadlock. The South Korean Government should take the initiative and invite the northern leaders to sit down with them to thrash out their differences. That would be an act of patriotism, and not one of opportunism or weakness. If they cannot accomplish their objective at the first meeting, they should meet a hundred and one times, or until a solution is reached under the spirit of compromise. No stone should be left unturned to defend the Korean people from self-destruction.[8]

When the United Nations turned to the task of setting up the machinery for restoration of peace in a unified Korea, it adopted an important resolution recommending that: (*a*) all sections and representative bodies of the population of Korea, South and North, be invited to cooperate with the organs of the United Nations in the restoration of peace, in the holding of elections, and in the establishment of a unified Government; (*b*) all appropriate steps be taken to ensure conditions of stability throughout Korea; (*c*) all constituent acts be taken, including the holding of elections, under the auspices of the United Nations, for the establishment of a unified, independent, and democratic government in the sovereign State of Korea; (*d*) United Nations forces be withdrawn from Korea except as necessary for achieving the objectives specified in subparagraphs (*b*) and (*c*) above; (*e*) all necessary measures be taken to accomplish the economic rehabilitation of Korea.

A major preoccupation of the Rhee government was a vendetta

against all advocates of peaceful unification of North and South Korea. But peaceful unification is a concept that the United Nations, the United States, and most other countries have consistently backed as the only alternative to enforced unification—which the Communists tried unsuccessfully in 1950 and which was outlawed by the United Nations. When North Korea, too, claimed to back this concept, Rhee's government considered the idea subversive. Former Premier Chang also proved unable to satisfy the South Koreans' longing for unification, although he was an advocate of peaceful unification.

The United Nations has called annually for elections under its own supervision in both North and South Korea. Today, however, the government in South Korea is no more freely elected than that of the North. Democracy has disappeared from the Korean Peninsula, at least for the present. In contrast to former President Rhee, however, the new Military Government accepts elections supervised by the UN throughout all Korea, not just in the North to fill parliamentary seats reserved for it. The Assembly has voted in committee to admit North Korean representatives to debate if their regime unequivocally accept the authority of the United Nations.

The United Nations

The fundamental objective of the United Nations in Korea is to establish a unified, independent, and democratic government for the whole peninsula. The division in 1945 at the 38th parallel was unacceptable to all parties concerned except as a temporary measure. The Korean conflict was begun by the North Korean attack on June 25, 1950. With the armed intervention of the People's Republic of China, the fundamental objectives of General Assembly resolution 376 (V) could not be achieved. The armistice that brought the conflict to a halt on July 27, 1953, was not a peace settlement; it was only an armed truce pending a true peace.

The United Nations Commission on Korea has set forth its basic difficulties and reviewed its efforts to attain some kind of settlement. The report deals with the establishment and organization of the commission and its terms of reference, its main activities, the political, economic, and social factors affecting unification and independence in Korea. The commission's summary and conclusions are as follows:

The embittered propaganda and hostile activities which now mark the relations between the two parts of Korea render the prospect of unification more and more remote. As long as the opposition of the Soviet Union to the efforts of the United Nations Commission to achieve the objectives of the General Assembly resolution continues, neither a relaxation of hostile propaganda nor any other measure can facilitate to a substantial degree the achievement of unification.

The world-wide differences between the United States and Soviet Union continues to be one of the basic factors underlying the present difficulties. Without a new effort by those powers to reach agreement on the question of Korea, no substantial progress toward the achievement of unification on the basis of the principles approved by the General Assembly can be made. From its very inception, the Republic of Korea has been confronted with many difficulties. It faced insurgent uprisings from within and was menaced by continuous clashes on the 38th parallel. While making due allowance for these factors, the Commission believes that a broadening of the Government's political base would allow it to meet these difficulties more successfully and so enable it to play a more effective part in achieving unification. The present Commission, like its predecessor, must place on record an acknowledgment that the situation in Korea is now no better than it was at the beginning, and that it has not been able to facilitate the achievement of the objectives set by the General Assembly.

From all appearances the Great Powers did not actually intend to solve the long-drawn-out problem in the United Nations General Assembly's debate on the Korean question, but simply to fight another round in the cold war—despite the disapproval of independent Asian and African nations. The outcome was a victory for no one but an exhibition of moral immaturity by those who consider themselves the elite of the world community. Children may argue harmlessly over marbles, but those who are vested with atomic power quarrel over human destiny at the risk of destroying all that is good. Hundreds of thousands of high-sounding words have been spoken on Korea's behalf in international forums, yet her people have not been given an opportunity to shape their own future. Thus Korea's misery and tragedy go on. The powerless little nation can do nothing but await the verdict of the United Nations General Assembly.

The United Nations is pledged to Korea's reunification, but it has not been possible to carry out the course of action. Korea is still divided. The case of Korea is still on the agenda not merely of the

United Nations but of the whole world. The United Nations cannot be insensible to the fact that the United Nations pledges have not yet been redeemed. The United Nations accepted a stalemate, but have not yet made a free, just and lasting peace.

The Korean question turned up again at the 15th session of the United Nations General Assembly which ended in December, 1960. The United Nations had been duty-bound to talk or at least show some concern about this unwelcome subject ever since 1947. As usual, each side involved in the Korean morass claimed it was right and the other wrong. They debated the question with chips on their shoulders or axes to grind, with no apparent intention of settling it. Except for the uncommitted nations of Asia and Africa and a few others, they discussed Korea along the old pattern of their political and economic alignments. Both sides simply followed their leaders in voting on the same perfunctory resolution of bygone years. Many were doubtless aware that such repetition would not solve the problem but they were afraid to deviate from the beaten path or initiate new ideas lest they be considered pro-Communist or un-Communist. They accomplished nothing after fighting another round of cold war over Korea, notwithstanding the "spirit of Camp David." They cannot help the Korean people unite the country or absolve their own responsibility until they rid themselves of bigotry, prejudice, and self-interest.

The Korean question remained unsettled after the fifteenth session of the United Nations General Assembly. Not even the customary multination resolution was passed, although a thirteen-power one was introduced which—as usual—reaffirmed past resolutions and the United Nations desire for peaceful reunification, called on the Communists to accept the Geneva principles of 1954, asked that the United Nations Commission for the Unification and Rehabilitation of Korea continue its work, and requested the Secretary-General to place the Korean question on the agenda of the next Assembly session. On the matter of whether Korea—or Koreans—should be invited to participate without a vote, however, the Korean question did receive different treatment.

On the question of future election for uniting Korea, the Soviet proposed for the establishment of a provisional assembly, based on "equalization of representation" between North and South Korea. But the West felt that such an arrangement would weigh heavily in favor of Communist domination of such artificial legislative creations. For North Korea has a population that is less than one-third of that in the South. Yet, according to Soviet proposals, these provisional assemblies would decide the conditions under which elections should be held, and they would prescribe the qualifications of electors. Western governments, on the other hand, have insisted that a prerequisite to the unification of both countries should be free elections, supervised by appropriate authorities, which would ensure the freedom of voters from force, pressure, or intimidation, and would safeguard the secret ballot and the accuracy of the results.

Professor Robert A. Scalapino, author of the Korea Section of the Conlon Report (United States Senate publication), stated:

> Speaking frankly, the unification of Korea appears to be a dim prospect at present. For more than a decade, two separate regimes have existed, each with its own bueraucracy, army, and political system. As is well known, moreover, these two *de facto* states have very unequal populations—nine million in the North versus twenty-two million in the South. Consequently, the Communists are unwilling to accept any democratic one-man and one-vote approach to the unification issue. They demand Federation in Korea as in Germany. This is wholly unfair and cannot be accepted.[9]

As the Senate publication graphically shows, the chances of Korean reunification in the near future are extremely remote despite the desires of the Korean people. There is no feasible method at present whereby Korea can be reunited, and two *de facto* Korean governments will likely continue for the foreseeable future. The Korean question will never be solved until that victimized nation is reunited. If the United States' preoccupation with South Korea is not accompanied by equal emphasis on the need for national unity, Asians may feel it sanctions the continued division of that helpless country.

Uncommitted Asian nations, with over a quarter of the world's population, refuse to recognize either Korean regime because they oppose division of innocent countries by stronger powers and want no part in hardening the division. Moreover, Americans should know that many economic experts believe South Korea alone can never attain economic viability because of its scanty natural resources coupled with its dense population. No regime in South Korea could last even a year without American backing. Can the United States guarantee the support of 22 million people indefinitely? It is also wishful thinking to believe everything will turn out all right just as long as the annual dole of several hundred million dollars is maintained and the Military Government stays anti-Communist. The American people must dismiss this hallucination. No nation prospers on charity or is contented with begging. South Korea is far from rehabilitated. About two and a half million people are unemployed and one million units of housing are urgently required. Inflation continues to spiral. Unless South Korea attains economic self-sufficiency—no one knows how—there is a danger of being conquered not militarily but economically by the North, with its richer industrial resources. People on both sides of the 38th parallel watch to see which side lives better.

American policy should not be based on temporary expediency. Winning of the East politically and psychologically demands that the problem of Korean unification be attacked with every facet of ingenuity. For the United States to continue its policy of silence while the Communist bloc—however insincerely—urges negotiations on unification, not only meets with Asian disapproval but also hands the initiative to the Communists. The homogeneous Korean people will not wait indefinitely for reunification. They will seize the first opportunity to free themselves from the unnatural situation imposed upon them. If the disillusioned people are reunited under nondemocratic influences, American policy, regardless of its good intentions, will be defeated before the watchful eyes of all Asia. A diligent search for every avenue toward unification will best serve the interests of the United States. This is a hard nut to crack, but Americans are noted for their imagination and initiative. No proposal guarantees success but surely it is better to keep on talking than not to. Perhaps statesmen might consider the creation of a political commission, with membership from both sides and from several neutral nations, to negotiate Korean reunification.

The Land of the Morning Calm, owing to its strategic location in East Asia, is an explosive pawn in the "cold war" between East and West. For few nations in the twentieth century has the fact of geopolitical location had more serious consequences than for the Korean people. Left to themselves, free of interference from their more powerful neighbors, the Koreans might have achieved unity and independence, profiting by contacts with social and political institutions of democracy. The native intelligence of the Korean people, the historic traditions, their cultural unity, the physical compactness of the peninsula, and the economic interdependence of its parts all favored such a course of progress. Unfortunately, Korea's strategical position—its close proximity to Soviet Union, Red China, and Japan—has forestalled such a consequence. The shooting has long since stopped. The cold war goes on.

It is important to think of freedom not only in terms of the freedom of individuals but also in terms of national freedom. Korea is a peninsula of such strategic value that it has for many years been the subject of big-power politics. Russia, Japan, and China have successively sought to use Korea to serve their own policies of aggrandizement. For a long time the Koreans have not been the masters of their own destiny. That should be ended. Courageous application of Korean reunification will hasten the completion of the United Nations mission and the termination of foreign occupation. Independence and unity achieved by exercising the right of self-determination will command the confidence of the Korean people and the respect of the world.

The leading nations, instead of trying to implement the Armistice Agreement's cardinal provision calling for withdrawal of all foreign forces and peaceful settlement of the Korean question though negotiations, indulged in mutual condemnation of military violations. When political settlement is reached, military problems will naturally cease. It is an understatement to say that the great powers plainly told the world they are not interested in freedom and unification of Korea but are chiefly concerned with advantages in their power struggle.

The absurdity in handling the problem has disillusioned the Korean and other independent Asian nations and heightened the tension in that region. The debates have been unproductive because the problem has been considered according to the interest of the Eastern and Western power blocs instead of meeting Korean needs and desires. These blocs have spoken for themselves, not Korea. The problem is at dead center between the East and West. If past performances are repeated there will be no solution, but only a worsening of the situation.

In light of the changing political atmosphere of the world and the injection of new blood into the United Nations, it is hoped the General Assembly will deliberate the problem with fresh ideas and approaches. No practical purpose can be served by rehashing the sterile arguments of the past. While it is not possible at this time to present a blueprint for Korean settlement, it might be appropriate to point out some possibilities for consideration by the statesmen from the entire member states of the United Nations. It is now crystal clear that neither side can dictate its terms upon the other; any settlement will have to be negotiated. Korean national survival and the reduction of international tension call for a rational settlement. The trend in this awakening world is moving toward realism. Progressive nations will no longer stick by the "hear no evil, speak no evil, see no evil" philosophy.

The solution of the problem ultimately rests with the Korean people. It therefore would be wise on the part of the United Nations to encourage a rapprochement between the two halves of Korea. There must be some accommodation between them, if not good will. If the great powers sincerely desire to maintain peace and reduce armaments, which weigh heavily upon the backs of humble men, they should work toward reuniting the divided nations to create a proper climate for fostering of a lasting peace. A divided Korea is not an asset to the great powers; it is an albatross around their necks, and a menace to world peace.

No people are free if they depend on foreign support for their existence. A nation divided against itself will perish. It is time the leaders in the North and South seriously considered whether the fringe benefits they derive from remaining in the cold war are worth the undermining of Korea's foundation—or whether they should obey the dictates of patriotism and reconcile themselves to bringing about national harmony. There is no time to procrastinate, because time is running out. No party can stay in power indefinitely at the expense of the people who have suffered long enough. There is no human dignity for the millions who are subjected to hunger, misery, and regimentation. A rejuvenated Korea will not tolerate further abuses. The opportunistic merchandising of East or West is not only short-sighted; it can bring only more chaos and bloodshed.

Neither the North nor the South can prosper as a nation without the other. If either—with its borrowed power—tries to subdue the other, it will invite self-destruction. The old proverb reminds that "When the lip is destroyed the tooth is cold." National unity is an indispensable requirement for Korea's survival and a natural desire of its homogeneous people which no power can stop. No one man or one side, alone, can restore Korea's divided house. All such adventures by domestic or foreign architects during the last fifteen years have brought disaster and tragedy. If the ruling parties insist upon mortgaging Korea's future to save the pawnshops of the great powers, the people might have to resort to divorce. Korea belongs to the 30,000,-000 members of her family. It is their duty to work together in rejoining the divided nation. If they fail they will be doomed. This imperative question of national unity should be thoroughly discussed among Koreans of all walks of life throughout the country. It has been delayed too long. It cannot be considered lightly. It is a serious matter of the nation's future—a choice between freedom and ignominy.

Regardless of their protestations and alibis, the vested interests under the aegis of their guardian powers have made it quite clear that they will reject any move toward national unity until they are sure of remaining in the saddle. But what glory and position will be left on either side if the Korean nation disintegrates? When this happens all will be over for the Korean people. True patriotism demands that leaders of both halves of Korea work for the independence of the country before fighting about political systems. It would be honest for the present governments to tell the nation their concept of patriotism. No titles or privileges should be more dear to them than the fate of their nation.[10]

The Korean people have lived together for centuries as one nation. They are one entity, ethnically, culturally, and politically. The present division of Korea did not stem from any difference among Koreans. Korean reunification and its admission as a free, independent country in the United Nations family would benefit not only Koreans, but peoples everywhere. Korea would strengthen the hope of peace and security for the entire world, and would signal one of the greatest triumphs yet achieved for the ideals and principles of the United Nations. On the other hand, no permanent peace can be achieved in the Far East without the unification of Korea. The United Nations has assumed the primary responsibility for establishing Korea as a unified and independent nation.

Workable plans for a righteous and just solution to the Korean question through peaceful unification have already been laid down in General Assembly resolutions. The United Nations Temporary Commission on Korea, and the United Nations Commission for the Unification and Rehabilitation of Korea, were established specifically to observe elections that would unite all Korea. The Korean people call upon the United Nations, guardian of freedom, justice and peace in the world, to do all in its power to implement its objectives stated above, and secure a righteous solution of the Korean question.[11]

The Korean problem was not solved by the truce, but remains one of the crucial issues of the cold war—one that will require decisions in the future fully as momentous as those in the past. The United States has been reluctant to maintain close relations with Korea but has been forced into recurrent commitments because of the strategic importance of Korea for the defense of America's own security. Korea is a clear testing ground for the United States and the Soviet Union in the world-power struggle between our antagonistic ways of life.

The Korean people are caught in the middle of a vast network of global conflicts. It is a test of the ability of the industrialized Western nations to deal effectively with the emergent nationalism, economic ambitions, and cultural stamina of Asia. It is a test of the ability of the United Nations to develop a world order based upon law. For more than a decade the Korean question has remained unsettled, to the great cost of the people of Korea and of the entire free world. During all this time the United Nations has insisted again and again that it is doing everything in its power to seek a "peaceful" solution. A smoldering fire should not be left unattended. It is time for action that lies wholly within the realm of peaceful decision by the United Nations.

Korea cannot be unified until there is reconcilation and agreement between the two antagonistic regimes under the harmonizing influence and advisement of the great powers and the United Nations. Every effort must be continued to bring a peaceful end of this tragic division in accordance with the principles set forth in United Nations resolutions, envisaging the achievement, by peaceful means, of a unified, independent, and democratic Korea under a representative form of government and full restoration of peace and security in the area.

One and a half million men are now poised behind the former Korean battlefront, the so-called cease-fire line at the 38th parallel. Some 50,000 American soldiers still are stationed in South Korea. Both South and North Korea will continue to remain impoverished by the necessity of maintaining large armed forces even though the great powers bear most of the cost. As mentioned above, Korea's resources are so divided that neither the industrial North nor agricultural South can become self-sufficient alone. It is impossible to resolve the question of United Nations membership for the Republic of Korea because of a Communist state sponsored by the Soviet Union in northern Korea.

Korea has figured in debates of every session of the United Nations General Assembly since 1948. While cliché and invective were abundant on all sides, a few independent voices were heard whose words—though not acted upon—may not have been totally lost. Unfortunately, not a single action brought Korea a step closer to the unification it needs so desperately. Korean political resolutions adopted by every session of the United Nations General Assembly did no more than reaffirm the existence of the problem of Korea. The great powers—neither prepared nor willing to effect the unification of this war-torn nation—once again failed the Korean people and aggravated international tension by leaving this festering sore unchecked.

The Korean political conference held at Geneva in 1954 also failed to achieve reunification. However, it was realized that the problem of a united Korea could not be resolved at one sitting or in a few weeks. The final settlement can be achieved only through long and unimpassioned negotiations under the guidance of forward-looking and practical statesmanship.

Voting in the United Nations reveals that the major Asian powers disapprove of the continuing East-West cold war over the Land of the Morning Calm. No nation, regardless of its power, can have a sound policy toward Asia without respect for Asian desires and rights in the solution of their problems. Inasmuch as the Korean question is of common concern to all Asia, Asian powers should be included in the deliberations, as well as the nations that participated at Geneva.

The good officers of these additional Asian powers might break the prolonged deadlock.

The West will captivate the minds of the Asian peoples if it boldly explores every avenue toward the liberation of a unified Korea. Simultaneously, the United Nations should vigorously press Soviet Russia and Red China for a peaceful unification of Korea. With the Soviet leaders busily representing themselves as messengers of peace, now is the time for the free world to launch a peaceful counter-offensive. It would be difficult to ignore such a move.

The reunification of Korea is the irresistible desire of every Korean, regardless of religion or politics. Every way must be attempted that might lead to this paramount goal on which Korea's future depends. Once again patriotic Koreans, in both North and South, as well as leaders of other nations involved, should carefully reconsider means of resolving this problem. Despite frequent utterances about reunification, many responsible leaders and spokesmen of vested interests on both sides of the 38th parallel do not seem to be working seriously toward this objective. The mutual distrust and enmity between the parties in power must be reconciled—regardless of political ideologies—if Korea is to survive as a nation.

The United Nations must share responsibility for the reunification of Korea, with the following principles as a guide:

1. A Korean settlement must be founded upon freedom and justice. Every nation has the right to determine its own way of life, its own political, economic, and social system, and to provide for its security with due regard to the legitimate interests of other nations. Justice requires that the Korean people be allowed to reestablish their national unity on the basis of this fundamental right.

2. The reunification of Korea is also a joint responsibility of the two great powers who in 1945 assumed supreme authority in Korea; it also requires the active cooperation of the Korean people in both South and North Korea as a whole, under conditions ensuring the free expression of their will. The unnatural division of Korea is a continuing source of international tension. So long as Korea remains divided, there can be no assurance of stability in Asia. The reunification of Korea in freedom is not only an elementary requirement of justice for the Korean people; it is also the only sound basis of a lasting settlement in Asia.

3. Only a freely elected all-Korean government can undertake on behalf of a reunified Korea obligations that will inspire confidence on the part of other countries and will be considered just and binding in the future by the people of Korea themselves. Such a government can only be established through free elections throughout Korea for an all-Korean National Assembly.

4. There should be no discrimination against a reunified Korea. Its freedom and security should not be prejudiced by an imposed status of demilitarization. Its government should be free to determine its foreign policy and to decide on its international association. It should not be deprived of the right recognized in the Charter of the United Nations for all nations to participate in collective measure of self-defense.

It is incomprehensible that America should lose interest in Korea's unification. The United States cannot continue indefinitely to underwrite South Korea politically and economically at the cost of billions of dollars, just as Russia cannot do so for North Korea. No nation can become free and independent on foreign aid. No matter how much material help may be poured into Korea, her people will be restless until their nation is unified and independent. If unification is not forthcoming peacefully through international efforts, it is quite certain they will take matters in their own hands at the first opportunity, regardless of consequences. No wise statesman waits for a crisis. The peaceful reintegration of Korea is an important key to peace in Asia. Deeply involved in the Far East, the United States cannot afford to overlook the importance of this problem or fail to seek a just solution. The longer the delay, the harder will be the untangling. The great good will America can garner in Korea and in all Asia will eclipse anything dollars can buy if its efforts succeed in reunifying that divided little country. All Asia is watching Korea's fate.

What will be called for is a practical United Nations politico-military resolution of the three most serious problems involving Korea: protection and assistance to an integrated North and South; judicious selection of responsible and reliable North Korean elements to cooperate with South Korean leaders in a unified Korea; and the maintenance of a protective interest in the Hermit Kingdom to ensure peaceful and democratic reconstruction. That the tasks ahead will meet with political and military resistance cannot be denied. The United Nations has demonstrated its willingness and determination to repel aggression in East Asia, but harder tasks lie ahead, for complacency and irresolution can set the East Asian clock back again.

There is no nation of Asia with which the United States has had as much heartening experience at making common cause as America has had with Korea. New Korea remains a growing symbol of progress, justice, and freedom, but this objective will be attainable only if the United States continues to make substantial commitments and consistent efforts for reunification.

When the United Nations shall exercise the principles laid down in its Charter, faith that "justice will prevail" permits the hope that the Land of the Morning Calm is not doomed to permanent division. A New Korea means a unified, independent, and democratic Korea.

Appendix I

A KOREAN CHRONOLOGY[1]

2333 B.C.–1122 B.C. Legendary dynasty of Tangun, a semi-deistic figure who, according to Korean mythology, founded the Korean nation by uniting the various primitive tribes into a single kingdom.

1122 B.C.–57 B.C. Period of Kija: introduction of Chinese culture.

57 B.C.–A.D. 668. Period of the Three Kingdoms: Silla, Koguryo, and Paikje. In A.D. 285 Paikje sent scholars, artisans, and craftsmen to introduce Korean culture into Japan. In 372 Buddhism entered Korea from China.

668–918. Korea united under Silla dynasty, with capital at Kyungju: notable for sculpture, architecture, and development of *hwarang:* a detailed code of chivalry.

918–1392. Koryo dynasty, with capital at Kaesong: period of Buddhist dominance; noted for production of celadon, classic ceramic ware of the Orient. In 1231 Genghis Khan invaded Korea, sweeping down as far as Kaesong. In 1234 metal movable type was invented.

1392–1910. Period of the Yi dynasty, with the capital at Seoul. During the reign of King Yi Sei-jong, a bronze rainfall gauge was invented in 1442—two hundred years before its invention in 1639 by Castelli of Italy; in 1446 King Sei-jong inaugurated *Hangul,* a phonetic alphabet of 26 letters. Colleges were established, literature and the arts flourished. Buddhism was minimized in favor of Taoism and Confucianism.

1592–1598. Korea defeated a Japanese invasion commanded by the warlord Hideyoshi. The invaders were defeated through the invention and use of the world's first ironclad war vessel, "the turtle-boat," by Admiral Sun-shin Yi. Exhausted by the war, Korea retreated into isolationism and became known as the "Hermit Kingdom."

1725–1800. Period of literary and artistic revival.

1882. Korea signed treaty of mutual friendship with the United States, thereby inaugurating trade and cultural relations with the West.

1895. Founding of "The Independence Club," by Philip Jaisohn, which sought to democratize and modernize the then decadent monarchy.

1905. Korea forced by Treaty of Portsmouth (ending the Russo-Japanese War) to accept the status of protectorate under Japan.

1910. Japan unilaterally proclaimed Korea a colony of Japan.

1919. On March 1 Korean patriots launched a "passive revolution," issued a Declaration of Independence, and established the Republic of Korea in exile, with headquarters in Shanghai; appealed to the Paris Peace Conference for recognition under the Wilsonian principle of "the right of self-determination of peoples."

1945. On August 15 Korea was liberated from Japan; the 38th parallel *de facto* division of Korea occurred; negotiations with Russia proved unfruitful.

1948. On May 10 elections in southern Korea were observed by the United Nations; a constitution was promulgated for all Korea, reserving 100 seats in the National Assembly to be filled by elections in northern Korea; on August 15 the Republic of Korea was formally proclaimed, with Dr. Syngman Rhee as President; on December 12 the General Assembly of the United Nations recognized this government as "the only legal government in Korea."

1950. On June 25 Communist troops launched a surprise attack across the 38th parallel; on the same date the UN Security Council called for withdrawal of North Korean forces to the 38th parallel; on July 5 the first American ground troops entered the conflict; on October 7 the General Assembly of the United Nations adopted a resolution calling for the expulsion of the invaders from the entire peninsula by force of arms, thus sending the U.N.-Korean armies onward into northern Korea; on October 20 Pyongyang, the north Korean capital, was captured; on November 26 the Red Chinese entered the conflict in great numbers, forcing the UN troops southward.

1951. On April 3, the UN troops pushed the Chinese Reds back across the 38th parallel; on July 10 negotiations for a truce began.

1953. On July 27 the Armistice Agreement was signed at Panmunjom; the Korean Government did not sign it but agreed to abide by the truce pending a promised political conference to unify Korea.

1954. At the Geneva Conference, April 26–June 15, the United Nations participants in the war and the Republic of Korea proposed the reunification of Korea based upon fair and free elections; the Communists refused.

1955. The UN Command noted that the arms-limitations provisions of the truce had been abrogated by Communist violations.

1956. Because of flagrant and continuous violation of the truce terms by the Communists, the UN Command suspended the provisions for Neutral Nations Supervisory Commission inspection teams in southern Korea.

1960. A student-led rebellion, protesting election frauds and corruption in government, led to the resignation of President Syngman Rhee and the establishment of a cabinet system of government. Posun Yun was elected as President and Dr. John M. Chang as Prime Minister.

1961. The ROK Army coup, headed by Major General Park Chung Hee, overthrew Chang's corrupt and inefficient government and set up the Military Revolutionary Government, announcing they would return to civilian democratic government in 1963.

1962. The ROK Military Government banned all political activity by former members of three defunct major parties and 36 minor political groups for six years, including former members of the National Assembly and provincial assemblies, Cabinet ministers, ambassadors, ministers, heads of formerly Government-run banks and corporations, and businessmen convicted of illegally building fortunes under the Rhee and Chang Governments. President Yun resigned in protest against a junta law barring civilian politicians from office for six more years.

Appendix II

New Law Concerning Extraordinary Measures for National Reconstruction[2]

Promulgated by the Supreme Council of National Reconstruction, and signed by President Yun Posun on June 6th, the Law, often called the Basic Law, prevails over the ROK Constitution, which was first written in 1948 and amended in 1952 and 1960.

General Provisions

ARTICLE 1: Establishment of the Supreme Council for National Reconstruction

The Republic of Korea shall establish the Supreme Council for National Reconstruction by way of the extraordinary measures intended for the reconstruction of the Republic of Korea as a genuine democratic republic, in order to safeguard the Republic of Korea against Communist aggression and to overcome the national crisis resulting from corruptions, injustices, and poverty.

ARTICLE 2: Status of the Supreme Council for National Reconstruction

The Supreme Council for National Reconstruction shall retain its status as the supreme ruling organ of the Republic of Korea, pending the establishment of a government following the recomposition of the National Assembly by means of a general election to be held after the fulfillment of the tasks of the May 16 (1961) Military Revolution.

ARTICLE 3: Basic Rights of the Citizen

The basic rights of the citizen under the Constitutional provisions shall be guaranteed within a scope that does not conflict with the fulfillment of the tasks of the Revolution.

Composition of the Supreme Council for National Reconstruction

ARTICLE 4: Supreme Councilors

(1) The Supreme Council for National Reconstruction shall be composed of the Supreme Councilors as elected from among the officers in active duty of the National Armed forces who determinedly uphold the cause of the May 16 Military Revolution.

(2) The fixed number of the Supreme Councilors shall not be more than 32 nor less than 20.

(3) The Supreme Councilors shall be elected through the recommendation of not less than five Supreme Councilors by majority vote of the Supreme Councilors duly seated.

(4) The Supreme Councilors shall be precluded from additional official posts except as the Head of the Cabinet and of military posts; however, the Chairman of the Supreme Council for National Reconstruction shall be precluded from any other posts except that of Head of the Cabinet.

ARTICLE 5: Election of the Chairman and the Vice Chairman

The Supreme Council for National Reconstruction shall elect one Chairman and one Vice Chairman from among the Supreme Councilors by majority vote of the Supreme Councilors duly seated.

ARTICLE 6: Functions of the Chairman

(1) The Chairman of the Supreme Council for National Reconstruction shall maintain order in the Supreme Council for National Reconstruction, regulate its proceedings, supervise its business, and represent the Supreme Council for National Reconstruction.

(2) When the Chairman is unable to execute his office for any reason, the Vice Chairman shall act in his stead.

(3) When both the Chairman and the Vice Chairman are unable to execute their office for any reason, the Supreme Councilor of youngest age shall act in their stead.

ARTICLE 7: Voting

Except as specifically provided for in this Law concerning the Extraordinary Measures, the Constitution, or the Law of the Supreme Council for National Reconstruction, matters on agenda items shall be determined by the attendance of a majority of the Supreme Councilors duly seated and by majority vote of the Supreme Councilors in attendance.

ARTICLE 8: Standing Committee

(1) There shall be established the Standing Committee of the Supreme Council for National Reconstruction in order to handle the affairs delegated by the Supreme Council for National Reconstruction within a prescribed extent.

(2) Necessary matters relating to the Standing Committee as mentioned in the preceding paragraph shall be stipulated in the Law of the Supreme Council for National Reconstruction.

Authority of the Supreme Council for National Reconstruction

ARTICLE 9: Exercise of the Authority of the National Assembly

The authority of the National Assembly under Constitutional provisions shall be exercised by the Supreme Council for National Reconstruction.

ARTICLE 10: Decision on Budget Bill

The Budget Bill shall be determined by the attendance of not less than two-thirds of the Supreme Councilors duly seated and by the majority vote of the Supreme Councilors in attendance.

ARTICLE 11: Exercise of the Authority of the President by Proxy

When the President is in default or unable to execute his office for any reason, the exercise of his authority shall be deputized by the Chairman or Vice Chairman of the Supreme Council for National Reconstruction, or by the Head of the Cabinet in the order of priority.

ARTICLE 12: Competency of the Supreme Council in regard to the Executive Matters

The following shall require decision by the Supreme Council for National Reconstruction:

1. Proclamation and termination of Martial Law;

2. Appointment and release of the Chairman of the Joint Chiefs of Staff, the Chief of Staff of each armed Force and the Commandant of the Marine Corps, and other important military affairs;

3. Awarding of honors and granting of pardons, commutation, and restoration of civil rights;

4. Approval for the appointment of the Prosecutor General and the Chief Prosecutors, the Chairman of the Board of Audit, the Chairman of the Inspection Committee, the Presidents of National Universities, Ambassadors and Ministers to foreign countries, and other public officials designated by law, and managers of important state-operated enterprises.

ARTICLE 13: Control of the Cabinet

(1) The authority of the State Council, as provided for in Article 72 (1), (2), (12), of the Constitution and elsewhere therein shall be exercised by the Cabinet under the direction and control of the Supreme Council for National Reconstruction.

(2) The Cabinet shall assume collective responsibility to the Supreme Council for National Reconstruction.

ARTICLE 14: Composition of the Cabinet

(1) The Cabinet shall be composed of the Head of the Cabinet and other Cabinet Members.

(2) The Head of the Cabinet shall be appointed by the Supreme Council for National Reconstruction.

(3) The appointment mentioned in the preceding paragraph shall be conducted by majority vote of the Supreme Councilors duly seated.

(4) The Cabinet Members shall be appointed by the Head of the Cabinet through the approval of the Supreme Council for National Reconstruction.

(5) The numbers of the Cabinet Members shall not be more than 15 nor less than 10.

ARTICLE 15: General Resignation of the Cabinet and Release of Cabinet Members

(1) The Supreme Council for National Reconstruction may obtain resolution on a general resignation of the Cabinet by the concurrence of not less than two-thirds of the Supreme Councilors duly seated.

(2) The Supreme Council for National Reconstruction may obtain resolution on a release of Cabinet Members by majority vote of the Supreme Councilors duly seated.

ARTICLE 16: Voice of Cabinet Members

The Head of the Cabinet and other Cabinet Members shall be authorized to attend meetings of the Supreme Council for National Reconstruction and state their opinions.

ARTICLE 17: Control of the Executive Powers Pertaining to the Administration of Justice

The major program of Executive Powers pertaining to the Administration of Justice shall be directed and controlled by the Supreme Council for National Reconstruction.

ARTICLE 18: Composition of the Supreme Court and Appointment of the Chief Justice and the Associate Justices of the Supreme Court

(1) The Supreme Court shall be composed of the Chief Justice and the Associate Justices.

(2) The Chief Justice and the Associate Justices shall be appointed by the President through the recommendation of the Supreme Council for National Reconstruction.

(3) The recommendation as mentioned in the preceding paragraph shall be made by majority vote of the Supreme Councilors duly seated.

ARTICLE 19: Appointment of Other Judges

(1) Judges, other than those mentioned in the preceding article, and the Director of the Office of Court Administration shall be appointed by the Chief Justice through approval of the Supreme Council for National Reconstruction.

(2) The Judges above and including the Chief Judges of the District Courts shall be assigned by the Chief Justice through the approval of the Supreme Council for National Reconstruction.

ARTICLE 20: Appointments of Heads of Local Governments

(1) The Provincial Governors, the Mayor of Seoul Special City, and the mayor of a city with a population of not less than 150,000 inhabitants shall be appointed by the Cabinet through the approval of the Supreme Council for National Reconstruction.

(2) Heads of the local governments, other than those mentioned in the preceding paragraph, shall be appointed by Provincial Governors.

Miscellaneous Provisions

ARTICLE 21: Amendments to Extraordinary Measures

Amendments to this Law concerning Extraordinary Measures shall be made through the recommendation of not less than 10 Supreme Councilors and by the concurrence of not less than two-thirds of the Supreme Councilors duly seated.

ARTICLE 22: Special Law, Revolutionary Court and Revolutionary Prosecuting Authority.

(1) The Supreme Council for National Reconstruction may enact special law in order to punish those persons who, prior to the May 16 Military Revolution or thereafter, take part in any antistate, antination, or counterrevolutionary activities.

(2) There may be established the Revolutionary Court and Revolutionary Prosecuting Authority, in order to conduct trials over the criminal cases prescribed in the preceding paragraph.

ARTICLE 23. Application *Mutatis Mutandis*

(1) Provisions on the National Assembly and those pertaining to the State Council in the Constitution shall apply *mutatis mutandis* to the Supreme Council for National Reconstruction and the Cabinet, respectively.

(2) The Ordinance of the State Council in the Constitution shall be issued as the Ordinance of the Cabinet.

ARTICLE 24: Relationship with the Constitution

The provisions in this Law concerning the Extraordinary Measures shall prevail over those Constitutional provisions which may conflict with them.

Supplementary Provisions

1. This Law concerning the Extraordinary Measures shall come into effect on and after the date of its promulgation.

2. The Supreme Council for National Reconstruction and the Cabinet in existence at the time of enforcement of this Law concerning Extraordinary Measures shall be regarded as having been constituted in accordance with this Law; and the Chairman and the Vice Chairman of the Supreme Council for National Reconstruction, and the public officials and the managers of the state-operated enterprises as appointed by the Supreme Council for National Reconstruction or the Cabinet, respectively, shall be regarded as having been elected or appointed in accordance with this Law; however, the concurrently assigned post in contravention of the provisions in the saving clause of Paragraph 4, Article 4, of this Law shall be released within five days from the date of promulgation of this Law concerning Extraordinary Measures.

3. The proclamations or decrees of the Military Revolutionary Committee or of the Supreme Council for National Reconstruction shall have the same effect as the provisions in this Law concerning the Extraordinary Measures or the laws pursuant thereto.

4. The Judges and the Director of the Office of Court Administration at the time of enforcement of this Law concerning Extraordinary Measures shall retain their office, pending appointment to be made in accordance with the provisions in Article 18 or Article 19 of this Law, respectively.

5. All pertinent provisions concerning the Constitution shall be suspended.

Treaty of Friendship, Commerce and Navigation Between the Republic of Korea and the United States of America[3]

The Republic of Korea, and the United States of America, desirous of strengthening the bonds of peace and friendship traditionally existing between them and of encouraging closer economic and cultural relations between their peoples, and being cognizant of the contributions which may be made toward these ends by arrangements encouraging mutually beneficial investments, promoting mutually advantageous commercial intercourse and otherwise establishing mutual rights and privileges, have resolved to conclude a Treaty of Friendship, Commerce and Navigation, based in general upon the principles of national and of most-favored-nation treatment unconditionally accorded, and for that purpose have appointed as their Plenipotentiaries.

The Republic of Korea:

    Cho Chung-Whan, Acting Minister of Foreign Affairs of the Republic of Korea,

and the United States of America:

    Walter Dowling, Ambassador Extraordinary and Plenipotentiary of the United States of America to the Republic of Korea.

Who, having communicated to each other their full powers found to be in due form, have agreed upon the following Articles:

ARTICLE I

Each Party shall at all times accord equitable treatment to the persons, property, enterprises and other interests of nationals and companies of the other Party.

ARTICLE II

1. Nationals of either Party shall be permitted to enter the territories of the other Party and to remain therein: (*a*) for the purpose of carrying on trade between the territories of the two Parties and engaging in related commercial activities; (*b*) for the purpose of developing and directing the operations of an enterprise in which they have invested, or in which they are actively in the process of investing, a substantial amount of capital; and (*c*) for other purposes subject to the laws relating to the entry and sojourn of aliens.

2. Nationals of either Party, within the territories of the other Party, shall be permitted: (*a*) to travel therein freely, and to reside at places of their choice; (*b*) to enjoy liberty of conscience; (*c*) to hold both private and public religious services; (*d*) to gather and to transmit material for dissemination to the public abroad; and (*e*) to communicate with other persons inside and outside such territories by mail, telegraph and other means open to general public use.

3. The provisions of the present Article shall be subject to the right of either Party to apply measures that are necessary to maintain public order and protect the public health, morals and safety.

ARTICLE III

1. Nationals of either Party within the territories of the other Party shall be free from molestations of every kind, and shall receive the most constant protection and security, in no case less than that required by international law.

2. If, within the territories of either Party, a national of the other Party is taken into custody, the nearest consular representative of his country shall on the demand of such national be immediately notified and shall have the right to visit and communicate with such national. Such national shall: (*a*) receive reasonable and humane treatment; (*b*) formally and immediately be informed of the accusations against him; (*c*) be brought to trial as promptly as is consistent with the proper preparation of his defense; and (*d*) enjoy all means reasonably necessary to his defense, including the services of competent counsel of his choice.

ARTICLE IV

1. Nationals of either Party shall be accorded national treatment in the application of laws and regulations within the territories of the other Party that establish a pecuniary compensation or other benefit or service,

on account of disease, injury or death arising out of and in the course of employment or due to the nature of employment.

2. In addition to the rights and privileges provided in paragraph 1 of the present Article, nationals of either Party within the territories of the other Party shall be accorded national treatment in the application of laws and regulations establishing compulsory systems of social security, under which benefits are paid without an individual test of financial need (*a*) against loss of wages or earnings due to old age, unemployment, sickness or disability, or (*b*) against loss of financial support due to the death of father, husband or other person on whom such support had depended.

ARTICLE V

1. Nationals and companies of either Party shall be accorded national treatment and most-favored-nation treatment with respect to access to the courts of justice and to administrative tribunals and agencies within the territories of the other Party, in all degrees of jurisdiction, both in pursuit and in defense of their rights. It is understood that companies of either Party not engaged in activities within the territories of the other Party shall enjoy such access therein without any requirement of registration or domestication.

Contracts entered into between nationals and companies of either Party and nationals and companies of the other Party, that provide for the settlement by arbitration of controversies, shall not be deemed unenforceable within the territories of such other Party merely on the grounds that the place designated for the arbitration proceedings is outside such territories or that the nationality of one or more of the arbitrators is not that of such other Party. No award duly rendered pursuant to any such contract, and final and enforceable under the laws of the place where rendered, shall be deemed invalid or denied effective means of enforcement within the territories of either Party merely on the grounds that the place where such award was rendered is outside such territories or that the nationality of one or more of the arbitrators is not that of such Party.

ARTICLE VI

1. Property of nationals and companies of either Party shall receive the most constant protection and security within the territories of the other Party.

2. The dwellings, offices, warehouses, factories and other premises of nationals and companies of either Party located within the territories of the other Party shall not be subject to molestation or to entry without just cause. Official searches and examinations of such premises and their

contents, when necessary, shall be made only according to law and with careful regard for the convenience of the occupants and the conduct of business.

3. Neither Party shall take unreasonable or discriminatory measures that would impair the legally acquired rights or interests within its territories of nationals and companies of the other Party in the enterprises which they have established, in their capital, or in the skills, arts or technology which they have supplied.

4. Property of nationals and companies of either Party shall not be taken within the territories of the other Party except for a public purpose, nor shall it be taken without the prompt payment of just compensation. Such compensation shall be in an effectively realizable form and shall represent the full equivalent of the property taken; and adequate provision shall have been made at or prior to the time of taking for the determination and payment thereof.

5. Nationals and companies of either Party shall in no case be accorded, within the territories of the other Party, less than national treatment and most-favored-nation treatment with respect to the matters set forth in paragraphs 2 and 4 of the present Article. Moreover, enterprises in which nationals and companies of either Party have a substantial interest shall be accorded, within the territories of the other Party, not less than national treatment and most-favored-nation treatment in all matters relating to the taking of privately owned enterprises into public ownership and to the placing of such enterprises under public control.

ARTICLE VII

1. Nationals and companies of either Party shall be accorded national treatment with respect to engaging in all types of commercial, industrial, financial and other activities for gain (business activities) within the territories of the other Party, whether directly or by agent or through the medium of any form of lawful juridical entity. Accordingly, such nationals and companies shall be permitted within such territories: (*a*) to establish and maintain branches, agencies, offices, factories and other establishments appropriate to the conduct of their business; (*b*) to organize companies under the general company laws of such other Party, and to acquire majority interests in companies of such other Party; and (*c*) to control and manage enterprises which they have established or acquired. Moreover, enterprises which they control, whether in the form of individual proprietorships, companies or otherwise, shall in all that relates to the conduct of the activities thereof, be accorded

treatment no less favorable than that accorded like enterprises controlled by nationals and companies of such other Party.

2. Each Party reserves the right to limit the extent to which aliens may establish, acquire interests in, or carry on enterprises engaged within its territories in transport, communications, public utilities, banking involving depository or fiduciary functions, or the exploitation of land or other natural resources. However, new limitations imposed by either Party upon the extent to which aliens are accorded national treatment, with respect to carrying on such activities within its territories, shall not be applied as against enterprises which are engaged in such activities therein at the time such new limitations are adopted and which are owned or controlled by nationals and companies of the other Party. Moreover, neither Party shall deny to transportation, communications and banking companies of the other Party the right to maintain branches and agencies to perform functions necessary for essentially international operations in which they are permitted to engage.

3. The provisions of paragraph 1 of the present Article shall not prevent either Party from prescribing special formalities in connection with the establishment of alien-controlled enterprises within its territories; but such formalities may not impair the substance of the rights set forth in said paragraph.

4. Nationals and companies of either Party, as well as enterprises controlled by such nationals and companies, shall in any event be accorded most-favored-nation treatment with reference to the matters treated in the present Article.

ARTICLE VIII

1. Nationals and companies of either Party shall be permitted to engage, within the territories of the other Party, accountants and other technical experts, executive personnel, attorneys, agents and other specialists of their choice. Moreover, such nationals and companies shall be permitted to engage accountants and other technical experts regardless of the extent to which they may have qualified for the practice of a profession within the territories of such other Party, for the particular purpose of making examinations, audits and technical investigations for, and rendering reports to, such nationals and companies in connection with the planning and operation of their enterprises, and enterprises in which they have a financial interest, within such territories.

2. Nationals and companies of either Party shall be accorded national treatment and most-favored-nation treatment with respect to engaging in scientific, educational, religious and philanthropic activities within

the territories of the other Party, and shall be accorded the right to form associations for that purpose under the laws of such other Party. Nothing in the present Treaty shall be deemed to grant or imply any right to engage in political activities.

ARTICLE IX

1. Nationals and companies of either Party shall be accorded, within the territories of the other Party:

 (*a*) national treatment with respect to leasing land, buildings and other immovable property appropriate to the conduct of activities in which they are permitted to engage pursuant to Articles VII and VIII and for residential purposes and with respect to occupying and using such property; and

 (*b*) other rights in immovable property permitted by the applicable laws of the other Party.

2. Nationals and companies of either Party shall be accorded within the territories of the other Party national treatment and most-favored-nation treatment with respect to acquiring, by purchase, lease, or otherwise, and with respect to owning and possessing, movable property of all kinds, both tangible and intangible. However, either Party may impose restrictions on alien ownership of materials dangerous from the standpoint of public safety and alien ownership of interests in enterprises carrying on particular types of activity, but only to the extent that this can be done without impairing the rights and privileges secured by Article VII or by other provisions of the present Treaty.

3. Nationals and companies of either Party shall be accorded national treatment within the territories of the other Party with respect to acquiring property of all kinds by testate or intestate succession or through judicial process. Should they because of their alienage be ineligible to continue to own any such property, they shall be allowed a period of at least five years in which to dispose of it.

4. Nationals and companies of either Party shall be accorded within the territories of the other Party national treatment and most-favored-nation treatment with respect to disposing of property of all kinds.

ARTICLE X

1. Nationals and companies of either Party shall be accorded, within the territories of the other Party, national treatment and most-favored-nation treatment with respect to obtaining and maintaining patents of

invention, and with respect to rights in trade marks, trade names, trade labels and industrial property of every kind.

2. The Parties undertake to cooperate in furthering the interchange and use of scientific and technical knowledge, particularly in the interests of increasing productivity and improving standards of living within their respective territories.

ARTICLE XI

1. Nationals of either Party residing within the territories of the other Party, and nationals and companies of either party engaged in trade or other gainful pursuit or in scientific, educational, religious or philanthropic activities within the territories of the other Party, shall not be subject to the payment of taxes, fees or charges imposed upon or applied to income, capital, transactions, activities or any other object, or to requirements with respect to the levy and collection thereof, within the territories of such other Party, more burdensome than those borne by nationals and companies of such other Party.

2. With respect to nationals of either Party who are neither resident nor engaged in trade or other gainful pursuit wtihin the territories of the other Party, and with respect to companies of either Party which are not engaged in trade or other gainful pursuit within the territories of the other Party, it shall be the aim of such other Party to apply in general the principle set forth in paragraph 1 of the present Article.

3. Nationals and companies of either Party shall in no case be subject, within the territories of the other Party, to the payment of taxes, fees or charges imposed upon or applied to income, capital, transactions, activities or any other object, or to requirements with respect to the levy and collection thereof, more burdensome than those borne by nationals, residents and companies of any third country.

4. In the case of companies of either Party engaged in trade or other gainful pursuit within the territories of the other Party, and in the case of nationals of either Party engaged in trade or other gainful pursuit within the territories of the other Party but not resident therein, such other Party shall not impose or apply any tax, fee or charge upon any income, capital or other basis in excess of that reasonably allocable or apportionable to its territories, nor grant deductions and exemptions less than those reasonably allocable or apportionable to its territories. A comparable rule shall apply also in the case of companies organized and operated exclusively for scientific, educational, religious or philanthropic purposes.

5. Each Party reserves the right to: (*a*) extend specific tax advantages on the basis of reciprocity; (*b*) accord special tax advantages by virtue of agreements for the avoidance of double taxation or the mutual protection of revenue; and (*c*) apply special provisions in allowing, to nonresidents, exemptions of a personal nature in connection with income and inheritance taxes.

ARTICLE XII

1. Nationals and companies of either Party shall be accorded by the other Party national treatment and most-favored-nation treatment with respect to payments, remittances and transfers of funds or financial instruments between the territories of the two Parties as well as between the territories of such other Party and of any third country.

2. Neither Party shall impose exchange restrictions as defined in paragraph 5 of the present Article except to the extent necessary to prevent its monetary reserves from falling to a very low level or to effect a moderate increase in very low monetary reserves. It is understood that the provisions of the present Article do not alter the obligations either Party may have to the International Monetary Fund or preclude imposition of particular restrictions whenever the Fund specifically authorizes or requests a Party to impose such particular restrictions.

3. If either Party imposes exchange restrictions in accordance with paragraph 2 of the present Article, it shall, after making whatever provision may be necessary to assure the availability of foreign exchange for goods and services essential to the health and welfare of its people and necessary to the avoidance of serious economic instability, make reasonable provision for the withdrawal, in foreign exchange in the currency of the other Party, of: (*a*) the compensation referred to in Article VI, paragraph 4, (*b*) earnings, whether in the form of salaries, interest, dividends, commissions, royalties, payments for technical services, or otherwise, and (*c*) amounts for amortization of loans, depreciation of direct investments, and capital transfers, giving consideration to special needs for other transactions. If more than one rate of exchange is in force, the rate applicable to such withdrawals shall be a rate which is specifically approved by the International Monetary Fund for such transactions or, in the absence of a rate so approved, an effective rate which, inclusive of any taxes or surcharges on exchange transfers, is just and reasonable.

4. Exchange restrictions shall not be imposed by either Party in a manner unnecessarily detrimental or arbitrarily discriminatory to the claims, investments, transport, trade, and other interests of the nationals and companies of the other Party, nor to the competitive position thereof.

5. The term "exchange restrictions" as used in the present Article includes all restrictions, regulations, charges, taxes, or other requirements imposed by either Party which burden or interfere with payments, remittances, or transfers of funds or of financial instruments between the territories of the two Parties.

6. Each Party shall afford the other Party adequate opportunity for consultation at any time regarding application of the present Article.

ARTICLE XIII

Commercial travelers representing nationals and companies of either Party engaged in business within the territories thereof shall, upon their entry into and departure from the territories of the other Party and during their sojourn therein, be accorded most-favored-nation treatment in respect of the customs and other matters, including, subject to the exceptions in paragraph 5 of Article XI, taxes and charges applicable to them, their samples and the taking of orders, and regulations governing the exercise of their functions.

ARTICLE XIV

1. Each Party shall accord most-favored-nation treatment to products of the other Party, from whatever place and by whatever type of carrier arriving, and to products destined for exportation to the territories of such other Party, by whatever route and by whatever type of carrier, with respect to customs duties and charges of any kind imposed on or in connection with importation or exportation or imposed on the international transfer of payments for imports or exports, and with respect to the method of levying such duties and charges, and with respect to all rules and formalities in connection with importation and exportation.

2. Neither Party shall impose restrictions or prohibitions on the importation of any product of the other Party, or on the exportation of any product to the territories of the other Party, unless the importation of the like product of, or the exportation of the like product to, all third countries is similarly restricted or prohibited.

3. If either Party imposes quantitative restrictions or the importation or exportation of any product in which the other Party has an important interest:

(*a*) It shall as a general rule give prior public notice of the total amount of the product, by quantity or value, that may be imported or exported during a specified period, and of any change in such amount, or period; and (*b*) If it makes allotments to any third country, it shall afford such other Party a share proportionate to the amount of the products, by quantity or value, supplied by or to it during a previous representative period, due consideration being given to any special factors affecting the trade in such product.

4. Either Party may impose prohibitions or restrictions on the importation or exportation of any product on sanitary or other customary grounds of a non-commercial nature, or in the interest of preventing deceptive or unfair practices, provided such prohibitions or restrictions do not arbitrarily discriminate against the commerce of the other Party.

5. Nationals and companies of either Party shall be accorded national treatment and most-favored-nation treatment by the other Party with respect to all matters relating to importation and exportation.

6. The provisions of the present Article shall not apply to advantages accorded by either Party:

(*a*) to products of its national fisheries;

(*b*) to adjacent countries in order to facilitate frontier traffic; or

(*c*) by virtue of a customs union or free-trade area of which it may become a member, so long as it informs the other Party of its plans and affords such other Party adequate opportunity for consultation.

7. Notwithstanding the provisions of paragraphs 2 and 3 (*b*) of the present Article, a Party may apply restrictions or controls on importation and exportation of goods that have the effect equivalent to, or which are necessary to make effective, exchange restrictions applied pursuant to Article XII. However, such restrictions or controls shall not depart further than necessary from the above paragraph and shall be comformable to a policy designed to promote the maximum development of nondiscriminatory foreign trade and to expedite the attainment both of balance-of-payments position and of monetary reserves which will obviate the necessity of such restrictions.

ARTICLE XV

1. Each Party shall promptly publish laws, regulations and administrative rulings of general application pertaining to rates of duty, taxes or other charges, to the classification of articles for customs purposes, and to requirements or restrictions on imports and exports or the transfers of payments therefor, or affecting their sale, distribution or use; and shall administer such laws, regulations and rulings in a uniform, impartial and reasonable manner. As a general practice, new administrative requirements or restrictions affecting imports, with the exception of those imposed on sanitary grounds or for reasons of public safety, shall not go

into effect before the expiration of 30 days after publication, or alternatively, shall not apply to products en route at time of publication.

2. Each Party shall provide an appeals procedure under which nationals and companies of the other Party, and importers of products of such other Party, shall be able to obtain prompt and impartial review, and correction when warranted, of administrative action relating to customs matters, including the imposition of fines and penalties, confiscations, and rulings on questions of customs classification and valuation by the administrative authorities. Penalties imposed for infractions of the customs and shipping laws and regulations concerning documentation shall, in cases resulting from clerical errors or when good faith can be demonstrated, be no greater than necessary to serve merely as a warning.

3. Neither party shall impose any measure of a discriminatory nature that hinders or prevents the importer or exporter of products of either country from obtaining marine insurance on such products in companies of either Party. The present paragraph is subject to the provisions of Article XII.

ARTICLE XVI

1. Products of either Party shall be accorded, within the territories of the other Party, national treatment and most-favored-nation treatment in all matters affecting internal taxation, sale, distribution, storage and use.

2. Articles produced by nationals and companies of either Party within the territories of the other Party, or by companies of the latter Party controlled by such nationals and companies, shall be accorded therein treatment no less favorable than that accorded to like articles of national origin by whatever person or company produced, in all matters affecting exportation, taxation, sale, distribution, storage and use.

ARTICLE XVII

1. Each Party undertakes (*a*) that enterprises owned or controlled by its Government and that monopolies or agencies granted exclusive or special privileges within its territories, shall make their purchases and sales involving either imports or exports affecting the commerce of the other Party solely in accordance with commercial considerations, including price, quality, availability, marketability, transportation and other conditions of purchase or sale; and (*b*) that the nationals, companies and commerce of such other Party shall be afforded adequate opportunity, in accordance with customary business practice, to compete for participation in such purchases and sales.

2. Each Party shall accord to the nationals, companies and commerce of the other Party fair and equitable treatment, as compared with that accorded to the nationals, companies and commerce of any third country, with respect to: (*a*) the governmental purchase of supplies, (*b*) the awarding of concessions and other government contracts, and (*c*) the sale of any service sold by the Government or by any monopoly or agency granted exclusive or special privileges.

ARTICLE XVIII

1. The two Parties agree that business practices which restrain competition, limit access to markets or foster monopolistic control, and which are engaged in or made effective by one or more private or public commercial enterprises or by combination, agreement or other arrangement among such enterprises, may have harmful effects upon commerce between their respective territories. Accordingly, each Party agrees upon the request of the other Party to consult with respect to any such practices and to take such measures as it deems appropriate with a view to eliminating such harmful effects.

2. No enterprise of either Party, including corporations, associations, and government agencies and instrumentalities, which is publicly owned or controlled shall, if it engages in commercial, industrial, shipping or other business activities within the territories of the other Party, claim or enjoy, either for itself or for its property, immunity therein from taxation, suit, execution of judgment or other liability to which privately owned and controlled enterprises are subject therein.

ARTICLE XIX

1. Between the territories of the two Parties there shall be freedom of commerce and navigation.

2. Vessels under the flag of either Party, and carrying the papers required by its law in proof of nationality, shall be deemed to be vessels of that Party both on the high seas and within the ports, places and waters of the other Party.

3. Vessels of either Party shall have liberty, on equal terms with vessels of the other Party and on equal terms with vessels of any third country, to come with their cargoes to all ports, places and waters of such other Party open to foreign commerce and navigation. Such vessels and cargoes shall in all respects be accorded national treatment and most-favored-nation treatment within the ports, places and waters of such other Party; but each Party may reserve exclusive rights and privileges

to its own vessels with respect to the coasting trade, inland navigation and national fisheries.

4. Vessels of either Party shall be accorded national treatment and most-favored-nation treatment by the other Party with respect to the right to carry all products that may be carried by vessel to or from the territories of such other Party; and such products shall be accorded treatment no less favorable than that accorded like products carried in vessels of such other Party, with respect to: (*a*) duties and charges of all kinds, (*b*) the administration of the customs, and (*c*) bounties, drawbacks and other privileges of this nature.

5. Vessels of either Party that are in distress shall be permitted to take refuge in the nearest port or haven of the other Party, and shall receive friendly treatment and assistance.

6. The term "vessels," or used herein, means all types of vessels, whether privately owned or operated, or publicly owned or operated; but this term does not, except with reference to paragraphs 2 and 5 of the present Article, include fishing vessels or vessels of war.

ARTICLE XX

There shall be freedom of transit through the territories of each Party by the routes most convenient for international transit:

(*a*) for nationals of the other Party, together with their baggage;

(*b*) for other persons, together with their baggage, en route to or from the territories of such other Party; and

(*c*) for products of any origin en route to or from the territories of such other Party.

Such persons and things in transit shall be exempt from customs duties, from duties imposed by reason of transit, and from unreasonable charges and requirements; and shall be free from unnecessary delays and restrictions. They shall, however, be subject to measures referred to in paragraph 3 of Article II, and to nondiscriminatory regulations necessary to prevent abuse of the transit privilege.

ARTICLE XXI

1. The present Treaty shall not preclude the application of measures:

(*a*) regulating the importation or exportation of gold or silver;

(*b*) relating to fissionable materials, to radioactive byproducts of the utilization or processing thereof, or to materials that are the source of fissionable materials;

(*c*) regulating the production of or traffic in arms, ammunition and implements of war, or traffic in other materials carried on directly or indirectly for the purpose of supplying a military establishment;

(*d*) necessary to fulfill the obligations of a Party for the maintenance or restoration of international peace and security, or necessary to protect its essential security interest; and

(*e*) denying to any company in the ownership or direction of which nationals of any third country or countries have directly or indirectly the controlling interest, the advantages of the present Treaty, except with respect to recognition of juridical status and with respect to access to courts.

2. The most-favored-nation provisions of the present Treaty relating to the treatment of goods shall not apply to advantages accorded by the United States of America or its Territories and possessions to one another, to the Republic of Cuba, to the Republic of the Philippines, to the Trust Territory of the Pacific Islands or to the Panama Canal Zone.

3. The provisions of the present Treaty relating to the treatment of goods shall not preclude action by either Party which is required or specifically permitted by the General Agreement on Tariffs and Trade during such time as such Party is a contracting party to the General Agreement. Similarly, the most-favored-nation provisions of the present Treaty shall not apply to special advantages accorded by virtue of the aforesaid Agreement.

4. Nationals of either Party admitted into the territories of the other Party for limited purposes shall not enjoy rights to engage in gainful occupations in contravention of limitations expressly imposed, according to law, as a condition of their admittance.

ARTICLE XXII

1. The term "national treatment" means treatment accorded within the territories of a Party upon terms no less favorable than the treatment according therein, in like situations, to nationals, companies, products, vessels or other objects, as the case may be, of such Party.

2. The term "most-favored-nation treatment" means treatment accorded within the territories of a Party upon terms no less favorable than the treatment accorded therein, in like situations, to nationals, companies, products, vessels or other objects, as the case may be, of any third country.

3. As used in the present Treaty, the term "companies" means corporations, partnerships, companies and other associations, whether or not with limited liability and whether or not for pecuniary profit. Companies constituted under the applicable laws and regulations within the territories of either Party shall be deemed companies thereof and shall have their juridical status recognized within the territories of the other Party.

4. National treatment accorded under the provisions of the present Treaty to companies of the Republic of Korea shall, in any state, Terri-

tory or possesssion of the United States of America, be the treatment accorded therein to companies created or organized in other States, Territories, and possessions of the United States of America.

ARTICLE XXIII

The territories to which the present Treaty extends shall comprise all areas of land and water under the sovereignty or authority of each Party, other than the Panama Canal Zone and the Trust Territory of the Pacific Islands.

ARTICLE XXIV

1. Each Party shall accord sympathetic consideration to, and shall afford adequate opportunity for consultation regarding, such representations as the other Party may make with respect to any matter affecting the operation of the present Treaty.

2. Any dispute between the Parties as to the interpretation or application of the present Treaty, not satisfactorily adjusted by diplomacy, shall be submitted to the International Court of Justice, unless the Parties agree to settlement by some other pacific means.

ARTICLE XXV

1. The present Treaty shall be ratified, and the ratifications thereof shall be exchanged at Seoul as soon as possible.

2. The present Treaty shall enter into force one month after the day of exchange of ratifications. It shall remain in force for 10 years and shall continue in force thereafter until terminated as provided herein.

3. Either Party may, by giving one year's written notice to the other Party, terminate the present Treaty at the end of the initial 10-year period or at any time thereafter. IN WITNESS WHEREOF the respective Plenipotentiaries have signed the present Treaty and have affixed hereunto their seals. DONE in duplicate, in the Korean and English languages, both equally authentic, at Seoul this twenty-eighth day of November, one thousand nine hundred fifty-six.

For the Republic of Korea:

For the United States of America:

PROTOCOL

At the time of signing the Treaty of Friendship, Commerce and Navigation between the Republic of Korea and the United States of America, the undersigned Plentipotentiaries, duly authorized by their respective Governments, have further agreed on the following provisions, which shall be considered integral parts of the aforesaid Treaty:

1. The provisions of Article II, paragraph 1 (*b*), shall be construed as extending to a national of either Party seeking to enter the territories of the other Party solely for the purpose of developing and directing the operations of an enterprise in the territories of such other Party in which his employer has invested or is actively in the process of investing a substantial amount of capital, provided that such employer is a national or company of the same nationality as the applicant and that the applicant is employed by such ntional or company in a responsible capacity.

2. The term "access" as used in Article V, paragraph 1, comprehends, among other things, legal aid and security for costs and judgment.

3. It is understood that Article V, paragraph 2 does not require a Party to enforce an arbitration award that is contrary to its public policy.

4. The provisions of Article VI, paragraph 4, providing for the payment of compensation shall extend to interests held directly or indirectly by nationals and companies of either Party in property which is taken within the territories of the other Party.

5. The term "public utilities" as used in Article VII, paragraph 2, is deemed to include enterprises engaged in furnishing water supplies, or in manufacturing and distributing gas or electricity, to the general public.

6. With reference to Article VII, paragraph 4, it is understood that neither Party is obligated to accord most-favored-nation treatment regarding rights to engage in mining on the public domain other than on a basis of reciprocity.

7. Either Party may impose restrictions on the introduction of foreign capital as may be necessary to protect its monetary reserves as provided in Article XII, paragraph 2.

8. The provisions of Article XVII, paragraph 2, (*b*) and (*c*), and or Article XIX, paragraph 4, shall not apply to postal services.

9. Article XXI, paragraph 1 (*e*) shall be construed to apply also to any company in the ownership or direction of which any third country or companies thereof have directly or indirectly the controlling interest. A Party is not obligated to permit nationals of the other Party to conduct business within its territories as representatives of a third country or nationals or companies thereof in contravention of laws generally applicable to all individuals.

10. The provisions of Article XXI, paragraph 2, shall apply in the case of Puerto Rico regardless of any change that may take place in its political status.

11. Article XXIII does not apply to territories under the authority of either Party solely as a military base or by reason of temporary military occupation.

IN WITNESS WHEREOF the respective Plenipotentiaries have signed this Protocol and have affixed hereunto their seals.

DONE in duplicate, in the Korean and English languages, both equally authentic, at Seoul this twenty-eighth day of November, one thousand nine hundred fifty-six.

For the Republic of Korea:

For the United States of America:

Treaty of North Korea with the Union of Soviet Socialist Republics[4]

The Presidium of the Supreme Soviet of the Union of Soviet Socialist Republics and the Presidium of the Supreme People's Assembly of the Democratic People's Republic of Korea.

striving to develop and strengthen the friendly relations between the Soviet Union and the Democratic People's Republic of Korea, the relations based on the principle of socialist internationalism,

wishing to contribute to the maintenance and consolidation of peace and security in the Far East and throughout the world in accordance with the aims and principles of the United Nations,

fully determined to render assistance and support to each other in case of an armed attack by some state or a coalition of states on one of the contracting parties,

being certain that the strengthening of friendship, good neighborliness and cooperation between the Soviet Union and the Democratic People's Republic of Korea meets the vital interests of the peoples of both states and will in the best way conduce to their further economic and cultural development,

have resolved with this end in view to conclude this treaty and have appointed as their plenipotentiaries:

The Presidium of the Supreme Soviet of the Union of Soviet Socialist Republics—Nikita Sergeyevich Khrushchev, Chairman of the Council of Ministers of the USSR,

The Presidium of the Supreme People's Assembly of the Democratic

People's Republic of Korea—Kim Il Sung, Chairman of the Council of Ministers of the DPRK.

Both plenipotentiaries after exchanging their credentials, which were found to be in due form and good order, agreed on the following:

ARTICLE 1. The contracting parties declare that they will continue to take part in all international actions aimed at ensuring peace and security in the Far East and throughout the world and will make their contribution to the cause of the accomplishment of these lofty tasks.

In case one of the contracting parties becomes the object of an armed attack by some state or a coalition of states and as a result finds itself in the state of war, then the other contracting party will immediately render it military and other assistance with all means at its disposal.

ARTICLE 2. Each of the contracting parties undertakes to conclude no alliances and to participate in no coalitions or actions and measures directed against the other contracting party.

ARTICLE 3. The contracting parties will consult each other on all important international issues affecting the interests of both states, being guided by the striving to contribute to the consolidation of peace and general security.

ARTICLE 4. Both contracting parties undertake to develop and strengthen the economic and cultural contacts between the Union of Soviet Socialist Republics and the Democratic People's Republic of Korea, to render each other all possible assistance and carry out necessary cooperation in the economic and cultural fields, in the spirit of friendship and cooperation, in accordance with the principles of equality, and mutual respect for state sovereignty, territorial integrity and noninterference in the internal affairs of each other.

ARTICLE 5. Both contracting parties maintain that the unification of Korea must be carried out on a peaceful and democratic basis and that such settlement is in line both with the national interests of the Korean people and the cause of maintaining peace in the Far East.

ARTICLE 6. The treaty goes into force on the day of the exchange of the instruments of ratification, which will take place in Pyongyang.

The treaty remains in force for the course of ten years. If one of the contracting parties does not declare one year before the expiration of this term its desire to denounce the treaty, it will continue to remain in force for the next five years and will be prolonged in accordance with this rule.

Done in Moscow on July 6, 1961, in two copies, each in the Russian and Korean languages with both texts equally valid.

For the Presidium of the Supreme Soviet of the Union of
Soviet Socialist Republics

N. KHRUSHCHEV

For the Presidium of the Supreme People's Assembly of
the Democratic People's Republic of Korea

KIM IL SUNG

Treaty of North Korea with the People's Republic of China[5]

The Chairman of the People's Republic of China and the Presidium of the Supreme People's Assembly of the Democratic People's Republic of Korea,

determined, in accordance with Marxism-Leninism and the principle of proletarian internationalism, and on the basis of mutual respect for state sovereignty and territorial integrity, mutual nonaggression, noninterference in each other's internal affairs, equality and mutual benefit, and mutual assistance and support, to make every effort to further strengthen and develop the fraternal relations of friendship, cooperation, and mutual assistance between the People's Republic of China and the Democratic People's Republic of Korea, to jointly guard the security of the two peoples, and to safeguard and consolidate the peace of Asia and the world, and

deeply convinced that the development and strengthening of the relations of friendship, cooperation, and mutual assistance between the two countries accord, not only with the fundamental interests of the two peoples, but also with the interests of the peoples all over the world,

have decided for this purpose to conclude the present treaty and appointed as their respective plenipotentiaries:

The Chairman of the People's Republic of China—Chou En-lai; Premier of the State Council of the People's Republic of China; and

The Presidium of the Supreme People's Assembly of the Democratic People's Republic of Korea—Kim Il Sung, Premier of the Cabinet of the Democratic People's Republic of Korea,

Having examined each other's full powers and found them in good and due form, have agreed upon the following:

ARTICLE 1. The contracting parties will continue to make every effort to safeguard peace in Asia and the world and the security of all peoples.

ARTICLE 2. The contracting parties undertake jointly to adopt all measures to prevent aggression against either of the contracting parties by any state. In the event of one of the contracting parties being subjected to armed attack by any state or several states jointly and thus being involved in a state of war, the other contracting party shall immediately render military and other assistance by all means at its disposal.

ARTICLE 3. Neither contracting party shall conclude any alliance directed against the other contracting party or take part in any bloc or in any action or measure directed against the other contracting party.

ARTICLE 4. The contracting parties will continue to consult with each other on all important international questions of common interest to the two countries.

ARTICLE 5. The contracting parties, on the principles of mutual respect for sovereignty, noninterference in each other's internal affairs, equality and mutual benefit, and in the spirit of friendly cooperation, will continue to render each other every possible economic and technical aid in the cause of socialist construction of the two countries and will continue to consolidate and develop economic, cultural, and scientific and technical cooperation between the two countries.

ARTICLE 6. The contracting parties hold that the unification of Korea must be realized along peaceful and democratic lines and that such a solution accords exactly with the national interests of the Korean people and the aim of preserving peace in the Far East.

ARTICLE 7. The present treaty is subject to ratification and shall come into force on the day of exchange of instruments of ratification, which will take place in Pyongyang.

The present treaty will remain in force until the contracting parties agree on its amendment or termination.

Done in duplicate in Peking on 11 July 1961, in the Chinese and Korean languages, both texts being equally authentic.

Plenipotentiary of the People's Republic of China

CHOU EN-LAI

Plenipotentiary of the Democratic People's Republic of Korea

KIM IL SUNG

Leadership: On the Revolutionary Process[6]

Introduction

At a time when the people and the armed forces are called upon to devote their whole energies to the task of eliminating accumulated evils and corruption, defending the Fatherland from internal and external aggression of the enemy, and reconstructing the country, the most urgent problem is the creation and establishment of a system of leadership which will guide such endeavors in the right direction. The establishment of leadership, as an essential social requirement, is the primary task requiring immediate attention.

The May 16 Military Revolution was an inevitable action, taken to drive out the so-called leaders of the past, who lacked firm leadership and consequently brought misery to the people, and the country to the brink of ruin. This moment will decide whether the country will rise or fall. To bring about the prosperity and security of the country, we must establish firm leadership quickly. Especially in a revolutionary era, leadership means that which is heroic. Assuming our society to be like a sea of oil, leadership must furnish the spark to bring about conflagration and sublimation. Among the people, indolence, egotism, the attitude of an on-looker, and fatalism must be burned out, and guidance must be provided to materialize the true desires of those who are led.

Character of the Leader

RELATIVITY OF THE LEADER

The perfect Leader, transcending both the led and their time, cannot be found among men. The value of a human Leader (not a deity) is largely determined by the degree and extent to which he can fulfill the demand of the led and of the age. Since perfection cannot be achieved due to the hard facts of reality, the capability of the Leader is therefore determined by his ability to narrow the gap between perfection and achievable conditions realistically appraised.

LEADERS OF THE PAST

Throughout the primitive, ancient and medieval ages, the Leader was variously conceived and defined as one who had an extraordinarily strong fist; one who was outstanding in physical attributes; one with special family ties or ancestry; or one who had attained heroic stature. In general, congenital rather than acquired abilities were emphasized, with the result that the position of the Leader was nearly always regarded as the result of fate and predestination. Thus, little scope was provided for competition in acquired abilities for the position of leadership.

The led regarded the Leader as a superman—an idol or a sacred and inviolable being. From the standpoint of the Leader, such reverent attitudes of the led was absolutely necessary to the maintenance of his position. In a time of crisis, the Leader was expected to bring about superhuman miracles or magical effects; human frailties or errors of the Leader were regarded with disgust and contempt rather than with sympathy and understanding.

Even in the 20th Century, backward peoples are prone to expect superhuman capabilities from their leaders, freely elected (at least in form). Faced with this contradiction, the leader's personal aides and close subordinates tend to establish a human curtain to interrupt the communication of opinion from below, while the communication of opinion from above too often takes the form of arbitrary orders. Thus dictatorship is fostered.

THE MODERN LEADER

In the modern age of well-developed democratic ideology, the Leader shares common interests with the led, and walks the same path—one step ahead of them. He is there not to arbitrarily command, but to represent and lead them toward the accomplishment of their true desires.

Since he is a representative, his position is not a priori but a posteriori; not fixed but fluid and creative. He breathes the same air with the led, and is quick to discover the most urgent desires of the masses. He is also expected to possess the ability to persuade the masses to accept methods which he believes are the best and most practicable. He must have the courage to lead, and the ability to secure the cooperation of the led. Brute strength or erudition are not necessarily attributes of the Leader.

Analysis of the Led

THE AGE WE FACE

The end of World War II brought about intensive rivalry between the forces of Red imperialism and the forces of democracy, as these human rights and individual freedom. The Red tentacles are being extended even today into many weak and unstable areas. Even in our country, the Red decay had begun to eat into the nerve centers. Prior to the recent revolution, our country was at the brink of disintegration because of the undermining Red Conspiracy. Notwithstanding the rallying calls of those in power, what lay ahead of us was slavery under Red dictatorship instead of human rights and individual freedom.

Our people embraced the ideology of liberty after liberation from the oppression and violence of Japanese imperialism. Democracy in our country flowered not with its roots in slow self-awakening, and development over a long period, but was suddenly thrust upon us by external forces. As such it lacked the spirit of autonomy and the sense of responsibility. It was comparable to a house resting on a shaky foundation.

The house finally collapsed. We must not blame the house itself as defective, but should be ashamed that we built it without laying solid foundations beforehand. Now we have reached the stage where we must reinforce the foundations all over again. This is one of the most important tasks for national reconstruction.

CONSTITUENT ELEMENTS OF OUR PEOPLE

Needless to say, there are some among our people who have a sufficiently strong sense of autonomy and responsibility to merit the full enjoyment of freedom and democracy. The majority of our people, however, are so steeped in the inertia of heteronomy that it has become second nature and their spirit of autonomy and sense of responsibility have been atrophied. As the result of freedom without responsibility, license, confusion, disorder, and destruction were created, and democracy, which should have been the basis for human rights, degenerated into a system of conspiracy, slander and false accusation.

Those in power, with their underdeveloped sense of responsibility, fell apart from the people, abused their power and authority, and amassed large fortunes in collusion with corrupt elements. Financiers conspired with politicians to secure loans by unjust means, evade taxes, and engage in smuggling and the expatriation of property. These evil influences were absorbed by the young people, who are like green buds growing out of the old tree stump, so much so that they aimed at success without moral foundation, cheap advancement in life, and indolence. Too many people relied exclusively on political backing, influence-peddling and devious maneuvering. Justice and the moral code fell to the ground; corruption, injustice, and immorality were rampant; and it was no longer possible to sustain the sick and diseased body politic.

Even though our people enthusiastically support the Revolution and the new start it provides, it will take long and arduous endeavors to eradicate the chronic evils of the people. These evils must be eradicated as quickly as possible. Yet, in our eagerness for quick success, we should not despair and abandon the effort without having paid the price due beforehand.

THE WISHES OF OUR PEOPLE
Our people wish to completely unify the Fatherland; secure our sovereign rights free from external coercion, manipulation or encroachment or any form of indirect aggression; to liberate ourselves from mankind's worst enemy, poverty; and to firmly establish genuine, free democracy based on universal prosperity, peace and mutual respect for human rights. In reality, however, our people have been going in exactly the opposite direction with vague expectations of windfalls, magic and miracles.

Required Attributes of the Leader Needed by Our Society

SENSE OF CAMARADERIE
The Leader should be neither an authoritarian nor a privileged personality standing apart from and reigning over the masses, but rather should share their destiny and be imbued with a strong sense of comaraderie. He must be prepared to experience their hardships and joys. He must be kind and humble in guiding the people; must personally set the example in tackling difficult problems; must give up personal considerations and be equipped with the sublime spirit of self-sacrifice for the sake of the people.

All power held by the Leader emanates from the people. There is neither power created by oneself, nor privilege endowed by Heaven. The Leader must be rooted in the masses and give up the pre-modern consciousness of privilege. Otherwise he will tread the same discredited paths of the RHEE and CHANG Myon regimes, and will be deprived of the ability to resuscitate the Fatherland.

CAPABILITY FOR JUDGMENT AND SOLUTION
The correct understanding of a problem is the key to its true solution. Medicine and treatment, however efficacious in themselves, may aggravate the illness if prescription and diagnosis are incorrect. When one discards the overbearing attitude, and embraces a sense of camaraderie with the people, he will then, and only then, be able to correctly grasp what is felt by the people, what they want and what they wish to avoid.

Since the desires of the led are not always rational, the Leader must be able to gently point out the contradictions or irrationality in the people's desires, and provide them with positive leadership to enable them to avoid these. In other words, he must be able to discern what aspect of the society is the cause of disease and harm to the health of the society. He must always be able to know exactly the permissible margin of necessary social evils, and the balance point of good and evil.

Approach to a problem is not always uniform or identical. It should be decided by the background, sincerity, energies, habits, attitudes and convictions of the led, and is subject to the influence of the ideological current of the age. The availability, or lack, of human and material resources necessary for the solution of a problem must also be taken into account. For these reasons, the Leader must have the sagacity to decide the priority ratings of different problems, and to judge what must be solved, and how, when and to what extent.

While passion and zeal are necessary conditions for the solution of a problem the method of solution should be flexible and elastic. Knowledge of facts is necessary for the solution of a problem. However, it is not to be expected that every Leader will be equipped with all specialized and technical knowledge, and it is for this reason that he must solicit and secure the cooperation of experts in their respective fields. Needless to say, he should have the ability to listen to and absorb their advice and counsel.

FORESIGHT

In addition to his capability to solve the real problem, the Leader must have the foresight to foresee future events, and to take appropriate steps to cope with them. It is still difficult, even in this age of scientific progress, to forecast the weather 24 hours ahead; so is it difficult for the Leader to plan ahead for a long period of time. It is all too true that he will in fact be unable to prepare meticulous plans to cope with all future events. Nonetheless, he must always entertain firm convictions regarding the basic objectives and the avenues of approach thereto, and must maintain an unswerving attitude and fortitude in overcoming any unforeseen obstacles, and thereby lead the people to the desired goal.

LOYALTY TO PRINCIPLES—THE CONSCIENTIOUS LEADER

Means may be revised to attain the end, but it is a virtueless and untrustworthy man who is so enslaved by the means that he deviates from the principles themselves. One surrenders his qualifications as a Leader when he disregards sound principles, and instead sways hither and thither as the occasion suits him. A politician who thus neglects his political duty cannot be condoned before the people.

He who is loyal to man is also faithful to principles. To be faithful to principles, he must be honest with himself and others. He must always guide himself and others. He must guide himself by a sense of justice and conscience, no matter whether the result brings praise or criticism. This is illustrated by the tale of an ancient monarch whose son committed an offense for which the prescribed punishment was the deoculation of both eyes, and who, to uphold the established law and to still save his son from total blindness, had one eye extracted from his son and from himself.

COURAGE

One who leads the people and opens the way for them must have the courage to accept the challenge of adventures and risks. Since he cannot have unlimited time at his disposal, he must see to it that all important matters are dealt with and disposed of promptly. Courage and decisiveness —these are indispensable attributes of the Leader. Courage and decisiveness have a strong power of persuasion upon the led, and so can be communicated to them with ease. Temporary failures are of no account, as long as these attributes of leadership can infuse the led with a power of revival.

BELIEF IN DEMOCRACY

The Revolution is aimed at completely overturning the former undemocratic system, and preparing the groundwork for a system of genuine freedom and democracy. It by no means intends to establish dictatorship or totalitarianism.

It is necessary, therefore, that the Leader, in the execution of the revolutionary tasks, should himself entertain strong convictions concerning democracy. He must be courageous in repudiating every form of dictatorship including Communist dictatorship. He must always breathe in harmony with the people; and do his utmost to infuse them with the spirit of genuine freedom and democracy.

To repudiate Communism, it is necessary to entertain firm anti-Communist ideologies. But these ideologies alone are not enough to win out against Communism and establish democracy in our country. To that end, we must achieve rational unity, which transcends democracy, and improve our living standard. When our country becomes more peaceful, more stabilized, and wins more international cooperation; when our national economy has achieved outstanding progress—then the superiority of our system will be proved.

The Leader ought to entertain firm anti-Communist ideologies and democratic convictions, and devote his whole energies to the preparation of a firm foundation for achieving a great leap forward politically, socially, and economically.

CONVICTIONS REGARDING OBJECTIVES
(a) Free Democracy and the Revolution
Free domacracy and revolutionary sovereignty ultimately emanate
from the people; therefore, it is our purpose to safeguard the people's
rights from encroachment. Even before the Revolution, the principle of
the sovereignty of popular rights had been institutionalized, and the
people's rights were guaranteed, at least theoretically. In practice, however,
the sovereign right was held by a few privileged people, and the general
public was not in the position to exercise their lawful rights. Moreover,
the national sovereignty itself was on the brink of collapse.

One may pose the question: "Is the Military Revolution in keeping
with freedom and democracy, or against it?" "A" cannot arbitrarily restrict the life of "B" when both are healthy and equal. But when "B"
contracts illness and receives therapy from "A," the latter may not only
restrict and regulate "B" 's diet but may even order him to be hospitalized.
The doctor may temporarily restrict the physical activities of the patient
for the sake of complete cure and recovery, and even force him to submit to painful surgery, when necessary. To save his life, it is sometimes
necessary to amputate bodily organs, which ordinarily would seem to vio-
late the law of physical well-being. Surgical operations are not pleasant,
but they can be accepted as a necessary evil—as a small sacrifice to save
the whole.

The Military Revolution was a kind of surgical operation. At a time
when the country was faced with imminent collapse and the people's freedom and sovereign rights. That operation was the Military Revolution.

Even as an act, taken to avoid imminent danger to one's or other's
life, body, or virtue can be justified, so an act taken to avoid danger to the
country and the people is justifiable at a time when undemocratic elements
were about to overwhelm the country, morality had reached the lowest
ebb, and corruption and injustice were rampant. Not only was this action
fully justified, but it was the people's bounden duty to carry it out.

Viewed from the standpoint of legal positivism, the Military Revolution may conceivably be regarded as an act of encroachment upon the
established legal order. However, it was the exercise of the people's in-
alienable basic right, which existed before the establishment of the legal
order and in fact constitutes the basis of the existing legal order. From this
viewpoint, the Revolution has both justifiability and legality. It is true,
nonetheless, that it was but a means to the end, and cannot in itself constitute the end.

Now we must bring genuine democracy to this land and realize prosperity and security. We must eliminate corruption and injustice, and put

the country and the people securely upon a foundation of justice. We must establish a correct order of human relations.

(b) Relationship Between Exercise of Force and Autonomy

The exercise of force, on the one hand, and autonomy, on the other hand, maintain a very sensitive balance (literally, are in an extremely sensitive disproportion. Tr.) with each other. When the led have a strong sense of autonomy and voluntarily fulfill their duty, there is no reason for the exercise of force. However, in the absence of such a strong sense of autonomy, the resultant evasion of duty—whether deliberate or not—and failure to positively observe and abide by established law and order, makes it mandatory to exercise heteronomous force for the maintenance of a minimum of order.

Such exercise of force should in all cases be utilized as a stimulant to evoke the sense of autonomy, and as the sense of autonomy gradually grows, the scope and extent of the exercise of force should be narrowed proportionately.

It is my belief that the exercise of strong force, in an extensive scope and over the required minimum time, is very necessary to bring order to this country, which has become a thieves' den ruled by disorder and confusion. It is also necessary to eliminate economic disorder, to bring into force powerful economic planning for some time. In order to eliminate all injustice and corruption and establish the moral code, firm and drastic measures must be enforced for some time.

The Leader should not become a sentimental doctor who removes the bandage to relieve the pain of the patient, and thus causes him to be permanently crippled. Until such time as the spirit of autonomy can be brought into force, the exercise of a powerful heteronomous force is mandatory.

(c) Scope of Exercise of Force

As a doctor should not give his patient more pain than is absolutely necessary for his cure and recuperation, so the exercise of force should not exceed the minimum necessary for the benefit of the led and the maintenance of order. The exercise of force must be avoided when other means are available to effectively achieve the objective. When our society has established the groundwork for normal progress, force—which is a means for abnormal progress—will be brought to a halt.

UNITY AMONG LEADERS

Unity among the Leaders is more important than unity among the led. Sociological researchers have revealed that juvenile delinquents are

more apt to be produced from a home where the parents are not in harmony with each other, than from an incomplete home with only a single
parent.

Should disharmony, division, wrangling and feuding arise among the
Leaders, should they expose the faults of each other instead of compensat-
ing for them, the led would again become a kind of juvenile delinquent.
At this time, when the country must be saved from the imminent danger
of disruption, lack of firm unity among the leaders will only bewilder the
people; and the country will be engulfed by the relentless penetration of
Red imperialism.

As regards the composition of the leadership of our country, it reveals
heterogeneity in many respects, although all its members have in common
a strong ideal and zeal for the accomplishment of the revolutionary tasks.
They vary as individuals. Some are mild in temperament while others are
radical. Some have been in positions of command, while others have led
staff careers. They are widely different in the type and scope of their
knowledge and experience. These heterogeneous elements are apt to
engender friction unless constant care is exercised.

The spirit of cooperation is the most important factor in preventing
friction, collision, and conflict, and in achieving unity and solidarity. Such
cooperation should always be based on commonly shared ideals. While
each should have firm convictions in his own ideals and beliefs, he must
nevertheless have the broadness of mind to listen to and accept others'
views, and not to despise or belittle others' abilities. Conspiracy and
slander, in particular, should not be condoned.

The attitude of cooperation with others, and the spirit of devoting one's
whole energies to one's given duties must be maintained at all times. We
must never again tread the track of the old regimes which, by their
factionalism, wrangling, slander, and mutual recrimination, disrupted the
government and endangered the safety of the country. We must courageously reject all forms of bickering over business interests, political feuds,
and wrangling over positions of authority and prestige. The creation of a
new humanity, to enable us to devote ourselves to the performance of our
duties in a pure and immaculate spirit of mutual cooperation, is the
quickest way to achieve national unity and solidarity.

SINCERITY AND ENTHUSIASM

The popular saying, "Sincerity can move the Heavens," does not
necessarily mean that the fervor of the weak can influence the mind of
the strong. It probably signifies that the sincerity and fervor of the strong

are capable of inspiring the weak with the sense of cooperation rather than fear and dread, and understanding rather than antagonism.

The Leader under a democratic system should exercise many times more sincerity than the Leader of a dictatorship. In spite of his human weakness and defects, the Leader can win both sympathy and understanding from the people by pouring forth his sincerity and enthusiasm.

TRUST

A Leader equipped with all the nine attributes enumerated above will easily win the trust of the led. Still, the relationship between the Leader and the led is never anything other than a relationship between human beings; and the most important requirement for the Leader to win the trust of the led, (who are humans after all) is his personality.

As mentioned previously, the leader must be equipped with the spirit of self-sacrifice, conscience, and ability to give examples to the led. Also, he must know how to cooperate. His personality must be noble, his moral attributes outstanding. He must keep his promises and must be more faithful than anyone else to the State and the people. His actions must always be based on justice. When and if all these conditions are fulfilled, the led will follow the Leader out of their own hearts.

Conclusion

Because of our past failures to establish correct leadership in the course of our 5,000-year history, we have been subjected to foreign incursions, sometimes divided internally, fighting, biting and scratching each other. Most of the time, the people were enslaved by poverty and misery.

Even the toppled regime could not have precipitated the country into such a sorry plight, notwithstanding its incompetence and ineptitude, had its leaders genuinely stood for and loved the people, and had they been fired with strong democratic ideals and sincerity. It is no exaggeration to say that the security of the country and the prosperity of the people ultimately depend on the establishment of firm leadership.

Truly important is the responsibility of the Leader who must lead the people towards the sacred goal of National Reconstruction. He must be able to overcome the present crisis, consolidate the foundation for national prosperity and security, and bequeath to the leaders of all future generations a genuine system of leadership which did not exist before. When such virtuous traditions have become firmly established, then and then only, will we have accomplished the tasks of the Military Revolution, which includes, among others, the reformation of the national character, reinforcement of national unity and solidarity, and improvement of the living standard of the nation, which still hovers at the lowest level in the world.

1961   GENERAL CHUNG HEE PARK

Park–Kennedy Joint Communiqué[7]

Following is the text of a joint communiqué issued by General Chung Hee Park and President Kennedy in Washington on November 14, 1961.

Chairman Park and President Kennedy concluded today a friendly and constructive exchange of views on the current situation in Korea and the Far East and various matters of interest to the Governments and peoples of the Republic of Korea and the United States of America. Foreign Minister Choi, Secretary Rusk and other officials of the two Governments participated in the conversations.

The two leaders reaffirmed the strong bond of friendship traditionally existing between the two countries and their determination to intensify their common efforts toward the establishment of world peace based on freedom and justice.

The chairman reviewed the situation in Korea which led to the military revolution of May 16 and set forth the achievements made by the revolutionary government.

He emphasized the positive steps taken by the Government for social reform and the economic stability, particularly the new Government's actions to reform the civil service, rationalize tax collections, abolish usury in local areas, increase employment opportunities, stimulate investment and expand both domestic and foreign trade.

He emphasized as well the positive steps taken by the Government in strengthening the nation against communism and in eliminating corruption and other social evils.

The president welcomed Chairman Park's full exposition of the current situation in the Republic of Korea and expressed his gratification at the many indications of progress made by the new Government of the republic.

The Chairman reiterated the solemn pledge of the Revolutionary Government to return the government to civilian control in the summer of 1963, as he declared in the statement made on Aug. 12, 1961. The President particularly expressed his satisfaction with the Korean Government's intention to restore civilian government at the earliest possible date.

The two leaders discussed the position of Korea in the maintenance of peace and security in the Far East, and in this connection reviewed the continuing contribution of United States economic and military assistance to the strengthening of the Korean nation.

Recognizing that the successful achievement of Korean economic development in accordance with a long-range plan is indispensable to build a democratic foundation and to maintain a strong anti-Communist posture in Korea, the President expressed great interest in Korea's draft five-year economic development plan. In this connection, he assured the Chairman that the United States Government would continue to extend all possible economic aid and cooperation to the Republic of Korea in order to further such long-range economic development.

The Chairman and the President discussed the problem of mutual defense against the threat of external armed aggression in the Pacific area. They recognized that the common interest of their two countries as bulwarks of the Free World against Communist expansion is deepened and reinforced by the fact that Koreans and United States troops are brothers-in-arms, standing side by side in the United Nations command for the defense of Korean soil.

The President reaffirmed the determination of the United States to render forthwith and effectively all possible assistance to the Republic of Korea, in accordance with the mutual defense treaty between the Republic of Korea and the United States of America signed on Oct. 1, 1953, including the use of armed forces, if there is a renewal of armed attack.

The two leaders recalled that Korea had been successfully defended against armed aggression by the first collective military measures pursuant to the call of the United Nations. They recalled the declaration by United Nations members whose military forces participated in the Korean action, including their affirmation that in the interests of world peace, "if there is a renewal of armed attack, challenging again the principles of the United Nations, we would again be united and prompt to resist."

The Chairman and the President reaffirmed their faith in the United Nations, and their determination to seek the unification of Korea in freedom through peaceful means under the principles laid down and reaffirmed by the United Nations General Assembly.

Chairman Park and President Kennedy expressed their deep satisfaction with their meeting and discussions and reiterated their resolve to continue to serve the cause of freedom and democracy, and to strengthen the friendly ties between their two peoples.

Bibliography

The following bibliography is intended primarily as an acknowledgment of sources and as a guide to further study. Only books published in 1955 and afterward are included. For publications on Korea before 1954, see the bibliography of *Korea Tomorrow*. Whenever the title does not clearly indicate the subject matter, a brief comment is supplied.

I. GENERAL BOOKS AND PAMPHLETS

Chung, Kyung Cho, *Korea Tomorrow: Land of the Morning Calm* (New York, The Macmillan Company, 1960, 3rd edition). A comprehensive survey of Korea's history, geography, customs, tradition, religion, arts, music, language, literature, culture, economic and political structure. It is also a commentary upon the contemporary problems facing its people.

Conroy, Hilary, *The Japanese Seizure of Korea: 1868-1910* (Philadelphia, University of Pennsylvania Press, 1961).

Goodrich, Leland, *Korea: A Study of U.S. Policy in the United Nations* (New York, Council on Foreign Relations, 1956).

Grosse Sowjet-Enzyklopädie, "Korea" (Berlin, 1956 [in German]).

Halthe, K. *Litt Av Hvert Om Korea* (Oslo, Norwegian-Korean Society, 1958).

Kim, H. W., *Korea, its people and culture of all ages* (Seoul, Hakwon-sa, 1960).

Lewis, John, *Reconstruction and Development in South Korea* (Washington, National Planning Association, 1955).

McCune, Evelyn, *The Arts of Korea* (Tokyo, Charles E. Tuttle, 1962).

McCune, Shannon, *Korea's Heritage: A Regional and Social Geography* (Rutland, Vt. Charles E. Tuttle Company, 1956).

Min, Yung Bin, *The April Heroes* (Seoul, 1960). A compilation of American and English reports on Korea's Student Revolution.

Park, Chung Hee, *Leader's Way* (Seoul, 1961 [in Korean]).

Park and Kang, *Korean History* (Tokyo, 1957 [in Japanese]).

Richard Allen, *Korea's Syngman Rhee* (Tokyo, Charles E. Tuttle 1960).

ROK Government, *Korea: Her History and Culture* (Seoul, 1955).

ROK Government, *The Military Revolution in Korea* (Seoul, 1961).

Truman, Harry S., *Memoirs: Years of Trial and Hope,* Vol. 2 (New York, Doubleday and Company, 1956). The Korean War is discussed on pp. 316-464.

Vatcher, William, *Panmunjom* (New York, Frederick A. Praeger, Inc., 1958). The Korean military armistice negotiations are discussed.

Weems, Clarence N., *Korea: Dilemma of an Underdeveloped Country* (New York, Foreign Affairs Association 1956).

Whiting, Allen, *China Crosses the Yalu* (New York, The Macmillan Company, 1960).

Whitney, Courtney, *MacArthur: His Rendezvous with History* (New York, Alfred A. Knopf, 1956). An account of the Korean War and the controversy between Truman and MacArthur are discussed on pp. 315-475.

UN General Assembly, *Report of the Agent General of the UN Korean Reconstruction Agency* (New York, 1955-1961).

UN General Assembly, *Report of the UN Commission for the Unification and Rehabilitation of Korea* (New York, 1955-1961).

UNESCO Korean Commission, *UNESCO Korean Survey* (Seoul, 1960).

U.S. Department of Defense; *Republic of Korea* (Washington, 1959).

U.S. Department of State, *North Korea: A Case Study of the Techniques of Takeover* (Washington, 1961).

U.S. Senates, *Asia* (Washington, 1959). Korea is discussed on pp. 109-188. It is known as the "Conlon Report."

II. PERIODICALS

Economist, London
Korean Report (*Korean Survey*), Washington
Korean Reporter, Palo Alto
Korea Review, Tokyo
Korea Times, Seoul
Korean Republic, Seoul
Newsweek, New York
New Korea, Los Angeles
New York Times, New York
Time, New York
Voice of Korea, Washington
Yalu, Charleston, South Carolina

Notes

The numbered footnotes are intended primarily as acknowledgments for sources of matter referred to in the text. The factual materials and suggestions in this book were derived from the *New York Times,* UN publications, the Conlon Report, the ROK publications, *Korean Republic, Korean Report, New Korea,* and *Voice of Korea.*

CHAPTER I. **Introduction**

1. *New York Times,* reports and columns on Korea, 1955–1961; Conlon Report, U.S. Senate, 1959; *Voice of Korea,* 1955–1961; *Korea* by L. M. Goodrich (New York, Council of Foreign Relations, 1956) p. 7.

CHAPTER II. **Old Korea**

1. "Korea and the Koreans," by George Fox Mott, *Korean Survey,* February, 1960, pp. 3-5, 12. Copyright by the American-Korean Foundation, Inc. Used with permission.

CHAPTER III. **Modern Korea**

1. *Korea's Syngman Rhee,* by R. Allen (Rutland, Vt., Charles E. Tuttle Co., 1960), pp. 12, 105.
2. *Ibid.*
3. *New York Times,* May 4, 1960.

4. *Newsweek,* May 16, 1960.

5. *Voice of Korea,* 1955–1961.

6. *Korean Republic,* Aug. 15, 1958; *Korean Survey,* January, 1961; *Voice of Korea,* May 3, 1956.

7. *Voice of Korea,* January–February, 1959.

8. *Voice of Korea,* April, 1960.

9. *Voice of Korea,* 1960.

10. "My Views on the Student Revolution," by F. W. Schofield, *The April Heros* (Seoul, Ilsin-sa, 1960), pp. 182-187; "April Revolution," *Korean Report* Nos. 1-2; *Voice of Korea,* May, 1960.

11. *New York Times,* May 2, 1960; *London Times Weekly Review,* April 25, 1960.

12. *New York Times Magazine* (article on Asian students), 1960.

13. *New York Times,* May 9, May 31, 1960; Report of the UN Commission for the Unification and Rehabilitation of Korea, 1960.

14. *New York Times,* April 28, 1960.

15. *Ibid.,* May 3, 1960.

16. *Ibid.,* May 9, 1960.

17. *Ibid.,* May 31, 1960.

18. *Korean Report,* 1960–1961, Washington; Report of UN Commission for Unification and Rehabilitation of Korea, 1960, pp. 9-10; ROK, *Unification of Korea,* 1961; Han Nae Bok, "April Anniversary in Korea," *Far East Economic Review,* May 4, 1961; ROK, *Military Revolution in Korea,* 1961.

19. R. Scalapino, "Tasks Ahead," *Korean Reporter,* March 15, 1961.

20. "South Korea," *Time,* March, 1961; "South Korea: Reform in Brown," *Time,* Feb. 17, 1961.

21. *New York Times,* March 21, 1961.

22. "April Anniversary in Korea," *loc. cit.*

23. *Ibid.,* pp. 208-211.

24. *Korea Times,* Seoul, Feb. 1, 1961.

25. "South Korea: More Things Change," *Newsweek,* April 3, 1961.

26. *Republic of Korea,* Department of Defense, (Washington, 1959), pp. 44-51.

27. *New York Times,* Sept. 3, 1960.

28. *ROK Army,* Vol. II, pp. 157-170.

CHAPTER IV. **New Korea**

1. ROK, *The Military Revolution in Korea* (Seoul, 1961); "What Made the Revolution Succeed," *Korean Republic,* Aug. 15, 1961; *New Korea,* May–July, 1961.

2. D. Walfstone, "South Korea Generals Strike," *Far Eastern Economics Review,* May 25, 1961, p. 348.

3. *Ibid.*

4. *Korea Photonews,* ROK, May, 1961.

5. *New York Times,* June 5, 1961, p. 7.

6. "What Made the Revolution Succeed," *Korean Republic,* Aug. 15, 1961.

7. *New Korea,* May–September, 1961; "The Revolution's First Two Months' Achievements," *Korean Republic,* Aug. 15, 1961.

8. *New York Times,* Aug. 20, 1961.

9. *The Military Revolution in Korea.*

10. *New Korea,* June 8, 1961.

11. "The Revolution's First Two Months' Achievements," *loc. cit.*

12. "New Life Created for Everyone, Thanks to Military Revolution," *Korea Republic,* Aug. 15, 1961.

13. "The Revolution's First Two Months' Achievements," *loc. cit.*

14. *New York Times,* Sept. 13, 14, 1961 (on Seoul).

15. R. T. Oliver, "Korean-Japanese Discord," *Korean Survey,* May, 1957, pp. 3-5, 12; *New York Times,* 1955–1961 (reports on Korean-Japanese relations).

16. UN Korean Reconstruction Agency, 1959; UN General Assembly, review of Mutual Security Programs on Economic Assistance: Korea, Thailand, and Iran.

17. "Conlon Report," U.S. Senate, 1959.

18. *New York Times,* March 4, 1961.

CHAPTER V. **Conclusion**

1. R. T. Oliver, *The Republic of Korea Looks Ahead* (Washington, Korea Pacific Press); *New York Times,* editorial columns on Korea 1955–1961; *Voice of Korea,* 1955–1961; Conlon Report; R. Scalapino, "Tasks Ahead," *Korean Reporter,* March 15, 1961; *Yalu; Korea,* by C. N. Weems (New York, Foreign Policy Association, 1960).

2. *New York Times,* May 31, 1960.

3. *New York Times,* 1955–1961 (Reports and editorial columns on Korea); *Voice of Korea,* Washington, 1955–1961.

4. "Korea," *Time,* Nov. 14, 1960.

5. *Reconstruction and Development in South Korea,* by John P. Lewis (National Planning Association, 1955), pp. 24-25.

6. *Yalu,* a periodical, January, 1961, Charleston, S.C.

7. *Voice of Korea,* 1955–1961; *New York Times,* 1955–1961; Conlon Report; *Korea,* by L. M. Goodrich.

8. *Voice of Korea,* March 31, 1949.
9. R. Scalapino, "Tasks Ahead," *Korean Reporter,* March 15, 1961.
10. *Voice of Korea,* Jan.–Feb., 1961.
11. ROK, *Unification of Korea,* March, 1961.

APPENDICES

1. *Korean Pacific Press,* Washington (up to 1960).
2. *New Korea,* Los Angeles, 1961.
3. *Handbook of Korea,* Chae Kyung Oh (New York, Pageant Press, Inc., 1957).
4. *Voice of Korea,* Washington, D.C., August, 1961.
5. *Ibid.*
6. *Leadership: On the Revolutionary Process,* General Chung Hee Park.
7. Park-Kennedy Joint Communique.

Index